MWARI:
THE GREAT BEING GOD

God is God

Gwinyai H. Muzorewa

University Press of America,® Inc.
Lanham · New York · Oxford

Copyright © 2001 by
University Press of America,® Inc.
4720 Boston Way
Lanham, Maryland 20706

12 Hid's Copse Rd.
Cumnor Hill, Oxford OX2 9JJ

Library of Congress Cataloging-in-Publication Data

Muzorewa, Gwinyai H.
Mwari : the great being God : God is God / Gwinyai H. Muzorewa.
    p.   cm
Includes bibliographical references.
l. God. 2. Theology, Doctrinal—Africa, Sub-Saharan. I. Title.
    BT103 .M89   2001   231—dc21   00-069085 CIP

ISBN 0-7618-1955-X (hardcover : alk. paper)

♾™ The paper used in this publication meets the minimum
requirements of American National Standard for Information
Sciences—Permanence of Paper for Printed Library Materials,
ANSI Z39.48—1984

Contents

ACKNOWLEDGEMENTS

This book devoted to God, could not have been completed without the sacrifice and help from several colleagues. The idea of this book was conceived over two decades ago. But, I guess this is now the Kairos moment!

First I wish to express my gratitude to my wife, Sue, who has always encouraged to "put it on paper, Gwin." I would still be carrying the ideas and concepts which now fill the pages of this book in my head (and heart!). Second, I must thank especially Professor Dorothea Solle who was a regular visiting Professor of theology at Union Theological Seminary, New York City (in the 1980's). Hailing from Hamburg Germany, she always challenged me to develop a lengthy treatise on "An African Concept of God." Professor Solle had a clear hunch that the African concept of God was more instructive than concepts flouting around, especially in the '60s, '70s, 80's. I am sure what she sensed then has not changed significantly, particularly in the United States of America. Both Professors Solle and James Cone helped to think about a God who ACTS in history. Both thinkers, co-teaching at Union, believed and advocated a God who cares for and liberates the oppressed and down trodden of the earth. This book, therefore, is intended to describing this God - the God of Africa who is the creator of the Universe.

To my several colleagues whose names I cannot catalogue here, I am extremely grateful because your literary works enriched me not only as a doctoral student and scholar, but as a "professing" author, i.e. an author who teaches what insights and inspiration he receives both from below and from above! In the same breath, I must appreciate the feminist school of thought (or theological perspective) because I learned from their theology something which, maybe, they did not intend to teach, namely that any talk about God which is gender-based tends to "limit" one's concept of God. Put differently, feminist theologians and what they argue led me to appreciate even more the fact that African concepts of God are genderless. Otherwise as a product of the colonial era and an academic product of the West, my mind had been "indoctrinated" to talk, think and even begin to conceived of God as "He." Thanks be to God, I caught myself during this project and have therefore intentionally decided to write about the God of Africa who is not limited... Thus, my favorite definition of the Supreme Being is: "God is God."

Finally, I am extremely grateful to the Lincoln University community. First, I thank Denise Williamson, one of the most efficient secretaries at Lincoln University, who typed this manuscript. In the same breath, I cannot find adequate words to thank Ms. Sue Chikwem who proof- read and even offered some thoughts that helped me in various ways.

How could I forget to thank God (although this book is about God) who is my creator, sustainer and redeemer? To God be the Glory, Honor, Dominion and Power, now and forever.

MWARI: The Great Being

The theme is MWARI: GOD. This book demonstrates that all God-talk, at least from an African perspective, can and should be done in non-gender language and non-oppressive tone. To discuss the nature of God (trinity) without being trapped in "mathematics" or "philosophy" is one aspect of the uniqueness of this book. Furthermore, to talk about God as "one among us" yet one who is God (not like any creation), and talking about the Divine revelation as an unparalleled Spiritual Power is another aspect that makes this book a must.

Mwari (God) makes reference to the One God, and the trinity is transformed from being a mathematical conundrum to being a useful doctrine which is instructive in its content, nature, character and "components." This book succeeds in destroying a mathematical image (created by the Trinitarian language), and replacing it with an analogy. Thus, the Treeness of God talks about the three components (or modes of being) without getting bogged down on the time (generation), seniority (Father-Son), and "threeness in one" mystery.

This book presents MWARI: The Great Being of the Bible, one who self-revealed to the African people, planting the pervasive spirituality of the Africans.

That God is spirit does not need to be demonstrated. What this book does is to present such a God as one who liberates the captive, the poor, the oppressed and lets all creation know that God is God.

Finally, the book presents an African spirituality that furnishes us with a life-affirming concept of death. Reading through these pages transforms one's attitude (and even understanding!) of death as life. African spirituality pervades the indigenous concepts of life, death and life-after-death. Furthermore, the book discusses major sources of the theology of all people of African descent. Black theology acknowledged as "more powerful", is appropriated within the umbrella of the theology of continental Africa.

Every student and scholar of theology, anyone who honestly believes in God, all feminist and womanist theologians, western theologians and eastern thinkers should find challenging notions of God in this book as the author revisits concepts of God's Godness. The book also discusses the Incarnation, gender of God, and the death at Calvary, in addition to the Trinity in its revisited form.

Introduction

Any knowledge of the nature of God is available to creation only when God self-reveals. This is true of humanity as well as any other creature. Human awareness and sense of not only the existence but presence of the Great Spirit God occurs through faith, experience and/or cognitive knowledge, all made possible through God's self-revelation. Discussions on the knowledge of God are endless because God continues to reveal who God is in various ways to diverse communities who then name God and develop attributes of the same. In sub-Saharan Africa, the majority of the indigenous names of the Great Being can be summarized and reflected in the names given to this Great Spirit God. Understood from an African perspective, expressed systematically in the light of the Scriptures and African spirituality, the Great Sprit is what has been described by the philosopher St. Anselm as "that than which nothing greater can be conceived."

Among monotheistic religions, Christianity claims to know God on the basis of five primary factors: 1. What God reveals to humanity in history (Revelation); 2. What the Word of God, that is, the Hebrew people's recorded witness of who God is and what God says, and does (Scriptures); 3. The Church's creeds and tradition convey who God is as the church professes its faith (Tradition); 4. Present personal or community experience of what God has done to manifest the glory of this Great God, which has helped us to believe that the Lord is God (Experience); and 5. Reason, whether aided with God's grace, revelation or scientific observation. To this list should be added two major sources of African theology, namely: African Spirituality and traditional religion (based on the primitive revelation of the Great Spirit God) of which even one of the more conservative theologians on the continent has said:

"It is now being recognized that African traditional religiosity is playing a major role in African understanding of Christian Faith, in the rapid expansion of Christianity, and in the nature of pastoral problems faced by churches especially in the rural areas. African Christians are discovering, often with passionate interest, that there are many religious and cultural points of contact between biblical and African backgrounds (Mbiti, 1974).

Christianity can actually freely utilize God concepts from indigenous religion because both religions believe in the same Great Spirit God. The significance of this commonality far exceeds the danger of elements of syncretism possibly incurred in the process. After all, it seems to be the nature of any religion to take on not only local color but philosophical thought-forms of the new environment it is launched.

Concepts of God are not the essence of God, but they help us to express in human language what we otherwise could not communicate to others or pass on to younger generations. Over centuries, traditional religion has developed its own concepts of this Great Being, which are necessarily tinted with the people's culture. And so, there is a great diversity of perceptions of who and what God is. When we share and reflect upon these perceptions, we create for ourselves an opportunity to increase our cognitive knowledge of God. African Christianity and the indigenous religion enjoy a common matrix within which the Great Spirit God is acknowledged.

If who God is were totally dependent on what we say about the Great Spirit, God would probably be nothing more than a fuzzy notion of reality named on the basis of respective human imagination. Furthermore, many people would, by now have probably given up the study of theology, and perhaps created some discipline like "spiritual anthropology," or "spirituality of psychology," or sociology of concepts of God," anything but the proper subject of theology. The God-talk and concepts in this book are based on the premise that the Great Spirit is the Unmoved Mover, the Uncreated Creator, which sustains all creation. Therefore these chapters do not seek to prove the existence of God. (This author cannot even imagine any being without God's prior existence!) The focus here is a discussion of who the Great Being is from the point of view primarily of select African sources such as: culture, indigenous religion, philosophy and experience. The book attempts to present God, the Great Spirit, in language free from sexist and gender limitations since the Great God is, in fact, beyond the limitations of the human language.

God would have been named everything but who God is, all in a vain attempt to know this Great Being through inappropriate means and forms of knowing. But God took the initiative to reveal who God is and that process is incessant. Every community has its local concepts of God, with some concepts being the same as, or similar to the biblical ones. Therefore, it could not possibly be merely a figment of human imagination. God has made God self known to humanity. There are many who believe that God is God in spite of humanity's faith or unbelief! At least this is the faith that encouraged me to write this book despite the fact that the topic has been addressed by countless authors. Also, many of my seminary students kept pushing me to "share your African perspective of God with us!" Professor Dorothea Solle, a committed liberation theologian from Germany, rather put me on the spot when she wrote this remark on one of my term papers at Union Theological Seminary: "we expect you to develop an African perspective of God as you have known this Great Spirit God in your culture" (Solle, 1980). Then I viewed these as moments of inspiration, not compulsion! Now, the experience borders on being a "revelation" of sorts.

I perceive my intended goal as presenting a specific African concept of the Great Being-the God of our culture. If the God who the Church preaches and teaches, in Africa South of the Sahara is the same that the traditionalist worshiped prior to the Christian era, can one not reconcile the two without condemning either one? There is one answer for me: maybe there has been too much polarized "God-Talk" rather than letting God talk through a people's cultural idiom. I hope that this study will probe deeper than mere comparison and reach the bedrock of African theology.

African theological concepts do not have to exclude biblical views of the divine. Although there is an appreciable overlap, cultural expressions, certainly the Western perceptions, cannot express or reflect African cultural presuppositions unless we participate in exhuming indigenous God-concepts. Neither can African cultural expressions be expected to be the medium of all Western concepts. To say, for example, God is "a great provider" is meaningful only to a community that has experienced at least once if not several times that God provides. Not every community that knows God, however, may know God as the provider. Some may know God as something else. I agree that for the purpose of knowing God, such knowledge is essentially the same. What is important is not what we know, rather it is the value of our relationship with who we know and what we have experienced. This is the criterion for the people of God who have developed a liberation theology. They not only know God, they enjoy a relationship with their God-the-liberator.

Thus each local community develops its own concepts depending on what event or phenomenon has led them to conceiving of God that way. Concepts of God that evolve in this manner need not be controversial because the community's experience itself documents and authenticates the attributes. A profusion of names, concepts and attributes can also create legitimately false impressions that there is a plurality of Gods. In past generations, this used to be a serious problem. Today, books by the broad minded thinkers like the author of <u>No Other Name?</u> present perspectives that deal theologically and critically with this topic (Knitter, 1986). With various forms of media and technology available today, the situation is expected to continue to improve.

On the one hand people do not generally encounter similar experiences of God because we live in different socio-political contexts and our responses vary. Also, some social atrocities have been committed in the name of religion because communities tend to respond differently in situations that present life-threatening signs, eliciting various types of reaction. Fortunately, we do not have to embrace all these concepts just because we believe in the same God. Neither are we expected to wage wars over our theological differences. But a systematic treatment of the subject does compel the theologian to develop a coherent and clear theological statement. In spite of this necessity, the tendency is that there are some concepts that appear to one group to be of little or no value at all, yet for others the same are central and crucial for their faith.

For instance, how is a young African Christian to interpret his or her concepts to a European or American white professor who does not either understand or appreciate the young person's worldview. How is he or she to earn a doctorate, for instance, in systematic theology, if the entire doctoral committee has a totally different concept of God from the candidate who is really at their mercy at the point of defending his doctoral thesis? Will the committee be patient or objective enough to listen to a totally different concept of God that this African student will present? Our knowledge of God is not only objective but subjective as well. The point is that valuable knowledge of God arise from one's experience not just from conceptual or cognitive knowledge of who God is. For the most part, both our human knowledge and experience of God is culturally based. This means we ought to really utilize our cultural conceptual tools to perceive and articulate our theology. However, systematic theology offers us a method of talking about the same reality unlimited by our socio-cultural uniqueness without, in any way, minimizing the importance of this diversity. The reality we experience is that communities differ even over the simplest claim that God is ONE. Strangely, there can be more discussion over the point of difference than about important attributes where there is agreement. One such controversy has been on the question of the three names used to describe God.

THE TREENESS OF GOD

Already this attribute may need to qualified before it can be accepted by the whole church, not to mention the whole group of "monotheistic" religions. The perennial question is: what does it mean to say "God is one?" By "One God," one must mean unity in a unicellular sense or else the Trinitarians would be uncomfortable with what is meant by "One." The Jewish people who believe in Yahwe (God) maintain that "One" means just that, with no qualifications, which Trinitarians would reject arguing that the One means the Father, the Son and the Holy Spirit. The Judaist community cannot endorse the "Three-In-One" concept of the One God. Heschel's book: Between God and Man states the Jewish position in simple terms: "You cannot ask with regard to the divine: Which one? There is only one synonym for God: One" (Heschel, 1959). Milton Steinberg writes in his BASIC JUDAISM, "Hear O Israel: the Lord our God, the Lord is One" (Steinberg, 1947).

The Moslems would join them and so would Africans who believe in the Great Spirit God. This is superior to all other spirits and divinities; in fact, there is no comparison. Before one argues that the *THREE* are *ONE*, one must believe that there is the ONE. The mystery about this ONE is that the same has been revealed to some communities as three. For the African people, the great Spirit God could appear in any form including revealing the Reality in three persons and the three persons can identify themselves as ONE. The Great Being ought to have that capacity. While the theologian must have the ONE without the three, he or she cannot conceive of these without *PRIOR EXISTENCE* of the ONE.

Consider this analogy. When one looks at a huge **TREE** from a distance, one generally sees a silhouette of the ONE tree. On approaching, one may see one, two, three or more huge branches. When one is finally under the huge tree where the stem touches "the ground of its being", only ONE huge stem is all one sees: ONE TREE! This is one way to express the "treeness" of God. It would be unreasonable to argue that "each branch is the whole tree." What is reasonable and natural is for one to say: I have seen "a tree" when in fact, one has only seen branches or even just one branch. It is also reasonable to say: there is a tree over there when one catches a glimpse of a trunk. We do not normally say, there is a tree without branches because such a detail is usually not called for. To talk of the "treeness of God" is more descriptive of God's ONENESS than to talk of the "three-ness" of the ONE God without being numerically contradictory. We could discuss character and identity of the DNA of the branches and their trunk, the sameness of the nature of the tree, same name, genderless status, fecundity, singleness of purpose, providential quality, personality, unmoving mover status, and so forth. Suffice it to note that the metaphor is richer than the Trinitarian arithmetic.

The sentiments with which we prefer to talk about God as a Person, are the very ones which tend to "muddle up" our spiritual vision. As far as I am concerned, talking about God as "numbers" (ie. The First, Second and Third Persons) is more "unperson" than using such an analogous language as we have done in this book. In Chapter Six where we discuss the Trinity, we have resorted to the traditional gender language only so that the three stand as T-H-R-E-E. Otherwise, the Great Spirit God as understood from indigenous perspective, cannot be thought of as "HE", or "SHE", or "IT." GOD is GOD.

If we could manage to go beyond the controversy surrounding the meaning of the Oneness of God, we would, even if we narrowed the circle to include Christianity only, encounter another set of controversial attributes and concepts of GOD. For instance, feminists and some womanists would protest against any notion of God as our "Father" and the Father of Jesus Christ our Lord and Savior. In fact feminists have attacked any sexist reference to God because they have experienced suffering due to sexism and hierarchical structures which tend to be oppressive. In THE DIVINE FEMININE: The Biblical Imagery of God as Female, Virginia Mollen Kott writes: "The Bible depicts God as a woman, not only carrying us in her womb and bringing us to birth in creation and redemption, but also sucking, the aspect of ourselves that remains always in infantlike dependency" (Kott, 1986). We do not care to repeat the traditional argument for the "fatherhood" of God, even as a "parent." The purpose for this book is not to demonstrate how God is "not Father", but to share an African perspective of who the Great Spirit God is - as experienced in African spirituality.

Right through her book, Kott's hermeneutics challenges the whole Christian theological tradition. Yet, interesting enough, the author bases her entire argument on the Bible! In fact, both feminists and womanists together (although these two factions do not always agree) have made quite an impact on the doctrine of God. I think African women involved in theologizing are still wrestling with the tension between the fact that truly the sexist language in the church is oppressive but "God qua God" is a liberating, benevolent and providential Spiritual Being! Since there are a lot more women than men in the Church, it is important that a meaningful and more inclusive doctrine be developed beyond this pendulum theology! But that would not solve all the theological problems with regard to sexism, because liberation theology has also made what already looks like a permanent dent on the doctrine of God. Yet oppression persists not only in society at large but even in the Church - the very House of the Lord!

Liberation theologians in North America, Latin America, Africa and Asia have protested against any doctrinal formulation that does not highlight the liberating mission of Jesus because they are dealing with the evils of hierarchical, socio-political and economic injustices and oppression manifested through classism, gender, tribalism, male chauvinism and racism. Throughout issues of feminism, liberation, liberalism and conservatism to mention a few, there is also an ingredient of process theology espoused by theologians like John B. Cobb, Jr. which claims that everything that was created, and even the Creator God, is in a process of becoming. His book PROCESS THEOLOGY: AN INTRODUCTORY EXPOSITION (1976) provides good reading on the subject.

In expressing theological ideas from all the groups and camps mentioned above, there is an overall question of perspective. The poor have their own "five senses" through which they experience who and what God is. So do the religious rich, capitalists, communists, humanists, socialists, and so forth. To further complicate the matter, it is obvious that every person has his or her own theological perspective. In this book, for instance, I maintain an Afro-centric perspective. It best expresses my perception of who God is, drawing from the indigenous cosmology.

In the midst of all this, on the one hand, it seems insane to attempt to develop another perspective of the doctrine of God, which might add to the confusion and fuzziness already there in print. On the other hand, because of all these varying voices and perspectives it is most compelling that this project be done in order to express a much desired yet neglected perspective. Therefore, the question before me is: who is God for the African people, mainly South of the Sahara? How does that "God language" fare on the "God-talk market place"? Also, since this is the God of all African people in diaspora, it is important to share our concept of God with all because we all belong to the same ancestry. Professor

John Mbiti notes that "The Herero believe that God dwells in heaven, but that he[sic] is omnipresent throughout the universe" (Mbiti, 1969). So, the assumption here is that there is some theological uniformity no matter how heterogeneous the concepts may appear to be. All people of African descent are bound by kinship ties to this Great Being-the God of our ancestors.

Although the objective of this book is to express (which is not by any means exhaustive) an African perspective of God, part of what inspired me to write on the subject is the pressing question: traditionally defined as all powerful, good and loving, what has the Great Being done lately that we can point to for the benefit of the believer and the non-believer so that we are reassured that God is still and always in charge? This was triggered in class at Union Theological Seminary when I took the course dealing with the question "Does God Act in history?" The question is a challenge especially to Christians who hold these attributes (among others) of God. What has the almighty and all-loving God done to speak to the dying, suffering and oppressed of the land? What has the Great Spirit done for the people of God who are in exile? How long should they live as hostages and refugees in their own world created just for them? Reflecting on these questions calls for a statement which articulates who God is.

My thesis simply phrased: "GOD IS THE GREAT ETERNALLY DYNAMIC, COMPASSIONATE SPIRITUAL BEING/POWER", a life-giving spiritual source or spring of all being whose essence is inestimable to humanity. We have often misconceived God through our anthropomorphic and finite language, thereby underestimating God's Aseity. God is not limited by our definition of who God is. To realize that there is so much more about God than humanity knows is additional knowledge of God. Appreciating how much we do not know about God is a kind of knowledge, and not by any means embracing the "ignorance is bliss" syndrome.

What concerns me the most is humanity's apparent general assumption that God is not anything more than what we say that God is! In spite of God's self-revelation, our knowledge of God is less than the fullness of God, yet sufficient for our faith, conviction and salvation. More specifically, for almost two decades, leading American theologians have addressed certain issues to no avail: God does not seem to be doing what we expect God to do; therefore, either: a. This God is not as all-powerful, all-loving and all-good as we had been made to believe. Put bluntly, God is not all-powerful, good, or loving or else all this evil around us would not threaten our very existence; or b. There is no such reality as God. God is nothing more than a figment of human imagination. Or, c. The God who is <u>not</u> all-powerful, all-good and all-loving needs humanity's help along to get things done. In other words, these voices are saying God is not God! My view is, maybe we are asking the wrong questions and making incongruous conclusions about God.

In order to do justice to any one of these conclusions, we need to know who God is and what God's purpose is in creating the universe of which we are a part. How do we know if what is happening has no bearing on the nature of God? Maybe we need to re-define our self-understanding in order to conceive of a God-concept that is not distorted by an anthropocentric myopia. God is known by the Africans as the Great Spirit "worshipped in spirit and in truth" (John 4:24). This also means, because God is spirit, humanity needs to perceive God through and in spite of cultural spirituality and materiality. The world must attempt to perceive God spiritually first, not merely anthropomorphically. An indigenous spirituality opens doors to the meaning of God in the Twenty-first Century. This is to be one of Africa's major contributions to the second millennium. Otherwise, we make the mistake of letting the world be led by the computer, a mere object of humanity's creation. The spirituality that has sustained the African people through enslavement and colonialism will see us through another millennium! Now is the time for the people of God to lead the world by this God-given spirituality.

Another series of theological debates has to do with God's all-powerful nature in connection with God's direct control of what is happening (or not happening when it should!) in the world today. For instance, if God, according to the Yoruba myth, "fashioned the earth" and all that it contains through the use of agents, but "closely supervised the process personally," why does the world seem to be falling apart? One response will have to be that the purpose of the creator is unknown to creation (no vision). So, there is need for spiritual leadership.

Dr. Mercy Amba Oduyoye of Ghana makes an important claim on behalf of the African people when she says "I do not know of any primal world-view of Africa that leaves our existence to chance". God is at work "making now a new thing" out of the chaotic old. We need to ask for a new meaning, not a new God. Oduyoye quotes: "God so suffered with our humanity and our suffering world that God did some things about the situation: while we were yet afar off...God looked out for us" (Luke 15:20). What is God doing today to deal with our contemporary situation?

I agree with the Cameroonian Jean-Marc Ela that it is necessary to come out from our ivory towers theologically speaking, to encounter the real Africa, to interpret the "today" of God in the daily life of our people, with an acute awareness of the problems posed by practicing faith in a given culture. We must stay in communion with the people of God, the only adequate subject of theology and faith.

To do this calls for uttermost faithfulness to God. God is a living God who even announces "I am who I am" (Exodus 3:14). It is counter-productive for us to conjure up a "God" who suits our finite specifications but then fails to save us from spiritual death. Rather, we are invited to seek the true, living God, the source of all being and suit that God's specification because that is our origin and source of livelihood. Mercy Amba Oduyoye has correctly stated that human beings, with all created things, participate in life whose source is the One God, a claim which places God in the center of all theology.

The majority of people of African descent are spiritual and believe that God is Spiritual Presence and Power whose sustenance they cannot do without. Yet today there are too many definitions of the "true" God. It is for this reason perhaps that Jean-Marc Ela's concern is to invite churches and Christians "to bring back God into our midst" and locate God at the heart of a new covenant involving all of us not only ritually but concretely. The invitation is indeed overdue as is the response. This is why the biblical prophet describes humanity as being "scattered like sheep" which do not have a shepherd (Isaiah 53:6).

Jean-Marc Ela is correct to note that in order for us to re-connect with our God who has always sustained us, it is necessary that we find an appropriate language (or song) that enables us to re-learn how to talk about God to our indigenous communities. We remind ourselves that traditional religion was propagated by word of mouth and the entire African population received it and has retained it from time immemorial. There is no reason why the Christian faith should fail to reach and touch the greatest number in spite of Islam, Judaism and traditional religion. The key however is to use a language that our people can understand, concepts that resonate and touch our feeling of total dependence on God. After all, Oduyoye correctly makes the point that what we in Africa have traditionally believed of the Great Spirit God who brought into being transcendent order, has shaped our Christian faith. If the people of African descent would take their spirituality seriously, the glory of Ethiopia would revisit African people everywhere. Professor Kwesi Dickson, an Old Testament scholar of Ghana, now head of the Methodist church, agrees with many other African academicians and leaders when he testifies that God is held very high in the thinking of the African, a fact which is evident from a study of the praise-names and from a consideration of how this relation to man is not only conceived by comprehended.

Furthermore, there is consensus among most African theologians I have consulted that in African thought, "God acts". Thus God is "held very high" because this Great Being God *ACTS*, thereby meeting the people's needs. Our people have no difficulty conceptualizing the Great Spirit (God) in action because among Africans, "the invisible is as real as the visible", the two are inseparable, and communicate with each other through appropriate symbols.

Although this book discusses the Great Being, the God who created the whole universe, it talks about that God according to this understanding. Put differently, Professor Gabriel Setiloane of the University of Cape Town, now retired, reiterates that African theology does not proclaim a new God, but a different perspective - - one peculiarly indigenous - - view of this One and Only MODIMO, SOURCE OF BEING.

Chapter One

Some Sources of African Theology

A careful analysis of African traditional religion's concepts of prayers, proverbs, myths, African experience, literature, the Bible and independent churches and singular events that have occurred revealing God's presence and acts in history (Revelation) can yield profound dimensions of African theology. Of course there are other sources but we shall limit our discussion to these few which are sufficient to make the point. We regard these as sources because they are a manifestation of the inspired word of God. God has made God self-known to the African people from time immemorial.

Many African theologians agree that the African religion has primarily a spiritual world view, consequently God is regarded as the Supreme Great Spirit. They also admit that Africans have always been very religious people. Professor John Mbiti, one of the leading scholars could not have stated it more poignantly when he said: "Religion is the strongest element in traditional background, and exerts probably the greatest influence upon the thinking and living of the people concerned" (Mbiti 1969,1).

However, only a few theologians attempt to tell us what African traditional theology is since this theology is more of a reflection and articulation about what God is doing and how humanity is responding to life's challenges in every age, communicated orally among the African people. Interest in the study of African traditional religion began in the early 60's and 70's, almost paralleling the rise of the Organization of African Unity (O.A.U.). That interest led to a serious study of Christian theology, especially as theology sought to address the oppression, poverty, colonialism and apartheid issues on the continent. Also, nationalists were raising questions which provoked theological reflection and articulation about the status quo.

John Agbeti, in his article: 'African theology: what it is' has a good discussion on this subject. He maintains that African traditional theology is to be distinguished from African theology. Dr. Fashole-Luke is another exponent of traditional theology as defined by Dr. Agbeti. Both Fashole-Luke and Agbeti have a good case, though divergent. Other African theologians are interested in TRADITIONAL religious concepts only for the purpose of interpreting "the meaning of Jesus Christ for the African world view" (Agbeti 1972, 5), not for the sake of formulating a theology for African traditional religion per se. For instance, John Mbiti begins one of this major presentations with these words: "In the last ten years or so, it has become fashionable to talk about 'African Theology', 'African Christian theology', 'Theologia Africana', etc...I have no wish to enter into a debate with any of these positions. I will use the term 'African theology', in this paper, without apology or embarrassment, to mean theological reflection and expression by African Christians" (Mbiti 1973, 33).

Mbiti does not wish to "enter into a debate" concerned with distinguishing between theology of "traditional" religion <u>and</u> Christian theology as it is informed by "traditional religious beliefs. Mbiti's position is most indictative of the fact that both the indigenous and the Chrisitan religious traditions are viable sources of our knowledge of God. In this chapter, we emphasize the importance of both TRADITIONAL sources from which theological interpretations are being constructed and CHRISTIAN sources (mainly the scriptures and Protestant church traditions).

DEFINITION

Dr. John Agbeti defines African theology as "the interpretation of the pre-Christian and pre-Moslem African people's experience of their God" (Agbeti 1972). A number of African scholars share the view that in doing 'African theology', traditional African religious concepts are given theological interpretation.

Agbeti implies in his definition that "talk about God" can happen without the aid of the written word (Scriptures) since TRADITIONAL God-talk is basically an oral theology. Most African theologians maintain that the traditional concepts and experience of God are distinct from the

Christian experience. For this reason, some scholars expect traditional theology to be different from Christian theology although the subject of discussion is the same: GOD. However, this is not the case since only one God is involved-the God of traditional religion is the same as that of traditional Christianity. Other scholars do not see the wisdom of separating the traditional concepts of God from the Christian. Like Professor Mbiti, Malcolm McVeigh, an expatriate in Kenya, now retired, dismissed the debate on the basis that the referent of both traditions is the same - God. Since African theology draws from both traditions it therefore renders Dr. Agbeti's definition invalid because it confines itself to pre-Christian and pre-Islam times. We may therefore define African theology as the interpretation, reflection and articulation of the African people's religious experience of, and their response to God in the light of the tradition of the self-revealing God. A definition of African theology must include the people's traditional knowledge and experience of the God of the African ancestors who also self-revealed in Jesus Christ and the Bible. When the traditionalists heard the scriptures read they said: what was written on our hearts is now in the scriptures.

There is continuity between traditional and Christinan theology since both share a vital component, namely a "living faith" in God. In some circles, traditional theology is sometimes thought of as a "preparatio evangelica". The two are continuous in that they are both reflective, with Christian theology revolving primarily around Christ, while traditional theology focuses on concepts of the Creator God, (whom Jesus Christ called "Abba") which were revealed to traditionalists before the incarnation. Given the African kinship concept, knowledge of the Great Parent is continuous with that of the son because the two are inseparable in essence.

When Agbeti says "there is a living faith in God" in traditional theology, we need to know that most of the sources of theology in African religion are oral, living memories handed down from generation to generation. Such sources as prayers, proverbs, songs, folktale, myths, experience to mention some, constitute major aspects of the African culture as well as African theology. Also, they convey truths that have been empirically verified over the generations, hence they are sources African scholars are taping in doing theology. Let us examine these one by one.

SOURCES OF TRADITIONAL THEOLOGY

a. PRAYERS

Prayers are a database for African theology because these are personal discourses by individuals talking to the Living God they learned of from their parents and ancestors. God revealed God self to the African people who have kept in contact with God through prayer, defined as talking to God, in order to ascertain and appropriate God's will for them in any given situation or circumstance. Prayer is loading one's burdens onto God; expressing one's ills to a listening and caring adjudicator. As discourse, then, theology is constructed based on what worshipers say about God, their expectation of God, their pleas to God, their thanksgiving to God and, indeed their entire livelihood in God. A look at such prayers easily reveals the African people's belief in God and their thinking about God, the Great Spirit God.

Prayer is also traditionally defined as "talking to God" for the purpose of either thanking, making a plea, crying unto the Lord, and so forth. Prayer is offered to the God in whom one has faith. Consider the following prayer from an East African community:

"God! Give us health" "God!! Give us raided cattle!"
"God! Give us the offspring of men and cattle" (Mbiti, 1975).

This prayer is only one of numerous standard prayers which portray God as the Provider. God is believed to be the source and Giver of all good things in life because God is in charge of the Universe and the fullness thereof. For instance, a people of Ghana say *"Asase trew, na Onyame ne panyin"* meaning "The world is wide but God is the master." This concept places God the Great Spirit at the "apex" of the universe. ("Apex" here does not refer to a vertical position, but to ultimacy). It creates a hierarchy with God viewed as above and beyond all. What is more, as Master, God is in control of the entire universe. God is God! Note that a prayer for good health, wealth and family indicates the people's faith in an imminent God, a God who cares about the people's well being on daily basis, not just on occasions. This comes to us from the tradition of the ancestors who experienced God as Almighty and the Great Provider, generation after generation. It is interesting to note that even "raided cattle" are given by God as a good gift because such raided cattle also enhance survival.

According to this thinking, God is the Sustainer in addition to being the Creator. From God we receive all our spiritual and physical requirements. For this reason, the Psalmist has said: "The Lord....restoreth my soul." It is no wonder African people generally hold the belief that God is the greatest healer...one who heals without the use of herbs or any form of substance or medication. It is also for this reason that even scientific doctors admit that they can only administer medicine but "nature" heals! By which they refer to the Divine mysterious power of healing. More and more Christian physicians mention God as the ultimate healer of disease, not to talk of the soul! By praying to God the traditionalist believes that God's word becomes concrete reality.

Thus, God is understood to be the provider whose benefits are tangible and are intended to meet the human at the point of need. Many Africans believe that their God is not a philosophical concept. For them, God is the spiritual Reality whose benevolence is tangible. "God..emerges as the clearest and most concrete spiritual reality." Prayer then is regarded as a very viable means through which "the word become flesh." Prayer, understood as "talking to a God who provides", is therefore a means through which Africans can communicate their survival needs to God, the Great Provider. However, to understand God's ways and dealings, one looks into "wisdom literature", i.e. African proverbs, as we will shortly do below. Another prayer - prayer for recovery - that indicates the centrality of God in traditional African reflection goes like this:

1. "O great Deng (God), let her live,
    Let her recover and escape from death,
    O great Deng, let her live" (Mbiti 1975).
    A husband praying for his wife's recovery says:
    "Thou alone, O God hast ordained
    that we marry women. Therefore
    grant that my wife, now sick,
    recover speedily" (Mbiti 1975).

Parents praying for their child's health would say this prayer:

2. "O God, thou art great,
    Thou art the one who created me,
    I have no other
    God, thou art the only one in heavens,
    Thou art the only one:
    Now my child is sick,
    And thou wilt grant me my desire" (Mbiti 1975).

In both these short but very precise prayers, it is clear that one who says the prayer is expressing total dependence on God. There is a clear relationship between God the creator, and a human being who has great faith in the Divine. It is not surprising that such dependency calls for absolute faith. Note that in saying such prayers there is no mediator. The worshiper is directly talking to God. Such a God could not be viewed as a distant God, but is immanent and transcendent at once. In sum, God is the object of the indigenous African prayer. All other things are merely aiding devices.

b. PROVERBS

Proverbs are another source of theology. Most African scholars would agree with the notion that African peoples "record orally" their great ideas and serious reflections in proverbs. In the absence of the written word in traditional religion, Dr. John Pobee says, Africans need to collect myths, proverbs, invocations, prayers, incantations, rituals, songs, dreams, and so on, because these contain or convey oral wisdom and theology. However, these materials need to be collected and interpreted systematically in order to produce a traditional theology.

In fact, there are some African theologians who believe that a proverb in African tradition is not only a didactical saying, it is a storehouse of wisdom and philosophy..a proverb about God is seriously a talk, a reflection on God which may result in books. It is African theology. And we may add what Mbiti says "It is in proverbs that we find the remains of the oldest forms of African religious and philosophical wisdom" (Mbiti 1970, 86) and God is one who gives us wisdom. King Solomon, in addition to all his riches, asked God for wisdom. Even atheists seek wisdom-an invaluable commodity.

Proverbs convey not only philosophical wisdom but theological knowledge as well. What does the reader think about such a proverb as this: "A creature is not greater than its creator" (Mbiti 1970, 87)? There is a decent number of African theologians who contend that African prayers and proverbs are loaded with theological insights. It is abundantly clear that Africans, apart from being imbued with the sense of religion, have also from time immemorial had a theology in their own way. The Ashanti have a proverb which says: "No one shows a child the Supreme Being," which means everybody knows of God's existence. Mbiti also informs us that there are various proverbs which are used to express the idea of God as the Sustainer of life. Sustenance is exercised through the mysterious, inaudible and invisible power of God.

For example, "The Herero hold that life of an old man is sustained by God, and death is caused by God calling him away" (Mbiti 1975). One after another, proverbs speak about life and God because the former is given by the latter. Other African peoples also hold God "to be the author and Sustainer of life." This concept is expressed in a proverb which says "God gives, God takes away." Various proverbs convey different philosophical and theological content, meaning and teaching about the Great Spirit God. Africans also have numerous oral collections of myths - stories told in order to explain and understand such concepts as the mystery of life and death, creation, the origin of sex, the relationship between God and humanity. As Benjamin C. Ray puts it: "Indeed, in African oral tradition myth and history generally overlap and shade into one another" (Ray 1976, 24).

c.   MYTHS

Regarding the value of myths as a source of theology, Mbiti said, "Myths are often the most effective means of keeping ideas circulating from one place to another and from one generation to the next" (Dickson and Ellingworth 1969). Consequently, much traditional theology is usually contained in an African mythical garb. In fact, many scholars agree that traditional African thinking tends to be mythical, bound up with the beginning of things, with Creation and the Primeval Age. Myths convey truth, as does theology, in a particular cultural matrix because their purpose is to teach and as such their content is theological. Mbiti tells us that Africans have a myth that says God created two sets of "first parents" so that the offspring from each set could marry from the other. This myth brings information to the African Christian who did not know how to solve the problem we are presented with in the biblical myth of Adam and Eve, our "first parents" (Genesis: 4:15-17).

The problem posed by the biblical myth is: after Cain had murdered his brother Abel, we are told he ran away, and married a wife! Where did this "bride"come from if all the children Adam and Eve had were Cain and Abel? Now, with Abel murdered, we only have Cain. The African myth teaches that God created two set of "first parents' whose children married. Whereas the biblical myth leaves room for a possible incestuous relationship between Cain and his mother, the African myth explains plausibly how the human race started. God is still the Creator! Well-thought African theology is expressed in myths, proverbs and folktales. When Africans do theology it is not for the purpose of being faithful to a Deity, but primarily for the sake of their own survival. Myths provide them with sound theology. Myths "constitute an 'original revelation', which is reacted in annually recurrent festivals, in a rhythm which forms the cosmic framework of space and time. The myths span the whole of existence, from heaven to the hut and the heart of individuals; in fact, from cosmos to clan" (Sundkler 1962, 100), as Bishop Sundkler noted in his little book.

d. AFRICAN EXPERIENCE

The sources we have discussed so far constitute the bulk of the database on theology. However, these sources are not conceived separately. They are created during the African peoples' experience of the divinity. For instance, a proverb may be "coined" on the basis of a series of experiences over a long time. This enriches experience as a source of theology. When several people experience God or a God-encounter is witnessed by a number of individuals or even the whole community, for generation after generation, that EXPERIENCE is "traditionalized" and incorporated into the body of the religious beliefs. Thus, the African themselves, through their own experience, are a very vital source of theology. African experience means what the people endure or encounter, or go through at the point of their Africanness. That is African experience. Only an African can experience "African experience." Based on this meaning of "African experience", one will have to argue that only Africans can construct a relevant knowledge of God within the matrix of African experience. This information then should come from various regions before we can draw meaningful theological generalizations.

Apparently, when Agbeti makes reference to African theology, he is talking about written theology. Yes, he may be correct, but we need to remind ourselves that the generality of theology is best based on its particularity. A key word in creating African theology is EXPERIENCE. Agbeti said, "The African traditional experience of the Supreme Being is...practical" (Agbeti 1972, 7). It therefore follows the experience of God, the peoples' reflection over such experience, together with their interpretation of it, is the content of African theology. The God we experience as people of African descent, and any revelation we may experience of that God is the content of theology. Experience does not negate reflective thinking. Earlier, scholars placed more emphasis on experience than on reflection. We believe that the two are of equal significance. One cannot reflect on "nothing" unless one intends to create "an armchair theology." Theology actually emerges from the peoples' experience and reflection. Reflection that follows experience is more fruitful than an armchair reflection divorced from experience.

Fortunately, the African people are more experience oriented than otherwise. Many theologians contend that in African theology, the acts of faith and reflection occur simultaneously because when a man throws to the ground his first morsel of food, it cannot be a thoughtless waste of food. He reasons that he should earn the good-will of the numerous ancestor spirits who are able to influence his life for good. When he arrives at a positive conclusion that it is meet to do so, so he does. Similarly, the ancestors reflect upon the actions of their sons who are experiencing what it is to be an African. They reciprocate amicably. African theology is talking to one's God in a communicative language, and God acting and responding to one's survival and needs.

Essentially, the content of theology consist in the message we receive from God when we approach the Supreme Being. Theology is the African way of life as it is understood in the community by members of that area. Since theology reflects a people's experience and this informs theology, it means that the African's daily activities could be interpreted as a theological manifestation. The symbolism of dropping a morsel of food for the ancestors and other spirits to receive, and the consequent reflection of the supposed interaction is theological. Such "communication" can only transpire when there is harmony in the community. Furthermore, such reciprocity indicates long life-wholesome living.

Of course not all experience needs to be theological. Experience which has theological dimensions has its bearing on the character of the God worshiped in Africa. Thus only certain experiences, such as religious acts can be interpreted as content of theology. Theology is the interpretation of peoples' experience of God, the Supreme Being or the Ultimate Reality and God's dealings with them in their history. A theology which distances itself from the people cannot be embraced by the African people of faith. Collectively we (the church) defined theology at the Abidjan meeting in 1969 as:

> "A theology which is based on the Biblical Faith and speaks to the African "soul" (or relevant to Africa). It is expressed in categories of thought which arise out of the philosophy of the African people. This does not mean that it is narrow in outlook. To speak of African theology involves formulating clearly a Christian attitude to other religions. It must be pointed out that the emphasis is basically on Christian theology, which could be expressed through African thinking and Culture (A.A.C.C. Abidjan 1969).

Although this definition was drawn up at the dawn of African theology, it highlights the most critical religious pulse-points namely the "soul" (or heart) and "culture" (social context or experience). (A.A.C.C. Abidjan, 1969). When the interpretation of the social and religious experience is done in the light of Jesus Christ, the result is CHRISTIAN theology. The latter is interpreted in light of Christ's teachings and the traditions of the Christian faith. When God reveals God self to the traditionalist, our reflection on such self-revelation of Divinity constitutes theology. Note that even when the means through which God is experienced are different, the product is the same: God with us.

AN EMERGING THEOLOGICAL PERSPECTIVE

African theology is a new perspective because it is concepts of God acquired through the scriptures which are interpreted in Afrocentric God concepts. This definition places our theology in the everyday African experience since "religion permeates all aspects" of African life. Theology, like religion "permeates all of life." Africans do not separate "theology" from "religion" since for them religion is "doing", "dancing", "singing", "eating" and theology is reflection on religious activity. Theology cannot be a matter of the "head" alone without the heart. In fact, this is the difference between a written theology and an oral theology. The latter still has to be processed through the head prior to "being saved" (to use computer language) in the heart, whereas the former is received cognitively and does not have to be "processed" in the heart. (Where I used the term "process" I could have said "digested spiritually.") This is why almost all Africans, tend to be spiritual people. For them religion is a phenomenon of the heart in the first instance.

Mbiti has expressed this precisely when he wrote: "To the Yoruba, God is known as 'he who sees both the inside and outside [of man], the Discerner of hearts" (Mbiti 1970, 3). From the very beginning, religion has always been a matter of the heart. The word of God touches the human HEART! In connection with the importance of "the heart," we note that mercy, pity and kindness are believed to "reside" in the heart. All we can say is, if God who is omniscient and omnipotent, is also "the God of mercy," should the human being not invest much in the heart? Most experienced adults agree that "when people turn to God (through sacrifice, prayer, or invocation) in moments of Crisis other need, they do so in the belief that he is compassionate and would take pity on them" (Mbiti 1970, 31). Some African scholars, therefore, do theology as a descriptive discipline, rather than reflective one. Mbiti's *Concepts of God in Africa* provides such an example. John Pobee, however, makes the case that African theology (by which he means traditional theology) is a reflective theology. It is not just: a "danced out" theology. Be that as it may, African theology resonates in the heart because we are both an oral traditional and a spiritual people of God. One hopes that Africans do not lose this quality since they are taking the character of written theology. If being systematic makes our theology foreign to our thought-forms, then it is better not to systematize it! The problem is that most African theologians, (even those who are also the exponents of traditional theology) seem to insist that theology be developed systematically in order to be valid. This expectation invites difficulties to the subject where crucial elements like "mystery" constitute courses of theology. How can a theologian present "mystery" systematically without sacrificing theology's essential content?

One would rather be unpopular if that is what it takes to keep African theology within the thought-form of African thinking. There are two reasons for this position. Firstly, the structure of African theology should be determined by its content. The content of traditional theology is structurally different from that of Western oriented Christian theology, which is based on the Graeco-Roman philosophical presuppositions. African theology is simply African. Secondly, the structure of African theology should be determined by an Afro-centric biblical modus operandi and hermeneutic. African experience and worldview distinguishes all Africans from all non-Africans. How we do what we do, and how we eat our food and how we raise our family - all this makes us who we are as a people. In other words, what distinguishes us from other cultures also distinguishes other peoples' cultures from ours. Unless these two criteria are satisfied, any talk about contextualization may not make African theology any more African or relevant to African needs than any other foreign theologies.

Since African philosophy is no longer formulating its tenets according to the rules of western logic, why should theology be compelled to formulate traditional truths according to Western methods? It seems to me that in order for theology to be a genuine African enterprise, it has to remain faithful to the indigenous philosophical thought-forms. It has to remain faithful to the African way of thinking, which is based on an African epistemology. This yields a distinctly traditional theology because one's method, more than source, generally influences the result. So, for best results, an African theologian must first re-discover this epistemology from the pre-scientific cosmology. Note that African epistemology is used even during the Twentieth Century because Africans are still operating within their cultural thought-forms - along with technology and science. By rejecting "Systematics" as defined in the Webster's theological dictionary, we are not necessarily advocating an "unsystematic" modus operandi. We are not dealing with opposites here. Our argument is, traditional theology should not be subjected to foreign methodologies because that does not produce desirable results. Let us bear in mind that when the Western theologies developed systematics, what they regarded as "sound philosophy," "psychology," "religious concepts," and "theological need," were all contextual and consequently, culturally defined. Theological ideas, like many disciplines, tend to be "culturo-centric". On this note, we turn to a discussion on the doctrines of the Trinity and Salvation - to be discussed from an Afrocentric perspective.

The doctrine of the Trinity in the Christian context teaches that "the Godhead consists of the Father, the Son and the Holy Spirit".

Mbiti reports that the Shona believe that God's unity exists in multiplicity. A form of God's Trinity or Triad is reported among the Shona and Ndebele peoples. In one area of the Shona, according to Mbiti, God is conceived as 'Father, Son and Mother'. Among the neighboring Ndebele, there is a similar belief 'in a trinity of Spirits, the Farther, the Mother, and the Son (Mbiti, 1970, 91-94). It is not clear whether this understanding is an influence of Christianity brought by the Portuguese or not. What we know for certain is that the Shona, Ndebele, Xhosa, Zulu and numerous African religious communities believe in the Great Spirit God, (in the singular, never plural).

First, it helps to substantiate the fact that God reveals God self to whoever God chooses in any form God likes. God revealed Divine nature to the Shona even before the historic Incarnation of Bethlehem. Could we then say that Christ was known in an African way long before 1 C.E.? What is the importance of the historical Jesus for traditional theology if Africans already knew of God-in Christ in pre-Christian ages? This leads to the question of the pre-existent Christ, which could only be consistent with the Great Spirit God who is the Living TRUTH. Africans know that as spirit, the Godhead is ageless, without boundaries and omniscient. It renders the Spirit Logos vunerable to an African Christology. Christ as God then emerges within the African culture as indigenous. It might call for a new definition, but the work of Christ in Africa would have to be re-discovered from time immemorial. It is little wonder that the babe Jesus (and his parents) would find physical refuge in Africa when King Herod sought to kill him.

Another concept that will need re-interpretation is the doctrine of salvation. Since Trinity implies the presence of Christ within the African culture, it makes sense to say that Salvation is an "in-built" mechanism in the African culture. Before Christ announced that his function was to save the world, African theologians believed that ancestors had some access to the knowledge of the immortality of the soul. This is why Africans kept contact with their ancestors, only to relinquish them when Christ announced that he would perform the tasks himself. Our belief in Salvation has always been confirmed by our belief that life does not end at the grave, but continues to live with God in a special relationship.

Salvation becomes a natural spiritual phenomenon which works through a specially God-ordained agent to rescue or save life, both spiritually and physically. For instance, a man who is washed away by a flood may be thrown on a tree-trunk which is lying across the flooded river. If his life is saved by the log, he can say: "were it not for that log, I would have perished." He rejoices that he has been saved somehow. Thus, salvation is not just spiritual. It is any limitless work of God through any divinely ordained means. Salvation is holistic. As that log had no power to "save" anyone, only the creator God used "that log" to physically "save" the man in God's *Kairos*. Africans who find themselves in this kind of danger would attribute such "salvation" to some spirit working through nature for humanity's salvation. This is the spirit which saves, or rescues, or redeems, and is none other than the mysterious HAND OF GOD.

In sum, God reveals Godself to the African people in various forms and modes of being. In each case, God is always working to enhance our survival. Theology is the very ACT of remembering or reflecting on "how we got over," information which is captioned in various database discussed here. Salvation is an event which accomplishes one's survival by external power. This means that one cannot save oneself. Such awareness leads many Africans to accept Jesus Christ the Savior because they realize the need for a SAVIOR. Now let us move on to a select and yet broader category of theological sources which are more widely recognized and accepted as such.

AFRICAN TRADITIONAL RELIGION

African religion is considered a major source for theology in Africa on the basis that God has revealed own self in African traditional life as a preparation for this revelation in Jesus. Many theologians interested in a relevant theology admit that indeed Africans knew God before the church was introduced to them. To be specific, God revealed Godself to the Shona of Zimbabwe as *Musikavanhu*, meaning the Creator of the human race. This is God!

One of the United Methodist church hymns (No. 176), composed by westerners and sold to us, is simply not factual, no matter how inspiring the music and the melody may be: "Ndakabarwa munedima Rekusaiziwa Mwari" (viz. I was born into a culture that does not know God.) The essence of this hymn is to highlight and praise the missionary who introduced the gospel to us. Of course we understand that most such hymns are translations of Euro-American Hymns, (and for sure most white people did not know God before Christianity! A good example is the Athenian Greeks who worshiped an array of gods.) Also, it is possible that lyrics were added to hymnal tunes by African converts who were eager to denounce their culture, religion and race because they had been led to believe that anything western including Christianity was necessarily good, whereas anything African including religion was necessarily evil. Unfortunately, the African did not reject such erroneous indoctrination since this message was brought by allies of colonial rulers. Instead, they went on to suppress their own resistance in order to be regarded as the saved ones.

Now, what was suppressed is erupting and is influencing the creation of a theology that seeks to emancipate the African believers so that they may be who God intended them to be. Our theologians declare that African theology sees Modimo/Qamata as the same as Yahwe of the Hebrews and the God of Christianity. The only thing it claims is that it has a different perspective of this one and only source of Being. This is why traditional religious concepts of God constitute an important theological database. It is therefore improper to call Africans "heathens."

A heathen is defined as "one who adheres to the religion of a tribe that does not acknowledge the God of Judaism, Christianity or Islam." Then the dictionary also says a heathen is "one who is regarded as irreligious, uncivilized, or un enlightened.

Based on the first definition, it would not be correct to regard Africans as "heathen" because they acknowledge the same God worshiped in Judaism. Relative to the second definition, Africans were regarded as "heathens" not just on the basis of their alleged lack of knowledge of God, but on the grounds that their civilization or culture was different from that of the white people who drew up the definition of the word. So, it is clear that white missionaries approached Africans (especially south of the Sahara) under the assumption that they were ungodly and needed to convert to Christianity. With these brief remarks, we have to return to our proper subject under consideration.

To make the point that Africans knew the same God that the missionaries came to "introduce", *God in Africa* authored by an expatriate, Malcolm McVeigh, has made it clear that "The God of African Traditional Religion and Christianity is in fact the same. The God who revealed Himself (sic) fully in Jesus Christ is none other than the one who continually made himself (sic) known to African religious experience. (McVeigh 1974)" We further agree with McVeigh's point that "It is simply no longer possible that God has left himself without a witness in the traditional religious heritage." Thus, traditional religious beliefs have tremendous value for African theology in that the native affinity to God in traditional life continues to find expression in the Christian context. What God said to our forefathers continues to be true for us today for the word lives eternally. This continuity between the God of traditional belief and the Christian God accounts for the prominent position which must be given to traditional religious concepts of God as a source of theology.

Note that African theology does not intend to re-convert the Christian to traditional religion. Rather it seeks to convert the "native" affinity of worshiping God to the "Christian" context provided that that leads to the deepening of our faith in God through Jesus Christ. Faith, not just culture, is the reason for conversion. African theology does not seek to uproot believers from their culture. To the contrary, it seeks to encourage the believer to live a life of faith that absorbs the total person.

Though very radical, it needs to be mentioned that there is no valid theological reason to <u>convert</u> to Christianity people who worship the same God who the Christians, Jews and Moslems believe in. The conversion from traditional religion to Christianity is merely ecclesiological, i.e. to worship God in the Christian fellowship. But we have to always remind ourselves that being church-goers is not co-terminus with knowing God or having faith in God. Conversion here would be from one method of worshiping God to another, rather than from one God to another since it is the same God in question. Put differently, conversion would mean movement from the indigenous to the western fashion of worshiping God. Again we could not agree with McVeigh more when he says "As Jesus did not come to destroy Judaism but to bring it to completion, even so he brings to completion the African religious heritage," without destroying the African culture (McVeigh 1972). Many missionaries - both African and Euro-American - did not seem to know the difference between cultural conversion and spiritual conversion. A little bit of incarnational theological understanding would help our overly jealous messengers of the gospel. One really must ask: is conversion desirable?

The African Churches need to convert from a Euro-American to an indigenous decorum in order to be relevant to the people. What the church gains in this process is the indigenization process of itself. Because the church often tends to "suppress rather than build on the spiritual insights of Africa" many African Christian groups have had to break away from such denominations in order to form congregations where they can worship in total freedom reflecting their culture. Such emerging groups are geared to meet the needs of the worshipers. When liturgy is African, worship becomes more meaningful. Yes, we maintain that what is African is naturally and logically more relevant to the people than what is alien to them. This fact becomes relative when the African has been transformed into being schizophrenic. There are some Africans who have lost their Africanity and have acquired foreign "culture" in the pretext of being Christian. Some people ask me: "Gwinyai, what is African?' Others argue that they are more comfortable with "western life style" than with the so-called African life style. Africans who do not know who they are and those who prefer cultures other than their own, will not appreciate what African theology has to offer. Neither do they appreciate who they really are. These stand in need of a special kind of conversion.

THE GREAT SPIRIT OF GOD AS CREATOR

As a source for theology the indigenous knowledge of God is acquired through God who revealed Godself through Jesus Christ. This does not change <u>who</u> and <u>what</u> God is. The revelation did not change WHO God is, or WHAT God is to us. There may be a difference between knowing and relating to God as "Father" (as Christianity teaches) and communicating with God as God the creator of all humanity. Of ultimate importance is that both traditional religion and the church acknowledge God as the creator of Heaven and earth, maker of all things. Thus, the two religions converge on this ultimate attribute of God: namely God as Creator. I maintain that this knowledge is not coincidence. It came through the revelation of God by God-ordained means. African religion is an important source because we can find in it information about what

God has done in the history of the people and how the Africans worshiped, talked about and reflected upon God.

If we accept the definition that a "source is" a "place or thing from which something comes or derives; point of origin" (American Heritage Dictionary) or "a person or place that supplies information," we can readily appreciate why we consider traditional religion as a source of theology. "God content" in indigenous religious thinking is based on God's self-revelation to the people of Africa. If then God had revealed Godself to Africans, that revelation is undoubtedly valid. Fortunately, to ignore the African witnesses doesn't necessarily nullify the fact of God's revelation which they are proclaiming. God is God, with or without a witness!

GOD IN PRIMITIVE REVELATION

Theologians acknowledge the revelation of God to the primitive African because, although the people were primitive, there is nothing primitive about Divine revelation. Furthermore, interested scholars understand that only Africans can express what God has revealed to them from an indigenous perspective. What God revealed to the Africans is exactly what the great Spirit God determined, or deemed necessary for such communities, at that time, and for a particular purpose. To require a clearer revelation, or the personification of God, is attempting vainly to run ahead of God. Furthermore, it makes sense to infer that the reason most of us accepted the Biblical message as the written word of God is precisely because we were already familiar with the idea of God in general and possibly, the ways of the Lord. For instance, we were already acquainted with the idea of supernatural spirits and divine intervention in our life. Therefore, when Jesus says in his prayer: "Not my will but thy will be done," we understand what that means (Matthew 26:39b).

To be a little more concrete, the claim that Jesus Christ was raised from the dead and today Christ lives with each one of us who believes in Him, is very consistent with the African spirituality and philosophy. Our point here is that traditional religious beliefs form a context within which the resurrection of the dead makes sense. "Death" and "resurrection" are two sides of the same coin. The dead and the living are two aspects of the same community. To live eternally, one must live then die. So "to die (in Christ) is to live" would be another example of African dialectic. God has revealed the fullness of life in the "life and death and resurrection" of Jesus Christ.

African spirituality and philosophy provide a theological matrix within which it makes sense to talk of "life after death," spiritual existence, being filled with the Holy spirit. Any reference to the spiritual guidance is more likely to be readily acceptable to African traditional thinking than to people who do not have the slightest notion of the reality of spiritual ontology. Thus, African spirituality renders believers vulnerable to the gospel of eternal life in God through Jesus Christ. Again, in Jesus, eternal living has been revealed to the finite humanity.

In most of the so-called mission churches, the dominant theology, liturgy and decorum is obviously western-oriented. However, there are other Christians who have made up their minds to break away from the so-called historic churches. (I prefer to call them mission-founded churches.) I believe that all churches constitute the catholic church which is historic, by which I mean "the church in the world." Even when a faction breaks away from the mother organization, the result is still the church (not sects) because there can only be ONE CHURCH in the world. Whatever the reasons for schisms in the church, Africa is now full of what are commonly referred to as "independent churches" led by people who experienced spiritual dissatisfaction in their worship. They break away from the mission-founded churches, and after a while they also experience a break away. It is an on going process. In a larger sense, break-aways are merely "sociological" but spiritually, there is only One Church with albeit diverse theological emphases and variety in polity, which makes them a good source of theology.

AFRICAN INDEPENDENT CHURCHES

The African independent churches are a major source of African theology. Independent churches have been defined as churches (which) represent a significant body of Christians who have already broken with the historic churches for a variety of reasons and who are in the process of adapting Christianity to thought patterns more in keeping with traditional Africa. Such churches decide what doctrine to embrace from the historic church, which rituals to employ to meet their needs, which sacraments to perform more regularly and how it should be done. These decisions influence their preaching, liturgy, rituals, teaching and ministry in general. Some of these independent churches withdrew initially from the mission-founded churches, which are linked with their "mother" churches in Euro-America. Some break away from other independent churches as we have noted earlier.

The indigenous churches enjoy their independence in many ways. The political and organizational structure that suits the socio-political needs is determined by themselves. Rome, or London, or New York has nothing to say about it. Such churches are also at liberty to determine what practices to adapt from the Christian tradition. They are free to compose and sing songs as they are inspired - very often using African traditional tunes and musical instruments. They were among the first to develop an Afrocentric hermeneutic and liturgical principles. Their list of items that demonstrate their freedom cannot be exhausted here. However, our current interest in these independent churches is that they provide theological insights based on, for example, traditional symbolism, values, proverbs and sayings that contribute to our knowledge of God.

One great concern of independent churches is to plant the gospel into their culture in such a way that the believers are comfortable to worship God more or less in a natural manner. For instance, some independent churches present Christ as one who takes the place of the traditional healer. For churches that have this "theology," the rituals they develop have symbolism such as a staff which is carried only by designated persons because it is sacred. Emphasis is on regular confession of one's sin in order to receive spiritual and physical healing through being tapped on the "heart" by the sacred staff. Couples who are unable to conceive are invited to present themselves to the "prophet" who is able to make the wife conceive by the ritualistic use of the staff. It is not difficult to preach a black Christ to these people because they "see" him every time! Also, that Christ liberates, forgives, blesses is common knowledge to such churches. Thomas Blackely, Walter Van Beek and Dennis Thomson in the book they edited make this point: "In the catechesis and liturgy of African churches, Christ is often referred to as the one true 'nanga [healer] because this is an image that the audience intuitively understands and at the same time is seen as rooted in scripture" (Van Beek and Thomson 1994, 79).

Indeed, the creativity with which most independent church preachers do their hermeneutics is such that most of their sermons turn out to be very Afrocentric. Their theology is the voice of the God of Africa speaking in an indigenous language to the people of the continent. These two authors are correct when they argue: "It can easily be shown that - at the level of folk theology - the n'anga symbolism is used over large areas of Sub-Sahara Africa. That paradigm is the medicine person, known in many Bantu languages by the "title n'anga or one of its cognates" (Van Beek and Thomson 1994,74).

Added to this paradigm are the ancestors, kinship, the community, totemism and a host of others. In sum, independent churches have reverted to indigenous God-concepts in order to experience God in truth and in spirit.

THE SCRIPTURES

The scripture is the most obvious source of theology in Africa, especially in the light of the emerging Afrocentric hermeneutics. By reading the scriptures for themselves, many believers are discovering truths which they had never heard from the missionaries' mouths. For this reason and others, we embrace the claim that the Bible is one major source for African theology. Of course, most Christian churches in various cultures also acknowledge the Bible as one of their major sources of theology. But we remind ourselves that, although we may all share the one source (the Bible), our interpretation may differ from one Christian context to another when the Biblical message is interpreted contextually. Most theologians agree that one's social context is bound to influence one's theological perspective. Or, one's perspective tends to influence one's theological interpretation of the Bible.

So, even if two preachers - one from a mission-founded church and another from an independent church - read the same passage from the same Bible, their sermons are least likely to be the same if their social contexts are different. Of course, this could be true with any two preachers, but our point here is that the difference between the two sermons is more likely to be contextual than exegetical or expository. In other words, what one preacher says from a given scripture passage is interpreted in the context and faith of one who is interpreting it. The original message is always there in the text, but when we come to the hermeneutics and application, a vast difference can manifest itself.

African theology is more closely related to the Biblical culture. Therefore, it is inevitable that most African scripture readers have predilection for the Hebrew culture. What an African understands from the scripture is determined by the one's cultural bias, which in turn influences and informs one's theological perspective.

The Bible also appealed to the African slaves in diaspora because when the Bible was introduced to them, they immediately identified with suffering slaves under the hand of the Pharaohs. More importantly, they met their Great Sprit God in the Old Testament readings. Thus, the scriptures continue to inspire the African believers as a viable source of theology. In sum, in each of these sources, there is a component that serves to connect or draw a relational thread which links the African believers to their Great Spirit God. That characteristic distinguishes African theology from all other theologies, Christian or traditional.

Chapter Two

African Theological Concepts of God

Theology is largely influenced by one's religio-cultural perspective and socio-economic context as well as by Scripture or revelation. Experience plays a major role in influencing one's particular concepts of God. Attempts to deal with, if not answer, economic, ontological, sociological and spiritual concerns often result in theology. A critical reflection on the African perceptions of who and what God is (as that is being constantly revealed to the people in various circumstances) is informative and necessary in this endeavor to construct concepts of God in a coherent way. This process is ceaseless because God continues to be. What God is doing also constitutes a major element of what ought to be the proper subject of theology. Also, we should always remember that any theological utterance need not be regarded as a conclusive statement on God. What God does is dependent upon and reflective of what and who God is. How any God-related data is interpreted depends on the community's experience and knowledge of God. Theology does not guide God; neither does it discover a hidden God if God were to hide. Rather, theology is our reflection on God's acts on what is happening in the world. It is against this backdrop that we attempt to articulate African perceptions of God. Following a definition of God, we will discuss the ultimate power of God, concluding with African American concepts of God that are both a carry-over and a modification of theology from the continent.

However, as an African I also believe that the African worldview could be our only foe as well as our friend in any theological enterprise. On the one hand, it could limit our perceptions of God to what we are culturally receptive; on the other hand, however, our conceptions could be broadened by insight from further reflection upon the cultural perspective. This is where African Christians need to constantly utilize the Bible, God's revelation of the Truth. Thus, what we know about God is revealed to us by God, the Great Spirit. Human reason serves to reflect upon and receive the revelation, albeit critically. Theology is then the construction and articulation of those insights in a coherent language in a manner that clarifies what God is saying. Again, our finite language could hinder the accurate expression of what our hearts and minds perceive of the Divinity's spiritual presence. However, it is not so much what we can do as what God chooses to do that is of ultimate consequence. God's aseity is inexhaustible. Furthermore, all attempts to define God fall short of the wholeness of God.

GOD IS GOD

The only discipline that can define God is theology, according to which one of the most comprehensive definitions of Great Spirit God is: God is God. God is that spiritual reality which is not only greater than, but sustains everything that constitutes the universe and beyond. God is Reality without a beginning or an end. God cannot be defined in terms of time, space or volume. The Shona of Zimbabwe have characterized this Spiritual Reality as Zimuyendayenda - a vast eternal Reality that transcends all and is not only imminent but forever eventual. The definition offered by Anselm that God is "that than which nothing greater can be conceived," merely points to humanity's idea of this Great Spirit God. It does not and cannot exhaust the essence of this Great Being. Anselm is counted among the world's greatest philosopher-theologians who made a tremendous contribution to Western philosophy and theology. It is highly unlikely that African beliefs were influenced by Westerners like Anselm because when the West was consumed in the debates and discussions relating to the question of the existence of God, Africans were already worshiping God who had revealed eternal divinity to them. Many serious thinkers admit that the conclusion the Westerners arrived at by use of the intellect is not necessarily discontinuous with what the Africans discerned primarily experientially but also cognitively and by faith. This theological coincidence is significant in spite of the fact that epistemology is culture-bound. We have to surmise that it is the universality of God rather than of human reason alone that connected the African awareness of Zimuyendayenda (God) and the Western consciousness of the same. This points to the TRUTH that transcends cultural diversity without sacrificing the integrity of particularity.

Anselm's statement expresses the general perception of who God is for the majority of Westerners, the Orientals as well as the Africans - both Christian and indigenous scholars. In my opinion, as I have implied above, it is unlikely that Africans borrowed Western philosophy or Westerners learned from the Africans who God is. That kind of communication was not available when Anselm made the statement. Anselm did not have contact with any African people regarding academic sharing of views. What is evident here is the apparent self-revealing phenomenon characteristic of the universal God. God does reveal divine glory to God's people everywhere. Anselm's statement, in my view, only gives a hint of who God is. It does not define God. Neither does it indicate a knowledge of, or an encounter with God.

African knowledge of God could enrich Christian theology today because Africans have long learned to approach the whole realm of God in spirit - first through their ancestral spirits, then through the Holy Spirit poured upon them by Christ who lives in spirit and truth. Africans acquire their awareness of God primarily experientially and also cognitively. The Ashanti proverb summarizes this well: "No one shows a child the Supreme Being". Professor Mbiti interprets this to mean "that everybody knows of God's existence almost by instinct, and even children know Him" (Mbiti 1970,38).

Do we still need to argue the belief that God's Godness is universal? To say God is "that than which nothing greater can be conceived" also means God is the Creator whose spiritual presence is universal. Many Africans believe that the statement about God subdues and transcends all creation in heaven and on earth. If there are creatures above the universe, they too, are rendered less than God because they owe their origin and existence to God although they may be above other creation. They may seem to be superior and may even be so on the hierarchy of creation. Yet God is greater beyond measure or comparison. This belief that no matter how great "heavenly" creatures may be, no matter how great some creatures of the sea may be, God is still greater, prepares the African believer to focus allegiance on God the Supreme Being in the face of various technological artifacts. All the African needs to establish in order to make the decision of who to worship is: is it a creature or is it God? If the answer is God, then the decision is made, followed by this instruction: Thou shalt not worship any "other" gods but God! (Deut. 6:4f). Also this spiritual discipline is re-enforced by traditional religious allegiance to one's ancestral spirit. It does not matter how great other people's ancestors are, one remains faithful to one's own because there is a relational bond between them. So, for the African, God is God because there is this non-negotiable creator-creation kinship bond. Many statements that attempt to postulate who God is signify that there was a time when everything that is created did not exist. Then this spiritual and intelligent reality we call God conceived and caused it to come forth! Using the Biblical imagery of God as the potter, God can give form to formlessness as the potter molds a vessel. Beyond what the potter can do, God brings anything into being out of nothingness (creatio ex nihilo)! This process from "nothingness" to somethingness" (or creation), has been labeled many things over the centuries in the Western World. In fact, not all philosophers attribute creation to God. Some do not even perceive any divine involvement in the whole event. Well, that would be very unAfrican because we cannot conceive of any other power or reality that has the capability to create the Universe.

While the Biblical tradition simply describes it as creation based on various myths, factions of the scientific age have explored several possibilities by which to give scientific accounts credibility but all has been in vain. For example, some attribute creation to the "Big Bang" theory, some call it "evolution," and a sector of the post-scientific age calls it "process." All these are attempts to describe the mighty work of bringing into being what was not - the transition from nothingness to somethingness.

I am persuaded to believe that God who is the original eternal living Being is therefore the source of all life since only God's aseity can be that way. God is the life-giving power which has been described by Paul Tillich as the "ground of Being." The Shona word which would attempt to accurately describe God, though still metaphorically, would be Manyuko - which I can translate for lack of better language as a "sourceless source" (or aseity) whose nature is to be, and serve as the cause of all that ever originated and existed. That first cause has no time reference. Thus God is conceived as Manyuko, because God is the author of life. Professor Mbiti expresses the thinking of most Africans when he writes:

> One of the titles by which the Akan refer to God, means "Excavator, Hewer, Carver, Creator, Originator, Inventor, Architect." They describe him as "the great Builder or Excavator who created the Thing; and as "He who alone created the World." These names emphasize God's position as the originator of all things. The one alone from whom they derive their architectural origin and shape. God is here pictured as the

artist of the Universe, carving it with omniscient skill and artistry (Mbiti 1970,45). (Appendix one lists various African names of God some of which express this description.)

Common among most African Christians is the belief that it is God alone who is the author of life even beyond temporal existence! Normally, when a person dies in a physical sense, the Western medical system generally closes the file, so to speak. But God resumes the individual's "file" at the spiritual level as life continues. Professor Kwesi Dickson one of Africa's Old Testament scholars is correct to say "Indeed, it might be said that in African thought death leads into life" (Dickson 1984, 193). African traditionalists like God, resume "the file." They have held this belief from time immemorial. Ancestology which was grossly misinterpreted by most foreign missionaries and anthropologists symbolizes a wealth of spirituality that could inform the Christian concept of "spirit christology" and trinitarian spirituality. Dr. D. E. Idoniboye, a Nigeria philosopher correctly pointed out that "the concept of the spirit in African metaphysics leads to a better understanding of the world around us" (Idoniboye 1973, 84). Suffice it to mention that the African concept of God does not allow time constraints to hinder the Godness of God since God is the Creator of everything including the commodity called time itself. Therefore I believe that it is not prudent to permit our finite concept of time to enslave our spiritual freedom to imagine the Godness of God.

Some Biblical witnesses, for instance, St. John, have endeavored to describe the beginning of timelessness, but such an attempt often leads people into difficulties. We experience difficulty in conceptualizing a timeless "beginning" because our minds are programmed to the calendar. Could it be mainly a matter of the language limitation, coupled with what finite minds can and cannot conceive? Or is it because we allow our finitude to narrow our visual capacity which only faith can stretch beyond the visual horizon?

Whatever the case may be, the African conception of the beginning is not adequately expressed by the phrase "in the beginning." I think it is difficult for the creature to be capable of conceptualizing the "ages" before time was created, because time is measured not only with but also by what was created. Prior to creation, "time", if there was time, might not have been a criterion or category for measuring anything. Also, the concept of "time" itself expresses a component of finitude even when we talk about eternity! The limitation I am pointing out has already been demonstrated by the whole calendar system, which describes time in terms of B.C.E. and A.C.E., before and after an event (the birth of our Lord

Jesus Christ). It seems to me that our time and language symbols are merely dots on "God's drawing board" with respect to the concept of <u>Manyuko</u>. The problem of time is further compounded with the tradition of linear mentality. However, on the whole it can be said that we Africans have a better tolerance of time. Whereas John Mbiti over exaggerated the matter when he said that Africans "have no concept of time," I would say we have a greater tolerance of time. This is the tolerance that gives us the view that both the "beginning" and "the eschaton" can at least be conceptualized as unfolding gradually.

What is important for Africans when thinking about the "beginning" of Creation is not to focus on time in terms of the calendar but to visualize the creator's power, potential and wisdom which transcends time and caused the beginning to eventuate. The mystery to reflect upon is how the Universe is such that it functions the way it does. This is what impresses the African believer in reflecting on: "in the beginning." Thus the believer is filled with a sense of awe, wonder, and amazement, and joins the Psalmist in the words: "O Lord, our Lord, how majestic is your name in all the earth!" Our imagination aided with revelation helps us to perceive God through God's own industry and technology.

In discussing our understanding of God, much of what can be said about the Divine derives from our attributes of God which express the formation of our God-conceptions. What God has done and is doing here and everywhere also affirms these conceptions. Consequently, our concepts are not abstract or merely speculative but experientially based on concreteness. They are based on what God has done, not on what the community idealizes in a God language completely divorced from reality. So, to understand who God is leads to characterizing God as the spiritual intelligence that creates, sustains, and preserves the whole Universe. God is an "actionful" Reality, a positively oriented force, a Reality we have to contend and reckon with because it defines our entire existence. Hence, we simply state: God is God. And of course, any attribute or any statement about who God is can only give us some understanding of who God really is provided that the statement we make is informed by revelation as well as any other sources at our disposal including the African worldview. However, we must always remember that any attributes tell us what God can do, or what God is not, but they never name the essence of God. At best we get partial information. For instance, to say: "God is the Creator," or "God is a Great Spirit" does not exhaust the essence of God. Africans, however, know who God is by admitting how much there is about God that they do not and CANNOT KNOW! This is part of the essence of African epistemology. That for us expresses part of who God is. Once an American friend told me: "Gwin, as long as you can count how much money you have, you aren't wealthy yet!" So it is with our knowledge of God. We are to know our God by how much more there is about God that we do not know in spite of God's revelation through Jesus Christ (Incidentally, I am not advocating "ignorance is bliss philosophy"). Not at all.

What this epistemology means is that Africans cannot make an exhaustive statement about who God is because such would be an understatement. We do not advocate the extreme. What we have said here is not to be misconstrued to mean that God is totally unknowable. We have faith in God because God has chosen to reveal God's own self to us for this purpose primarily, i.e. that we may know God. However, knowledge of God is different from scientific knowledge of an <u>object</u> (Isaiah 55:8-9). Unlike our scientific knowledge, the knowledge of God increases our spiritual self-awareness and cognizance of our finitude. In other words, we cannot "master" God through our knowledge of God. To know God is to understand the true definition of life and that which gives a humanizing orientation to life. We know God in part in order to gain some perceptions on where we originate from and our destiny, all of which is contained within the meaning of "God" when this is defined as our <u>Manyuko</u>. Put differently, the better we know ourselves, the more we begin to understand who God is. Such knowledge liberates us from finite anxieties and suffering, because then we receive knowledge that comes from God. In God, we have our security because we are within God whose <u>aseity</u> ensures us eternal life. Outside of this state of being, there is fear and consequent self-destruction and ultimately spiritual death-that is death to God, (complete detachment from the Source of life.) God through Jesus Christ is the only Savior because God alone can draw humanity out of its habitual narcissistic tendency. Thus life is more purposeful when one believes in God because it is God who not only creates, gives, sustains, saves but provides it. However, this anthropological perspective is not to be misconstrued as self-contained in and of itself. It can only be developed in the light of who God is as Creator.

THE MENDE MYTH

The teaching that God is the transcended Spiritual Being seems to arise from peoples like the Mende of Sierra Leone who believe that God has removed God's own self from among human beings because human activities usually tend to be inconsistent with the life and nature of the Divinity. Of course, the Mende had to conjure up a myth which expressed for them a deist understanding of the nature of God (see our discussion of the Mende in chapter 5). Myth attempts to explain who God is but cannot exhaust the subject because, in my view, the moment we think we have "fully" defined God, we would not be talking about <u>Zimuyendayenda</u> (ever being transcendent God). The finite cannot grasp the infinite in its entirety because it is impossible unless through revelation. Note that the Mende have given us a perspective different from that of Western Christianity regarding the relation of the first people to God, their Creator. The Mende are described in the myth as so <u>obedient</u> to and <u>dependent</u> on God that they always asked God for deliverance, strength, guidance, and material supplies, and they always worshiped God the Creator. God withdrew from them because God was "worn out" according to their myth! God wanted them to exercise freedom with responsibility as they enjoyed full dependence on God. It is my view that this paradox has more profound meaning than the paradox where the creature and creator seem to engage in an endless battle, with the creature apparently having it his or her way all the time.

The Mende give us a fresh approach to the doctrine of the original sin because according to their understanding, the first family of human beings was not expelled from the presence of God (or from the Garden of Eden as the biblical myth has it). Rather, it is God who decided to make Godself hidden to humanity as humanity became increasingly dependent upon God, just as God can choose to reveal Godself when humanity is groping in the dark! To say God "withdrew" tends to distort the African concept of an omniscient and omnipresent God. Rather it would appear that as humanity became more narcissistic and completely surrounded itself with self-love, it lost sight of Divine presence which is always there to gird the entire universe including humanity!

Viewed this way, God continues to be universal (omniscient and omnipresent); God's initiative is forever at humanity's disposal, and the challenge remains before us. Since there is death (i.e. there is no life) outside of God, if such an 'outside' were conceivable, the African elders decided that wisdom lies in seeking permanent, spiritual contact with God. Whereupon God in Jesus Christ re-revealed God's own self in order not only to save us but to assure an eternal kinship. Appearing in the form of humanity like us, God has drawn our attention significantly. In other words, God as creator wished for God's creation to mature and be independent, within God's love. This, I believe, portrays quite a different picture of God, and it also indicates a continued relationship, since kinship is not temporary, with God always taking the initiative.

Furthermore, the Mende myth possibly gives us a clue to why the African church is growing rapidly today. Simple. Africans are responding well to God's initiative. The operative phenomenon is that God is revealing Godself to humanity which is constantly seeking God's blessings, making alien the idea of a remote God, or deism.

This view implies a rather sharp contrast to the commonly held Western view that "man is rebellious" against God. Such is not the "God-humanity" relationship in our theology. Paul Tillich refers to "sin" as "the power of estrangement from our true being" (Tillich 19,225). It may very well be that Tillich, a theologian of culture, is speaking for his race. The Caucasian Westerners tend to be rebellious against God to the point where they postulate the death of God! But that is not the case with the majority of African believers, including the African American people in Diaspora whose clear form of rebellion is against any dehumanizing social forces such as slavery, racism, and oppression. And God has taken sides with us as God would with the suffering of the world, regardless of race (Exodus 3:1 and Luke 4:18-21).

I perceive a serious lack of consistency in a theology which argues that humanity-(God's best creature!, made a little lower than the angels [Psalm 8:1-9])-is by "nature" rebellious to its creator. To contend that humanity is rebellious "by nature " is to imply a flaw in creation which would be a commentary on the Creator. What God created was GOOD (Genesis 1:31). Our African concepts of God do not depict a Creator God who could make errors, as it were, mistakes that went unchecked! (Isaiah 55:8-9). For the same reason, I no longer accept the whole doctrine of original sin. Unfortunately time and space do not allow me to debate it here. It needs a separate treatment, especially in the context of the doctrines of Grace, Creation, Omniscience and God's foreknowledge.

The God-humanity relationship exists because God as Creator necessarily enjoys the prerogative and initiative to reveal Godself to us whenever God wishes to communicate a vital message, or to conceal God's own self by virtue of God's invisible presence and mystery. Furthermore, this explains why and how it is that God takes the initiative to reveal Godself, not humanity. It is indeed a mystery that no matter how much humanity may want to physically see God, it may only succeed if God decides to reveal Godself in God's grace. Again this makes God

God, in spite of God's own revelation recorded in the Scripture. In other words, one may say God is always available to us on God's own terms for the purpose of meeting our need.

This reminds us how impossible it is for humanity to manipulate God, and how any claims to "fully define" God must be at best too ambitious, if not sheer vanity. Unless we accept "the mystery," we may be tempted to "create" a god whom we can "fully define" and still attribute mystery to the god. Many 21st century theologians are likely to fall into this trap, especially in America and Europe where almost any phenomenon must be interpreted in terms of science and technology-not mystery. African believers actually expect God to be "mystery" and they have a problem understanding the "Godness" of God without the element of mystery. In fact, the African tends to attribute to God anything which must be characterized as "mystery' since God is the ultimate mystery.

Also, because God and the first human communities "lived" in harmony according to various African and Semitic traditional myths, the human soul deep down longs to be with God. Consequently, ideally, humanity should keep searching for God. What I am saying is probably what St. Augustine's <u>The Confessions</u>* refers to when he discusses the soul's search for the beatific vision.

Therefore, we are more inclined to believe that the first human beings (whether they committed particular sins which undoubtedly must have occurred, or not) were not rebellious against God, as we are told by most Western theologians and preachers. The Adam and Eve Story is blown out of proportion. My view is, when this couple sinned, God continued to sustain them while they were yet sinful. I concur with the view that sin is primarily a human to human as well as human to God matter. For instance, with reference to the sin of racism or oppression, that God has not "zapped" the oppressor does not indicate God's approval of the status quo. God continues to sustain the sinful oppressors as God does with everyone else. In fact, it seems that God even blesses them (of course not for being oppressors), but because it is God's nature to sustain creation. However, it is also possible that some oppressors may not attribute their blessings to God but to their own wisdom and hard work. There are others who believe that what they are doing is in accordance with God's will if they prosper, and it is against God's will if misfortune befalls them. In Africa, "everyday the Nandi pray to God for the safety and prosperity of their cattle" (Mbiti 1975, 65). God is involved in every aspect of the African people. Dr. Paris is correct to note: "scholars have always agreed that religion permeates every dimension of African life"

(Paris 1995, 27). To add on to this, a leading African scholar also said: "secularity has no reality in the African experience" (Mbiti 1970, 203). Evidently all this seems to point to the question and meaning of God's involvement in human affairs. God has the primary responsibility to sustain life. However, this does not mean God is indifferent to humanity's sinful ways. Through the Scriptures we already know how God has judged oppression, murder, injustice and all sin. We should not confuse God's forgiving nature for moral permissiveness. God is good. Africans believe in this God who acts in history, a God of history, a God who intervenes, a God who expects moral people.

We create a vast false theological canyon, I think, when we indicate that when the first human beings sinned they were thrown out of the Garden and had to fend for themselves! As Jesus revealed it, God does not throw sinners out. Rather, it is SIN that God hates. I contend that there cannot be existence apart from divine sustenance! Furthermore, God does not sustain us because we are righteous but because we are God's creation whom God loves unconditionally. This is the meaning of John 3:1b: "God so loved the world...", a message the church has short-circuited by defining "believe in him" to mean joining the Christian church and not belief in God who transcends church walls.

However, the nature of our life is such that our lifestyle and our thinking are not the same as God's (Isaiah 55:8-9). We spend much of our life living differently from how God lives; and although God has given us the knowledge to distinguish between good and evil, we still frequently fail to live righteously. We should not blame our failure on God, (which we do if we believe that humanity is evil and rebellious by nature). Rather God's presence (if we are aware of its gracious nature) always makes us realize who we were created to be and to who we ought to turn in order to live eternally beyond our narcissistic cocoon.

The sad truth is we often choose to disobey God in the interest of pursuing our own whims! This gives us a basic notion of what sin is-departure from communion with God, alienating ourselves from the source of meaningful life. Sin is unbelief. In the process, naturally, our intended communal life with God is strained so much that we tend to end up living "as if there was no God." Sin also leads us to harm our humanity, consequently threatening our own peaceful existence. To use street language: sin is when humanity "stink." In short, sin destroys life. Theologically speaking, humanity is lost into extinction and non-existence when it attempts to live outside the Divine WORD, i.e. living in communal and sustaining relationship with God. Once humanity loses kinship with the Creator, it is dead. This is the result of unbelief. Unbelief becomes so serious that the very idea of the presence of God becomes extinct in our consciousness. Ironically, at that point, it is the creature (rather than the Creator) which dies (and stinks!). By "death" here, I mean becoming spiritually detached from God who is the "ground of our being," as Paul Tillich would say. Thus we die many times and the spirit of God that is life giving and vitalizing constantly re-vamps (draws) us from our state of death. By the way, most theologians would agree that only God can bring the "dead" back to life again in this sense. No one can bring oneself to life. Only God can because God is the restorer of life. This is why the Psalmist says: "He (the Lord, my shepherd) restores my soul" (Psalm 23).

DEATH AFTER LIFE

Death after life occurs when a human being ceases to be "human" and becomes "inhuman" by totally detaching the self from <u>Manyuko</u>. In spiritual terms, when a person detaches the self from the <u>source</u> of life that person is dead. The Shona would say, for instance, "Mahachi is no more." Since it is God who takes the initiative to seek and find such non-persons like Mahachi from their lost state (our death state), God through God's grace redeems the dead and re-instates completely. Even after our spiritual death, God as life-giver can re-instate life (Isaiah 1:18).

In spite of this effort on God's part, some people continue to stray all their life until their physical death (which is a given for every human being). Then the soul has to encounter God's glory which is what the Christian scriptures refer to as the Judgment Day (Matthew 25:1f). Hence, from an African traditional view, though a decisive event, physical death is regarded not as an evil because it is merely an ontological metamorphosis.

ONTOLOGICAL METAMORPHOSIS

This process (death) is a critical spiritual event which brings closest to us the feeling of total dependence on God the giver of life. Africans believe that death is a sacred state because the spirit is in the presence of God in a special context, different from the everyday presence of God in our temporal life. Most people tend to revere the human spirit when it has taken on this new relationship with God. Of course, many do this out of fear and awe. But death brings us closest to the meaning of a holistic life as mortal beings in the presence of the immortal Being.

In all cultures death is a common occurrence, which God has ordained in God's justice and human ontology. Every human being ought to experience what I call ontological metamorphosis. I realize this view is not popular at all, but the fact is, all human beings must ultimately resume the original spiritual state and commune life with God, where they will live eternally with the Creator. So, death is ideal because it is our only way ordained by God for us to "return to our point of origin," (a complete cycle). The completion of this cycle culminates in perfection. This thinking again confirms the significance of non-lineal concept of life and existence. Lineality signifies an eventual destination whereas cycle denotes endlessness or perfection. It also signifies eternity. This is the essence of the African concept of death-eternal life. Perhaps I need to caution my readers that this view of death does not necessarily negate the goodness of life. If it seems like it relegates life, it is only because this approach to death is too difficult not only to conceptualize but to accept.

Death is really humanity's major turning point on its ontological journey to the state of eternal living. In this state, (death) it is no longer possible for the individual to defect. It is the beginning of a steady communal spiritual life with God. Such existence is characterized by spiritual permanency in the state of perfection. The question is: how does one get on this path to perfection?

THE DEATH-LIFE THEORY

Over many years of talking about death, I have developed a death-theory. Here it is. Every day in our life, unconsciously we are actually seeking the location on earth where our spirit enters God's Great Spirit, wherein to inherit eternal life. When we situate ourselves most strategically in order to engage the ontological metamorphosis and return to "the place of origin," that is when death happens. Now this theory assumes that death is an integral part of life within which, in context of God's aseity, human life secures an eternal beginning to which there is no end. This theory does not espouse a philosophy of determinism but a sense of culmination. Included in this theory are all forms of death including accidental, suicidal, and natural.

All deaths by natural cause including illness and old age fit into this theory. One reason that leads our thinking to this theory is that one notices that when one "escapes" death, say from an automobile accident, what would have killed one tends to cease to be regarded as evil, but if one gets hit then it becomes an evil. By this we really mean that death is evil, but I have indicated in this book that it is not. According to my theory, it is the result, not what causes it that is evil. But if we pursue that thinking to its logical acme, namely that death is only a "change of status" on our ontological journey to perfection, and since perfection is the highest good, then death is most ideal.

According to this theory, no one knows the time when death comes under normal circumstance. Blaming death on the devil or God is simply humanity's way of expressing fear of death which most people generally regard negatively. Furthermore, this theory does not allow us to associate death with pain or anything negative because not everything that is painful is negative for instance hard work, childbirth pain is not to be regarded as evil. Furthermore, we experience pain only in life, not in death. That God in Jesus Christ brought back Lazarus' life does not mean God did not approve of death (John 11:17-44) as we hear from most Christians. God's miracle and "parable" of bringing Lazarus to life actually means bringing him to God in the very presence of all who were there! We have just argued above that real death is life away from God who is "the ground of all being". So here, God in Jesus, calls Lazarus to come to Him. That is the point of that holy incident! In fact, the Lazarus incident is the apparatus of the theory I am proposing here.

The event was intended to communicate the message: God in Jesus said, "Lazarus come forth!" Come to whom? To God! Yes, we also hear that Jesus wept for Lazarus because he loved him (John 11:35). As a true human being and Very God, Jesus was filled with compassion. So, he cried because he empathized with all who were present including Lazarus's sister Mary and the rest of the family. Again this reveals God's never-failing presence even beyond death. (Note that this interpretation is based on an Afrocentric exegesis.)

When Jesus was on the cross he also cried as any normal human being might have. Life on the cross was painful. But Christians believe that death on the cross was a blessing to all humanity, because when death came to Jesus, there was no more crying, no more pain..."for the former things have passed away!" So Jesus Christ of Nazareth cried until his life went through the ontological metamorphosis into a peaceful state. Also, Jesus himself uttered: "It is finished" - getting ready to move on. He did not cry because death was evil or more powerful than God on whom he was totally dependent and in whom he was fully secure. His crying expressed his humanity as did his death.

Finally, in addition to the forgiveness of sin on Good Friday, the goodness of death becomes apparent in the resurrection. According to our theory of death, Christ's death was good because his blood would cleanse the sins of the world; death for each of us is good also, though for a different reason. It brings us into an ideal spiritual communion with God, a state that we hardly reach in our physical life.

This understanding of the importance and goodness of this ontological metamorphosis has been suppressed throughout the Christian tradition in the West because its meaning is very bitter to human beings. Yet, I believe it is the only truly meaningful explanation of why every person must die no matter how saintly, rich, young, professional, famous, committed to family or loving anyone may be. Also, we have seen some people we think should not outlive the saints, but they do by the grace of God! According to our theory, then, death does not have anything to do with evil overpowering God. Those who have a problem with God's omnipotence experience difficulty because they are dealing with a wrong premise. (See below). With reference to Jesus' death, the reader is invited to regard it as an inseparable aspect of Jesus' life. Furthermore, we do not need to measure faith or lack of faith on the basis of longevity of life. Most people would like a long life. However, only those who know the true meaning of death according to this theory, sing: "And I can't feel at home in this world anymore!"

When Christians grasp this truth about death, they will cease to mourn as if they do not believe in the God and Lord of life and death. They will even begin to appreciate the variety of ways in which we all "cross the river Jordan" and resume life in our original spiritual transcendent communion with God.

Of course, the truth of the matter is that our sentiments for this life tend to frustrate us and make us even more miserable. No wonder Buddhism teaches the Four Noble Truths according to which once we overcome our self-imposed suffering we are set free to enjoy Nirvana. As I have cautioned the reader earlier, all this is not to deny the beauty and fullness of our temporal life. Rather, this theory seeks to extend the beauty of life into eternity! This theory affirms the wholeness of life sustained by God's aseity which alone can transcend all finitude and invite us into eternity.

GOD: THE ULTIMATE POWER

One attribute that has been challenged lately by some Western scholars is the claim that: God is all-powerful. According to Langdon Gilkey, theologians like Hartshorne deny "the absoluteness and aseity of

God in every respect: God's perfection and even God's necessity do not involve God's absoluteness;" and Whitehead argues that "in order that God be good and we be free... God must be radically distinguished from the principle of ultimate reality, from the force and power of reality......" (Gilkey 1984, 77-78). Gilkey also notes that according to these process thinkers,

> Thus finitude of God, in the sense that God is not the source of finite reality in all its aspects but rather that God is only one of a number of correlated and primal ultimate "factors" constitutive of finite actuality, is not asserted by a most important school of contemporary Christian theology. Needless to say, this is new in the tradition (Gilkey 1984, 78).

In my opinion, these process philosophers' definition of God and evil may have necessitated this conclusion which many Christians including myself find difficult to accept because of the traditional definition of who God is and also because the argument advanced by these philosopher-theologians does not seem to be persuasive. What has persuaded the process philosopher-theologians to define God does not move me to look for another way to define God. I think that God cannot be defined adequately by just what humanity expects God to do but that and also by what God expects humanity to do in situations where people are asking the wrong questions and expecting their own pre-conceived answers. My plea to all believers has been well expressed by theologians who have argued: "let God be God!" For this reason, I feel more comfortable with this definition: God is God.

However, many theologians still uphold the traditional view that God is all-powerful (omnipotent) in spite of the difficulty they face in trying to explain why God does not, in their opinion, intervene when things are not going well for God's people. I have heard many bereaved people protest angrily against God: "If God is all-powerful, God should have not allowed this disaster to happen!" Since these words come out of people who are experiencing great pain, anger, desperation, and hopelessness, maybe we should not take them literally. It could be the human way of crying: "My God, my God, why have you forsaken me" (Matthew 274b) But more critically, these words reflect humanity's limited definition of what it means to say God is all-powerful.

Certainly "all-powerful" does not mean only operating within our human definition of power. If "all-powerful" means God operates according to how God chooses to, then we need to seek to understand what God wills, rather than expecting God to do only what we can understand, worse still, what we desire. After all, human desires are often self-deceptive and transitory. We do not know what we really desire! We make a serious error if our judgment of who God is, is based on what we want in life. Our sense of pleasure or pain cannot be the criterion by which God is defined because these are creation and God is the Creator! Furthermore, being "all-powerful" does not cause or compel God to do anything but only makes it possible for God to act at God's own judgment and free will.

In discussing God's omnipotence in connection with death in particular, since most people rank death highest on the list of evils humanity experiences (Also, we have just made a serious critique of death in the foregoing pages), it is appropriate to bring it to its logical conclusion. The power of death only lies in God's power because God is the Lord of death.

Why does God not protect humanity against what humanity regards as its ultimate "enemy"-death? It seems to me that God could have created us in such a way that we would not have to experience ontological metamorphosis. If it is true that angles do not die, it means that God could create beings which are capable of living eternally (Genesis 16:7-16) without change of status. So, dying is not something that God could not deal with in order to show not only God's power but mercy and justice. Therefore, "death" is simply an inappropriate phenomenon and criterion by which to assess God's omnipotence, justice and mercy. Also, according to the Bible, man was not initially created as mortal. In fact, before the fall from grace there was no death! There are more challenging forms of God's power such as creating the Universe, being God, being eternal, to mention a few.

Many have argued that most deaths are caused by natural law. For example, if I fell from the twentieth floor of a high-rise building and splashed straight on the pavement, it is most likely that I would die on the spot! Or if a hungry wild lion saw an elderly religious woman praying under a tree, it would most probably devour her and she would die that way with prayer on her lips! What would stop death from occurring in either of these cases? If death did not occur in either case, we would conclude that it was nothing but a miracle-the supernatural work of God, as was the case with Daniel in the lions's den (Daniel 6:16). In fact, if the natural thing did not happen, namely dying on the pavement and dying in the mouth of a hungry lion, respectively, that would also be a manifestation of God's power! Those who do not accept the concept of "supernatural" events will spend as long a time as it would take to establish a scientific explanation. As for the majority of Africans, it has always been the tendency among believers to designate as divine mystery or protection by the spirits, any events that are beyond finite comprehension. It may well be the case! But do all mysteries originate with God? Should all mysteries be used to explain what God is doing in history? Could there not be other sources of mystery which have no bearing on God? A positive answer to these rhetorical questions would be quite reasonable if we acknowledge that mystery is not only defined by what we cannot understand or explain.

According to the Shilluk belief, what they cannot account for is explained as the work of Juok (God) as we have noted earlier. Rather than conclude that Juok does not have ultimate power, they attribute ultimacy to God because the definition of God entails ultimacy. Many African communities share this view. The Lele attribute all the complicated events to their Mingehe (spirits which have always been spirits since their creation) whose angel-like function is to perform certain "supernatural" works which humanity cannot handle or account for. Such work is believed to be still too mundane to attribute to God. The tendency among these communities is that mysterious phenomena, to which the West would quickly assign a scientific explanation, are generally attributed to the Mingehe. Anything beyond that is attributed to Njambi (God) who is believed to be all-powerful. That belief is held in spite of everything else that goes wrong in the world. For most of these communities, it is inconceivable that there could be any form of existence greater than God.

To attribute everything to God means that God must provide solutions to even mundane problems according to our finite desire, definition and conception of reality. We need to bear in mind that God is not accountable to us but to Godself which is the meaning of aseity or Manyuko. Even what appears to most people as destruction or evil (e.g. accidental death of a young father or mother leaving toddlers without support), needs to be conceptualized as originating from human finitude. I agree with Professor Peter Paris, a leading African American ethicist that "it is important to point out that whenever they (Africans) were faced with suffering of any kind, traditional African peoples became preoccupied with the quest for relief: a two-directional search that centered on God as the agent of relief and on themselves and others as the cause of their misfortune" (Paris 1995, 45). Thus, from God Africans expect only goodness. Paris continues: "evil is thought to have its origin in human wrongdoing, which in turn cause some form of imbalance to occur between the human community and the realm of spirit" (Paris 1995, 45).

Like the spirit world, God is consistently Divine and God's ultimate power is used for the good of all. God will not self-destruct, or contradict or have second thoughts on God's own work.

We run into a serious theological problem when we define God in such a manner that God's thoughts concur with our thoughts as a condition for God to be our God. God is God. Rather our thinking should concur with God's because God is our God, creator of the Universe. In his critical prayer while facing death, Jesus said, "Father, let this cup pass, but not my will but your will be done." Part of the purpose of the revelation of God in Jesus Christ is to enlighten us. For example, "Good Friday" is truly good not because Christ was crucified, but because the ultimate "God-act" - God sacrificing Godself and receiving the sacrifice - occurred for the benefit of all creation. If it were not for the "Sunday Morning News," (Luke 24:2-7), who would have made sense out of the crucifixion, death and burial of Jesus Christ given our very negative attitude toward death? Not many at all. In fact, some people still do not understand why Jesus, the Son of God, had to undergo the suffering and shame he experienced in his temporal life.

Another concern raised by the skeptic is: Why does the all-powerful God let people go through excruciating pain which many people sometimes endure when they are nearing their death? Again death is generally associated with pain, which as we have already pointed out, is illogical. It is interesting that people do not raise the same question about the pain usually related to the birthing experience. Could it be possible that it is because they appreciate that for which such pain is to be endured, namely having a baby? And yet "birthing pain" is rated most excruciating! So, as I have mentioned earlier, our understanding of death is basically influenced by our attitude toward it, which is negative. In this book the author contends that death is positive because it is part of the fullness of life for those who are liberated from narcissism, concupiscence and sin.

We experience the ontological metamorphosis in order to return to our original spiritual communal state which lasts eternally. To talk of "original spiritual communal state" does not mean that God is shut off from us in our temporal life. It means that in terms of the form of existence, we finally unite with God when we are in our spiritual state. For this reason, most Africans tend to be a spiritual people in this life anticipating the next, thus maintaining spiritual continuity and wholeness. This is what an African philosopher, D.E. Idoniboye, means when he says: "spirits are the one entity that remains constant in all African belief-systems" (Idoniboye 1973).

It is a common belief among Africans that life originates with God who is our <u>Manyuko</u>. Because God has invested the highest premium conceivable in humanity, God sustains humankind forever-that is through our temporal existence and spiritual eternal life. Consequently, in history we live in the presence of God, but in eternity we live in communion with God. (Living in union with the Divine is different from living in the presence of the Deity in that in the former we live in a state of sinlessness). That state of existence is irreversible. Also, in that form and state of existence, we participate in and identify with God's perfection in its fullness. Being in union with God is the real eternal life; being totally obedient to God is a life of the Kingdom! Thus humanity is potentially a reflection of God which is why God in Jesus Christ took on human nature in order to reveal the eschaton. In processing this, one has to be careful not to confuse the flow of logic. Humanity reflects God but God does not reflect humanity which was created in God's image. God created humanity but when humanity creates a god, that is idolatrous.

In a discussion on the African doctrine of God, we have to talk about death because in understanding our own spirituality we begin to comprehend God's spirituality which is a major dimension of the essence of the nature, character, and being of God. When we begin to understand who God is we understand ourselves more if we subscribe to the theology that we were made in God's image. We reiterate, image here has nothing to do with physical features! When God revealed Godself to us in a human and divine form the intention was that we understand ourselves in the light of the purpose for which God created us. This lays the ground for the possibility of fellowship and kinship with God in this life and that to come.

Thus God reveals God's nature to humanity in order to draw us to the kind of kinship spirituality exemplified and manifested in the Trinity: a life of not only community but communion, selfless love, sacrifice, gracious service, faithfulness, unity, "solidarity" and ultimate power. God unites with struggling people in their spiritual journey. And where two or three are gathered in the name of God, in the pursuit of life of which only God is the author, ultimate liberation is achieved and guaranteed. Thus God constantly draws us to God's own self, in order that we discover our wholeness. We have to lose ourselves to God in order that God may install us to the fullness. God is our point of life-orientation because God is <u>Manyuko</u>.

When our humanity is at the verge of self-destruction, we can regain our personhood by reverting to the source (God) who restores our soul and provides a re-orientation. Once that illumination sparks in the individual, its momentum towards freedom is not only resumed but accelerated. Liberation originates with God when God's spirit "opens windows" within us and it culminates in God in whom the ontological metamorphosis reaches perfection. In most cases political, racial or cultural protest are outward manifestations of the inward struggle for spiritual liberation which originates from God's spirit which offers us total freedom. The presence of God that liberates also sustains persons especially under extreme pressure. A case in point is the dehumanizing conditions of slavery such as were experienced by the African slave community in the middle passage and in the American colonies. This people developed a concept of the liberating and caring God due to what they experienced during and after slavery. Paris correctly says of Africans everywhere: "Their Christian belief that God wills that the good of all peoples should be realized in community (that is in harmony with others) is both commensurate with and expensive of the African traditional understanding of God" (Paris 1995, 45).

SOME AFRICAN AMERICAN CONCEPTS OF GOD

Any discussion on the African concepts of God must also include how Africans in Diaspora (African Americans in North America and the islands) perceive God because their God-concepts originating from the continent were put to test during plantation slavery in North America. For the most part, African American concepts of God are essentially the same as the African with only contextual variations necessitated what the suffering slaves went through including the dehumanizing conditions of racist America which still persist in North America. Professor James Cone, a major voice not only in black theology but third world theologies, devoted a whole chapter in his book to a discourse on black peoples' doctrine of God (Cone 1970).

From the very beginning of that chapter to the end, all African American theological scholars agree with black theology's presupposition that God is a Spiritual Reality, and not just some nebulous spiritual entity. Black theology has been defined by its architect this way: "Black theology is an attempt to analyze the nature of that reality, asking what we can say about the nature of God in view of his self-disclosure in biblical history and the oppressed condition of black people" (Cone 1970, 107). Cone immediately refers to "God and his (sic) participation in the liberation of the oppressed of the land..." (107) because he believes that the living God acts on behalf of the oppressed and the dehumanized in history. Not only is this position biblically based, it is highly political and revolutionary. Black theology believes in a God of Power. God is the ultimate power to whom black people appeal. If African Americans did not believe that their God had ultimate power, they would not appeal to such a God for their liberation. The African Americans believe in a God who has a record of "setting slaves free"-the God who cares so much that liberation of the downtrodden is non-negotiable. This is the God who set the children of Israel free from the Egyptian bondage.

Because Cone speaks from the perspective of only the African people's experience in North America, doctrine of God and Jesus Christ his has been criticized for being rather racially exclusive. The author was consciously focusing on his own people's experience of God in order to speak from a particular social context. In connection with God's spark in the heart and mind of the suffering, Cone endorses our contention when he says "...for God has stirred the soul of the black community, and now that community will stop at nothing to claim the freedom that is 350 years overdue: (108). And once the Divine illumination occurs, nothing will hinder the dream from unfolding; not racism, not slavery, not ignorance, not even death upon the tree (whether lynching or crucifixion) would stop the will of God who said: "Let my people go." Note that the word "my" renders Cone's perspective in *God of the Oppressed*, both exegetically and hermeneutically appropriate.

Another black voice on the subject, Professor Major Jones, author of *The Color of God: The Concept of God in Afro-American Thought*, is correct when he says:

> In contrast to Western psychological and theological ideas that set God apart as the Totally Other, Black Theology has concerned itself less with the question "Does God exist, and how?" than with the question "Does God care?" God-talk within the Black religious tradition has spoken of God as coextensive. The nature of God in the Black religious experience is both to "be" and to "let be" (Jones 1987, 21).

The character of the God of the African American is the same as that of the African in that caring for the suffering is a priority. There is an experiential kinship between God in Diaspora and people on the African continent. This is not by coincidence. The people of African descent have faith in a God who guarantees them security and protection. I agree with Dr. Paris that: "One of the most important marks of continuity between Africans on the continent and those in the Diaspora is their common belief in a transcendent divine power primordially related to them as the creator and preserver of all that is" (Paris 1995, 33). Most Africans are not deistic in their theological outlook because God is not just transcendent but transcending, revolutionizing human conditions that need to be transformed (Exodus, 3:f). In fact, the majority of African American theologians do not believe in a theistic or deistic God who removes Godself from the people who God loves so much that God paid a very high premium in Jesus Christ. Africans on the continent and in Diaspora believe in a God who hears the cry of God's suffering people and comes down and not only set them free but provide their "daily needs." This is how God makes Godself known. That is why African Americans believe that God has power - power to deliver! The African community in Diaspora, like the rest of the Africans on the continent, worships a God who not only deliberates but also liberates the people from dehumanizing living conditions of racism, oppression and marginalization. Theirs is a God who acts justly and with MIGHT.

In our African spirituality, we decidedly believe in a God who acts in history because ours is a living God. For instance, Cone talks of

> "the reality of the biblical God who is actively destroying everything that is against the manifestation of human dignity among black people...'" a God who "has stirred the soul of the black community...."; a God who "has decided to make our liberation his own" (Cone 1970, 108-9).

Black theology believes in "a God of revolution who breaks the chains of slavery" (Cone 1970, 112) and colonial thrones throughout the African continent. This is also the God who, for the Africans, causes rain to fall, wind to blow, and the sun to shine-a God who is pro-life in its wholeness, i.e. both spiritual and physical.

The doctrine of God according to African American black theology, teaches this:

> The destiny of black people is inseparable from the religious dimensions inherent in the black community. One theological way of describing this reality is to call it general revelation. This means that all men have a sense of presence of God, a feeling of awe, and it is precisely this experience that make men creatures who always rebel against domestication. The black community is thus a religious community, a community that views its liberation as the work of the divine... (Cone 1970).

God created African people to be free to become who they can be though they have been forced to live in diaspora. The point of this lengthy quotation is to make it clear that for African people in Diaspora as well as on the continent, God is a part of the community with which God has a kinship relationship which nothing can ever disentangle, no, not even enslavement or colonization. God is a reality present among us! God is powerful because of what God has done and can do. African attributes of God express what God does and so indicate who God is. Indeed, God is the lifeline of those who are made to suffer because of the color of their skin. Thus, in God, the black community has a foretaste of eternal life, a feeling which inspired the "Negro spirituals", as well as the blues! In *The Spiritual and the Blues*, Cone says:

> To be a child of God had present implications. It meant that God's future had broken into the slave's historical present, revealing that God had defeated evil in Jesus' crucifixion and resurrection. The black slave could experience now a foretaste of that freedom which is to be fully revealed in the future (Cone 1972, 92-3).

According to Cone, the black scholars' hermeneutical principle for the African understanding of God is quite different from the general protestant interpretation espoused, for instance, by Karl Barth or Paul Tillich. Although Cone agrees with these white theologians as far as the biblical truth that Jesus Christ is the Son of God, thereafter, there are critical points when there are radical differences. For instance, Cone parts ways with these white scholars the moment he articulates who God is, what God has done, and why Christ came to this earth! Although these theologians use the same source-the Bible-their theologization is influenced by their social context. For Cone: "the point of departure of Black Theology is the biblical God as he (sic) is related to the black liberation struggle" (Cone 1972, 115). Blacks know God because God remembers them and struggles with them in their battles for liberation. Tillich and Barth would not share Cone's point of departure, since they have never experienced the marginalization, oppression and racism which Cone experienced..

Cone shares two hermeneutical principles which are generally operative in the construction of the doctrine of God by black people:

3. As a Christian theology, black doctrine of God arises from what the Old and New Testaments say about the

revealed God. We knew God through Jesus Christ who is the revelation of God. And we also know God whenever God chooses to reveal God's own self to us. The ideal that God has revealed freedom to be creative and to seek to fulfill God's purpose for creating humanity as an inseparable component of a full humanity is a goal that Black people seek to realize as did Christ.

4.   In black theology God is known because God is actively involved in the liberation of the oppressed blacks everywhere. This point is not unrelated to the first one. Because Jesus reveals how God cares for the oppressed, the suffering, and the poor, we can begin to understand who God is by living a life of faith in Jesus Christ. God in black Theology makes Godself known through God's work of the liberation of the oppressed (Exodus 3:1-22), which leads to a full humanity. Thus God is humanity's point of orientation because God is the author of life (Cone 1972).

It is because God is believed to be actively involved in the life and death of the black people that Cone refers to God as "black like us." Although Africans on the continent do not ordinarily talk of a "black" God or an "African" God, they do not conceive of a God who is not dedicated to their welfare. Africans talk of a God who is a Spirit Being just as their ancestor spirits identify with them in their spirit state. Thus there is a concrete identity between God and God's people. Africans talk of "our God." They do not know a God who is not in solidarity with them. On the continent we cannot conceive of a God who does not identify with God's own creation. Regarding God's caring concern, Dr. Paris also supports the understanding that "by maintaining distance from nature and humanity the deity manifests divine care" (Paris 1955, 30). Therefore, for us God is a Great Spirit with whom our ancestor spirits team up and commune in providing for our needs. In fact, the Mende of Sierra Leone name God "Ngewo," Great Spirit or Great Ancestor (Setiloane), because, as part of family the major function of ancestors is to fend for and protect the family.

In his book, *African Tradition and the Christian God* Fr. Charles Nyamiti also makes the point that "Another African factor from which the Christian could take much profit is the teaching that God is Ancestor"

(Nyamiti 1970, 16). The concept that God is our ancestor has great ramifications because ancestors are believed to have committed themselves to the welfare of the living. They also insist on good morals! Evil is punished.

Thus, the African American doctrine of God can be summarized in two words: God cares. This statement embraces the concept of an active God; a God who is with us; a God who is alive and one on whom we necessarily depend because God is all-powerful, omnipresent, and all knowing in a way only God can be! God is the <u>Manyuko</u> of all existence.

We have explored a significant range of similarity between the African doctrine of God and African American theology, discovering that both teach that God acts in history because God is, a statement based on experience. We have also mentioned that God is involved in seeing to the welfare of suffering humanity; God is inseparable from creation though the two have their own separate identities, with God as author. God is spirit who wills to bond together all African people in love and solidarity in their struggle to survive (in the case of the oppressed blacks in Diaspora).

With respect to solidarity, most African communities are united through their ancestral links and belief in a caring God. Africans in Diaspora are further unified by their common plight under the yoke of racist oppressors who dehumanize them because of or on the basis of the color of their skin. The white oppressive system in general seems to lack the humane capacity to understand how God can create blacks, whites, and yellows all in God's own image. Consequently the system claims to be superior, thereby unfortunately in fact, losing its status of equality by committing the sin of unfounded Pride (which gave rise to apartheid in South Africa, for instance). In *The Color of God: The Concept of God in Afro-American Thought*, Dr. Major Jones concurs with our view when he says:

> Both in African and Afro-American thought, God, as an "outstanding reality," has a central place, because he is equated with human existence itself. For Black people, aspiring to God is the same as aspiring to one's future, for the future is grounded in God's being (Jones 1987, 22).

This thinking has a direct link to African traditional belief in one's future as being together not only with one's ancestors but with one's offspring and God the Creator, all primarily in one dynamic spiritual existence." [Josiah U. Young has authored an important book entitled: *Black and African Theologies: Siblings or Distant Cousins*, 1986].

There are many other spiritual similarities between traditional religious beliefs and Judeo-Christian beliefs although many African Christians are hesitant to accept the fact because most have been spiritually disoriented by Western concepts. The African and African American concepts of time, presence, and reality all contribute to the African doctrine of God who is a Spiritual Living Being.

CONCLUDING OBSERVATIONS

To conclude this discussion on an African concept of God, a salient point needs to be reiterated, namely that most Africans believe in the One God who is a dynamic Spiritual Creator. They give God numerous names in different languages but all the names point to the same Reality. *(See the charts on African names of God). This is undergirded by the African philosophy of naming that an object or person is named because of what the object or person is, and not so that the object or person may become what it or the person is not. Something is named because it is that which it is. In the case of God, God is named because of who God is as revealed to us by God's own self. Consequently, the most adequate definition of God is: God is God.

One major reason that compels us to reckon with this point is that henotheism in Africa is not polytheism. Africans everywhere believe in One God who is the Spirit that sustains everything in the whole universe. A variety of names of God merely points to different ways of worshiping, knowing and relating to the Only One living God who is the ultimate reality. Put differently, God the Creator is the Ultimate and yet there is a plurality of human ways of acknowledging, naming, worshiping, and of course interpreting (theologies) that God. This diversity should not be tampered with even by systematic theologians who tend to be faithful to an argument, even at the expense of truths of ultimate Reality, if such truths do not seem to conform to the theologian's method and/or system of thought. In modern pluralistic society, Christianity has to be more than just ecumenical in its activities. The church must be at one with other religions whose God is identical with the Christian God, if it is to present God who revealed Godself through Jesus Christ. Jesus did not come pointing to himself but to God who is Spirit and Truth, Lord of the Universe. For all to become one flock under one shepherd (John 10;16), we have to recognize various theological and religious perspectives of God's mission to salvation. Moreover, if Christ is the ultimate revelation of God, as many Christians argue and believe, Christianity ought to "draw" together all the God-oriented believers rather than alienate them on the basis of a provincial theology and technical expression of the aith. Jesus instructs clearly in his words: "If they are not against, they are for us!"

True religion is not achieved only by teaching the unGodly in the name of the Christian religion, but by being just peaceful, Godly and loving a neighbor the way God says we ought. (Mark 12:31, James 2:8, Exodus 20:17). But how can there be peace when the oppressed are suffering at the hands of those who call themselves "Christian?"

Our cultural interpretation and expression of the Gospel does not need to prevent the good news from incarnating in other communities (John 10:16). Christianity cannot declare a monopoly on the theological interpretation of God. Worse yet, the Church in Euro-America should not assume the monopoly of not only the Word of God but even knowledge of God. A statement by a Protestant theologian, Professor Owen C. Thomas gives the impression that we can only know God through the Western culture, which is misleading. Apparently speaking on behalf of many Western theologians Thomas says: "We can approach the Bible only in the light of the history of Western culture from the first century to the twentieth century and especially in the light of the cultural situation of the present" (Thomas 1983, 54). I would have thought that in light of the present global state of the faith, every expression of faith in God needs to be heard because the Kingdom of God is amongst us (Luke 17:21), i.e., the whole Church and even beyond the walls of the Church.

The coming of high technology and materialism has tended to mislead many so-called First World nations into assuming that they can be independent of not only other human beings but even God; that they can control, invent, destroy, sustain, and preserve the material so well that they really do not need God if God does not seem to be accountable to them; that if they need a god, they can simply "assemble" one and worship a convenient god and then "disassemble" after use! Such idolatrous thinking must be displaced by the age-old belief and truth that there is One Living God and no other (Deut. 6:4). There is the only God who was first known and worshiped in Africa, and no other.

One hope that Christian traditional views juxtaposed with the African Christian and traditional beliefs in God, will complement and strengthen each other in their affirmation of faith, and thereby enrich the Church's God language and the believers' God-consciousness.

Hear ye oh universe, the Lord our God is One-East and West, South and North. How I wish that that divine unity would influence human beings into building one people with total obedience and commitment to God so that in the end, we are one people of the One God in our cultural diversity.

Chapter Three

God: The Soul of Our Spirituality

African spirituality is among major sources of theology in Africa South of the Sahara. It provides a rich spiritual creedal which calls for a careful theological formulation. Furthermore, there is a general consensus among scholars that there is a close resemblance between the Hebrew and African spirituality. Thus, spirituality as a source of theology compliments Scriptures - (another major source of theology) - the former arising from indigenous religion while the latter is the inspired word of God.

Usually there is tension between the Word of God and cultural practice, yet culture is the matrix within which the Word of God is planted. St. Augustine's treatises on, for example, "the original sin," "the trinity," "grace" or "baptism," were attempts to answer questions that were arising in the early Church vis-a-vis culture. Consequently, it is apparent that our spirituality is a major source for theology. African spirituality could be thought of as a "theocentric spirituality" because God is the center. Our spirituality begins and ends with God, the Great Spirit, God the source of life. It is for that reason that we have designated this chapter God: the Soul of our spirituality.

As a spiritual discipline, there is no better source of theology than African spirituality, interpreted and understood in the context of both traditional and Christian concepts. The entire spirit world, according to professor Michael Gelfand, author of *The Genuine Shona*, ultimately connects to God the Great Spirit. In enumerating all the spirits which constitute the spirit world of the Shona, Gelfand is absolutely right when he says: "all are under the great omnipotent God (Mwari)." (Gelfand 1973, 133).

Crucial to African spirituality is the presence of the spiritual in the material - a co-existence intended for a liberative purpose. The spirit embodies a host with a particular mission just as God incarnated in order to save humanity. Thus, African Christians understand, and in fact aspire to being "spiritualized" beginning in this life. The spirit world is welcome not just to but in us!

So, when the Lusaka declaration by the Church says "we no longer live for ourselves but we live for Christ who lives in us.," (A.A.C.C. Lusaka), what is at stake is an expression of African spirituality. The spirit of Christ and the Holy Spirit is welcome within us, for a divine purpose to be conceptualized through our spirituality.

The people of African descent are used to addressing their ancestor spirits as forefathers and foremothers, because the spirit world and the physical world belong together. So the African people (church) continue to relate to the living Christ not just because he rose from the dead but "because he lives." African spirituality renders the people spiritually receptive because "the words expressed by the possessed individual are derived from the spirit world and therefore constitute the truth" (Gelfand 1973, 13). So, when Jesus said: "The spirit of the Lord is upon me..." (Luke 4:18) that claim authenticated the presence of truth and reality.

Thus, belief in African spirituality is an entire ontological world view which takes spiritual reality as an integral part of a holistic life. For the African, Christ provides a bridge as do the ancestors, between the spirit world and the physical world. No science or technology has replaced this way of thinking and perception of reality for the Africans for whom spirituality is part of African identity. In many respects, our spirituality has helped us to retain salient human sense of value which other cultures have lost due to the influence of science and technology when this is given a paramount role at the exclusion of humanizing values.

Now let us focus on specific instances of spirituality, such as the Shona practice of *Kurova guva*, meaning a special ritual related to the cleansing of the spirit of our dead loved ones, and consequent ancestral installation rites, common in many communities south of the Sahara.

THE PRACTICE OF KUROVA GUVA

Kurova guva is a Shona and Ndebele peoples' attempt to deal with the issue of life and death, God's time and the concepts of eternity and the immortality of the soul. Kurova guva is a human endeavor to comply with God's plan of eternity. The practice provides us with a concrete example of African spirituality. What the Shona call, <u>Kurova guva</u> the Ndebele call <u>Umbuiso</u>, meaning "bringing the dead home in their community."

ARE THE DEAD LIVING?

African people are among thousands of communities who do not forget the graves of their loved ones. Some cultures put flowers on the grave every year. Others actually seek a "living dialogue" with living-dead relatives. Is this normal? A story is told of a white missionary in central Africa, who always took flowers to the grave of one of the early missionaries who had died while serving the church of Africa. One day, this expatriate met an African who also had always carried special ritual millet (grain) porridge to his great-grandfather's grave. The missionary asked: "Sir, won't you get tired of taking food to your ancestors who never come to eat it? When do you think they will ever come to eat that stuff?" The elderly African paused a little and then responded: "When your missionary friend comes to acknowledge the flowers you place on his grave yearly, my ancestor will also come to eat this food."

There was no further dialogue. The two parted in a pensive mood, most likely thinking about the brief and brittle conversation they had on the meaning of their respective rituals. The interesting observation regarding this practice is that both the white man and the African proceeded with their mission anyway, showing how seriously committed they were to their beliefs. For us, the important point to note is that the "dead" are indeed believed to be "living", hence these various practices. This belief that the "dead" are "living" sheds much light on the concept of everlasting life. Apparently, death is not regarded as an end but merely a "change of environment and mode of existence" as we have discussed in chapter where I have described death as a state of "ontological metamorphosis."

In Zimbabwe, this practice called "<u>kurova guva</u>" involves rituals to bring the "spirit of the living-dead" back in the community. In fact, there is a reciprocating occurrence. The ritual is believed to make it possible for the spirit of the junior ancestor to mediate between the spirit world and the physical world. This means that the practice involves both "sending" and "receiving." By virtue of this activity, we must infer that the dead are living since they actually get involved in their family affairs.

Now many Christians in my country are involved in the practice of "kurova guva" but they are not sure whether it is allowed by the Church whose burial ritual reads: "The spirit has departed - gone back to God who gave it, and the flesh goes back to dust where it came from." If Christian leaders condemn the traditional practice, what is the theological reason? If they allow it, what is the theological justification. If we just let it go, why are we indifferent on the matter? Furthermore, as the people of the light (Jesus Christ), we should take the initiative to teach the correct practice to our people who may be living in darkness, if this practice is regarded as pagan. However, the question is: are the dead living? The answer must be positive based on the behavior of the living.

In this book the author maintains that Kurova guva is an aspect of African spirituality which is a major source of African theology. This ritual implies that the dead are living in spirit form which the physical world has had to reckon with can dialogue and interact with.

KUROVA GUVA

"Kurova guva", a religio-cultural practice, is the final stage in a series of traditional burial ceremonies. The primary purpose of "kurova guva" for most people is to formally bring back home the spirit of the dead person so that he or she may resume certain responsibilities such as protecting or punishing the living members of the family when necessary. The living-dead also serves to advise the family on any crucial matters that may arise within the family. Advice from the living-dead is believed to be valuable since they are in the spirit world with God who is believed to be omni-present and all-powerful. The practice is also observed in order that the spirit may be accepted by those gone before into their community. In all this, we must bear in mind that the living members of the family do not, as some mistaken people think, deify the spirit. The living-dead are venerated but not worshiped. We note that Africans are the only race that never worshiped idols as an end in itself. Unfortunately, our ancestors veneration was misconstrued to signify idol worship. True, all ancestor are addressed in the prayers, but with instruction or mandate to "take our prayers' to the Great Ancestor, the Great Spirit, God.

Whatever is done to revere, (kuremedza), remember, or respect, and appease the spirit, a distinction is maintained between musikavanhu (God) and this spirit which was itself created, preserved and restored by Musikavanhu so that it may be where God is. Once this creature-creator relationship is understood properly, there should not be any confusion regarding the intention of the whole practice.

If the traditional practitioners seem to fear the spirit more than Musikavanhu, it is only because they realize that Musikavanhu can work through (and also in spite of) their living-dead spirit to either bless or make the living face the consequence of their actions. In other words, the traditional African believes that God can use these spirits as creaturely agencies since the African believes that the spirits are closer to God, who is the source of all supernatural power than are the living. Our spirituality does have a cognitive dimension.

It is true, however, that African spirituality tends to lump together the two spiritual forces. Yet there is a clear distinction in essence, origin and function. The only similarity is that both are spirit. The ultimate difference is that one is a creature, the other is the creator God. For example, I used to think that American Christians worship both the national flag and the Christian flag, since they fly both in Church. Some friend was kind enough to correct my misconception. You see, as their pastor, (Mediapolis, Iowa) I had asked the church layleader to remove the national flag from the altar and fly it outside where it belongs! I got the lesson of my life!

Regarding reverence of the ancestors, consider this example. Most law-breakers tend to fear a police officer as if he/she is one who passes judgement on their offence. They seem to not be aware of the judge himself/herself, better yet the law itself. God is like the law, ancestors are like the police officer. The two are distinct, yet continuous.

The judge and the law itself are quite in the background. By analogy traditionalist seem to fear the spirits more than the Great Spirit/God, although they know that the latter is the ultimate Reality. Another example which serves to demonstrate two points at once is this. There are some parishioners who give large amounts of money to the Church only because they love their pastor, yet they can be indifferent about their commitment to God to whom the pastor points. The point is although such people do not worship the pastor, their actions make it seem like they in fact do. The pastor advocates what God wants, yet the pastor is not God.

People who give large amounts to the Church because they love the pastor really are ultimately giving to God because that is the proper theological understanding behind the whole idea of the offertory. There are some members who do not know that when they give gifts in church, they are giving to God. Why have we not heard voices challenging such acts expressing doubts as to whether these people are aware of what they are doing? It has been our observation that theological reasons are often left in the background in most religious practices.

After all, how many parishioners know the exact theology behind every sacrament they receive in the Church? How many understand the theology that undergirds the creeds we recite every time we assemble for worship? The answer to all these rhetorical questions, if one were to be honest and realistic, is: very few indeed. It is not true that one needs to understand the theology to benefit from the practice. Faith is enough! Why do we seek to under-estimate the African ingenuity and traditional theology? African spirituality is a parable for eternal life. Traditional beliefs allude to this doctrine by way of ancestrology. The issue is, relevant to our people's spirituality, kurova guva is a important form of spirituality because it anticipates eternal living-i.e. living with God endlessly.

One thing is made clear by this practice: Africans engage in it because their spirituality informs them that death is never the end of life. Life goes on-gravitating toward God. In this discussion, we hope that by understanding African spirituality both the traditionalist and the Christian develop, not only an appreciation but insight into the subject.

WHERE DOES THE SPIRIT GO?

Kurova guva also exposes an answer to the question: Where does the spirit go? The answer is simple. It goes to be with God who is everywhere. There are no geographical limitations to the activities of the spirit of the living-dead. One may challenge the Christians because they do not really know what happens to the spirit when their beloved dies. The scriptures give us at least two different views without reconciling them. On the one hand the Church community commends the spirit to God who gave it. On the other hand the same community visits the grave every year until Jesus comes back to fetch all those "sleeping" in their graves! Yet, the church teaches us that when we die the spirit goes to heaven to be with God; on the other hand, it teaches that the "dead" are only "asleep" in their graves! On the resurrection day, the trumpet will sound and the graves will open to release the dead. The Church has not resolved this contradiction-whether the spirit goes to God immediately or it awaits the resurrection day when Christ comes again. To not care to resolve this indicates that there are many more matters which Christianity has not, and cannot address, yet it is too arrogant to learn from traditional religion. The same community spends much money on the coffin-an earthly home-which the spirit has abandoned. Why? Like us, the Hebrews have a holistic ontological world view. The Church community believes that God takes all the spirits they commend to God. However, some realistic church people admit that, they do not know what happens to the spirit once it departs from the physical body. Rightly so, they leave it all in the "hands" of their God who is in heaven. Apparently, the traditionalist shares with the Christian the belief that death is not the end of all existence. It is, as we mentioned earlier, merely a change in mode of existence and environment. The two traditions part ways where African spirituality is able to account for the whereabouts of the spirit whereas the Protestants cannot unless they are willing to learn from African spirituality.

PROTESTANT CHRISTIAN VIEW

When the Church talks about Heaven, what is described sounds very much like some affluent suburban community. Does anyone know what it is like really? Be that as it may, many Protestants hold a CERTAIN VIEW which they express through their sermons, hymns and rituals, especially burial rituals. Traditional spirituality's input is the view that life continues beyond death. Furthermore, the living-dead are actually active in their spiritual abode. They work with God. The Protestant Christian view can only be enriched if it embraces the traditional insight that when someone is dead, he or she has gone to another world. After all, the bible is not clear on the matter. The United Methodist Church has a hymn which clearly makes the point: ("Pano handi musha wedu, tinoziva imwe nyika tinoenda nekufara, uko tiri kudaidzwa"..., meaning this world is not our home, we know another world where we are glad to go and we are being called there). Christians are divided on this matter. Roman Catholics believe that the spirit of the dead may wait in purgatory until the day of judgement, whereas most Protestants hold the view that after death, the spirit returns to God who gave it in the first place.

However, African Christians in Zimbabwe, both Catholic and Protestant often experience incidents which contradict their Christian belief, namely interacting with the spirit of the departed one way or another.

Here I shall cite only one incident which should make the Christian uncomfortable regarding the belief in life-after death. It involves an unquestionably Christian people - the Chieza family. Sekuru Timothy Chieza's grand-daughter had a dream in which his late wife mbuya Chieza, a staunch Christian woman who died some time back and had a "Christian burial" said: 'Muzukuru, imba yangu iri mumvura,' translated: my grand child, my house is immersed in water. The granddaughter shared this rather disturbing dream with grandpa (Sekuru) Chieza, who just ignored the whole thing at first (as a well-trained Christian should!) The second and third time, the granddaughter had the same dream: "Muzukuru imba yangu iri mumvura."

Apparently, there was no peace in the grandchild's mind: "I thought grandma went to heaven. What is this?" We note here that in traditional spirituality, dreams do not cause any commotion at all. People generally pay attention if dreams seem instructive. Mr. Marima who was our Conference Layleader, and Mr. Chieza decided to check mbuya Chieza's grave to see whether it was in order. The two went to the exclusive cemetery (only Christians are buried at Mutare Mudhara,) and found the grave flooded by the water which was over flowing from the Mutare irrigation ditch. So they fixed it and thereafter mbuya Chieza did not come again in the dream. This means, either mbuya is watching her earthly home from above or from within. There may be other possibilities.

One question which comes to mind is: If Mbuya Chieza could communicate with one of her loved ones living today, could she not communicate with those who went before? Other questions are: Where does her spirit dwell? Is she not with us almost in the sense that we believe Christ is with us though with a different function? Was a truth not revealed in what the grand-daughter dreamed? Is that not some kind of revelation of the truth that death is not the end and that the dead are recognizable in their "human" body though they are in their spiritual state? This is the spirit in which traditionalists bring Mudzimu home. The process involves recognizing the presence of the living-dead in certain family matters. Would practitioners be violating humane principles if they gave her a place in the home? Did God not bring his Son Jesus Christ back home (Jerusalem) and ultimately where God is? To revisit the question: Where are the spirits of those who have been given Christian burial? African spirituality through kurova guva can give us some definite clues. This author believes that the answer to most of these questions is very crucial and essential for relevant Christian theology? Thus, African spirituality informs Christian theology. We may draw spiritual insight from kurova guva, a practice which enables the thinker to reconcile the problem which even the New Testament does not answer coherently.

Some Christians hold memorial services for their departed relatives. The purpose of these memorial services is not clear to this author if it is not celebrating "the beginning" of eternal living in the spiritual state. On the one hand the practice seems to contradict the

Christian belief that when a Christian dies the spirit goes to another world as we have already pointed out. On the other hand, in essence the practice of holding annual memorial services is not very different in its spirituality from kurova guva, because in each case we recognize the spiritual continuous presence of our loved ones. Most people would agree that generally, both Christians and traditionalists do not "bury and forget." They continue to remember their departed. Of course there may be different explanations and interpretations of the significance of memorial services. But the following facts cannot be disputed:

5.   Africans, Christian or indigenous, believe that death is not the end of our lives. The spirit transcends the physical body. (This could be a basis for the doctrine of the resurrection of eternal life. Our spirituality provides the context for this doctrine.)

6.   God is spirit. Our living-dead also become spirit like God, though not the same as God. There are differences in nature, quality, character and function. It suffices to note that this informs the doctrine of creation. The spirit returns to God who gave it in the first place because there is some commonality between the two-the creature and the creator.)

7.   Both Christians and traditionalists in Zimbabwe believe that there is Musikavanhu (Umdali) (God), the creator of humanity. And, there is an everlasting kinship relationship that binds the two eternally.

8.   Both religions also teach that some day we will die and hopefully join those who have gone before us-hence the idea of a heavenly community with God at the throne. According to African spirituality, this community is always in existence except that then it will be more evident.

On the basis of all these observations, or some of them, we can conclude that practice of "remembering the dead," whether in the form of a more general "memorial service" or the concrete ritual of "kurova guva", has spiritual significance and meaning which informs Christian theology. We get the feeling that some day we will be together in a different world and context. Also, our knowledge in that state will possibly be a different kind of gnosis and awareness, (as St. Paul says in I Corinthians 13:12) from what we know in this present reality.

Another serious theological question is invoked by this concept. If we believe that our loved ones, though dead, are still with us in a "spiritual community," does that not suggest that they are awaiting judgement? Or, does it suggest that they have been judged already? Is God already using them as divine agents to do the work God wants them to do? Are they waiting for general resurrection? Where is this "other world" where we believe the spirits of the dead belong? Are the spirits in fact already with God who is everywhere? Has geography anything to do with this "other-worldly" reality?

There are no easy theological answers to these questions, but African spirituality helps us develop theological insights on these matters. We also are aware that theological claims we make in these matters may only be our deep-seated psychological desires and anxieties. This author believes that there is a definite plan which God has worked out for our spirits. There is no randomness in God's design. The most likely possibility is what God has revealed to us in Jesus Christ-namely that the human soul (spirit) must return to God who gave it. It is not our beliefs that determine where the spirit ends up. Rather it is what God has provided from the beginning of creation. We prefer to call this God's plan of salvation, rather than predestination. This is the central role played by Christ who is Very God. Thus, Christ is the spiritual leader.

IS JESUS CHRIST OUR MODEL?

As Jesus Christ lived, died and now lives eternally, so will we. This is the sense in which Jesus Christ is the way, the truth and the life. Whosoever believe in him will not perish because, though they die, yet shall they live eternally. To say Christ is "the way" is not to create a bottleneck, but to open up a path for "whosoever believeth!" Because Jesus Christ is:

1.　　　The example of God's plan for a full humanity and eternity;
2.　　　The way to being with God and the truth of God;
3.　　　The revelation of God.

we have to regard his life, death and resurrection as the paradigm for humanity. Christ is the way to God and the way of being in God because he and God are one. We need to remind ourselves that Jesus Christ is not what he is because of what we believe him to be. Rather, he is who he is because he is the Son and Revelation of God - he is the Christ. The church cannot "colonize" Christ because the church itself is only one colony in God's kingdom. So, we must have a correct meaning of Christ as the way.

Consider this example: Death is the way for all and the gate for all to exit this world and enter another world. The amazing phenomenon is: whether one knows the fact of death or not, he/she will "walk the way of death," and walk it the correct way! Similarly, whether one knows Christ or not, Christ is still the way to God because He and God are one. We should remember also that we do not motivate God, but God motivates us through God's love and grace. So, on the matter of salvation, God in Christ takes the initiative to save all human beings because all are crated in God's image. According to African spirituality, whatever sins we commit in this life will have to be done away with in order that the spirit may proceed to being with God.

Furthermore, death which comes to both the rich and the poor, young and old, Christian and other, male and female, may be God's peculiar manifestation of Divine justice. It is God who instituted it in the sense that it is in the package called life. However, we Christians know how much we "differ with God" on that matter! By this I mean we are often shocked by death and surprised at certain people's death. But DEATH remains the only way through which human beings leave this form of life and enter another. We do not have to accept death to die. We suspect that we may experience similar shock, surprise or disgust, when we find God organizing our spirits around the throne of Grace not as the world would want, or know. Again, since Christ, our Paradigm, had to die before he could be exalted, so we too must follow suit and regard death as ontological metamorphosis in life as a whole. Lived out in the ritual of kurova guva, African spirituality regards death as necessity. Christ's death was necessary for our salvation. Every one's death is also necessary in order for each one of us to proceed in the business of life. We learn from Christ's fullness (humanity and divinity) that a whole life includes living and death, with death as "ontological metamorphosis." Death emancipates us for eternal salvation in community with God. Right through this discussion, we have developed the sense that African spirituality is a mode of life which God has provided us in order to walk the path of life eternally.

SIMILARITIES AND DIFFERENCES BETWEEN CHRISTIANITY AND TRADITIONALISM

The difference between these two religious belief systems is that traditionalism regards life-after-death as a continuation of a form of life, while Christianity sees death as a discontinuity between this life and beyond. For the Christian, the spirit of the dead is believed to have nothing to do with the physical affairs of this life. Yet the spirit of Mbuya Chieza said: "My house (grave) is immersed in water!" Is this "house" not material? To be realistic, we just have to recognize the presence of the spirit of the dead and the need to dialogue with the same. At least, the Church does not have to despise the concept of the living-dead which, in fact, furnishes us with a solution to the problem presented by the Bible. Unfortunately, this difference is only theoretical. In practice, most Zimbabwean Christians and traditionalists believe that "the dead" are living a different form of existence. I know this because many talk to their living-dead; they address them and ask them to give them guidance when they are in crises.

There is another distinction between these two traditions. The Christian view maintains that after death the human spirit returns to God who gave it. This is consistent with another Christian belief that at the end of time, all souls will gather for judgement - the good will then be admitted into God's Kingdom, while the bad souls are sent to eternal hell fire. There is a sense of finality which Christians believe was set by God. For the traditionalist, the final stage is not until all sins are forgiven, all souls cleansed and sanctified - made suitable to live with God eternally. Regarding forgiveness, African spirituality has devices meant to "remove sin" so that one may lead a normal, healthy life. The Genuine Shona says:

> "every person is forgiven past offences when he dies. The spirit is never reminded in the spiritual world of the bad he did in his lifetime. His name is cleared and he is remembered in this world as long as his descendants remain on earth" (Gelfand, 1977, 137).

This is also true of women.

If the world that is evil knows how to forgive, what more will that great ancestor, the spirit of God forgive! This is why in Shona spirituality, there is no concept of hell, but not because they are an amoral society! Sin is forgiven. That God, our loving, gracious and merciful creator will let sinners burn eternally, is a questionable theological perspective. However, what is clear is that in many African traditions, there are no concepts of judgement day, hell or heaven. God continues to "work" with God's creation forever. The evil are cleansed by their community in order to qualify to join the eternal world of God's community where God "further" cleanses and sanctifies them, confirming the forgiveness from the community. Traditional theology knows only one world consisting of this physical world and the spiritual world which is understood to be a continuation of this. History is linear, yet it makes a complete circle of perfection. There is not a concept of a community of spiritual bodies. The living-dead simply continue their responsibilities of fending for their families although, this time, they are in a spiritual state - almost superhuman, yet not God. This idea compares with the Christian idea of the communion of the saints, except that in the case of this communion the saints are locked up somewhere, whereas in the former case, the "saints" are deployed to work among their loved ones. Again here African spirituality offers more insight into life after this earthly living - one where the history of salvation "concludes" with a happy never-ending hereafter.

Given the theology of African spirituality and ontology, our world view does not include hell. Traditional theology questions the concept of hell as eternal punishment inflicted by God upon those who disobeyed God while they were living. The reason is, it seems, that punishment is cruel and uninstructive because it is endless. Our merciful and forgiving God would not let us suffer eternally as that would be either a flaw or failure in God's plan of salvation. The African concept of God presents so to speak, a technical "knock out" to the concept of hell. Would God have created people without a purpose at all? Traditional spirituality believes in the God who ultimately makes things right. This is the meaning of such attributes as: Almighty, compassionate, good, just (one who justifies what is unjust), invincible and so on. The author of *African Thought, Religion and Culture* has poignantly expressed the general African traditional understanding regarding life beyond death. Agreeing with other African scholars, he said: "The majority of African peoples do not have the belief in judgement after death and as such do not expect any form of reward in the here-after" (1991, 89).

Professor Mbiti also supports the above statement when he says: "For the majority of African peoples, the hereafter is only a continuation of life more or less as it is in its human form" (Mbiti 1969, 161). Eternal punishment is not God's way to deal with sinners. God in Christ showed us how God deals with the sinners.. Calvary showed us how God deals with the sins of the world. Rather, hell is place or category where the souls that are incapable of receiving God's mercy, forgiveness, or loving kindness due to being spiritually dead belong. It is not a place of punishment. Therefore, such souls do not suffer eternally. In fact, such souls cease to exist, and so we cannot even talk about "souls" in hell. They become spiritually extinct.

The African theological perspective which rejects the idea of hell as punishment, is more consistent with a proper understanding of Gehena, which is a place of refuse located in the Kidron Valley, West of the city of Jerusalem. There is no need or intention of redeeming any rubbish that has been dumped in "Gehena." Gehena is the final destination of the useless, the "spiritually dead." Moreover, the spiritually dead in Gehena cannot even strive to get out because they are dead. In fact, there is no striving or struggling. That death is different from "the-living-dead concept." So, for Africans in Zimbabwe, the dead are living and there is no hell for those who die in sin. Both the good and the sinful are cleansed, justified and sanctified consistent with the nature of God.

This theological perspective does not contradict what Jesus Christ taught and meant. Yes, the dead souls should be thrown in hell fire because they are no longer capable of receiving God's grace. Thus, hell is not punishment. One cannot punish non-existence.

It is important to make this point in order to challenge any Christian theology that teaches a tradition of punishing sinners because such is not consistent with the forgiving spirit of Christ. More critical is the fact that the Church has painted God (and we believe wrongly) as a merciless God who punishes the people who sin and rewards those who do good. This is what ancestors may do, not God. To say that God punishes the sinner eternally, we believe, is misleading. What the Bible actually teaches is that God "hates" sin. It is evil that God does not accept. We do not believe that God will "throw away the baby with the bath water!" as the saying goes. The reason Jesus Christ came to the world was to demonstrate that God's attitude toward a sinner is redemptive, not vindictive. Every time the Jews presented Jesus with a "sinner" this is what he tried to teach them - salvation, justification, not punishment. Christ died so that the sinner may be saved. Even the scriptures tell us that God is concerned about saving the sinner. God strives to separate the human being from the sin. Once that separation has taken place, God burns the sin eternally. The parable of the lost sheep demonstrates the point. In traditional religion, it is a goat without blemish which is thrown away, not the person who is cleansed. This symbolic separation of the "sin" from the one who committed it is also reflected in the Easter event. After the sacrifice, using Jesus Christ, God took God's son back, having cleansed the sins of the whole world.

We are convinced that people should choose to do good not because they FEAR to be thrown in hell, but *OUT OF THE WILLINGNESS TO DO THE WILL OF GOD*. There is no way the Church can scare people into loving God meaningfully! Rather, the Church can educate people so that they understand the love of God, whom they may choose to love with all their heart, mind, strength and soul. This is accomplished when the Church teaches that God is Love, good, merciful and just. Traditional theology teaches that:

> "God is called Friend, or the Greatest of Friends. This is an image which shows great confidence in God. People feel at home with him, believing that he (sic) is trustworthy, faithful, close to them and ready to help them just as a true human friend would do... They know he (sic) is always there for them." (Mbiti 1970, 49).

In Zaire, some people have a saying: "rejoice, God never does wrong to people". Such is basically the traditionalist's concept of God vis-a-vis sin.

We take this position regarding life after temporal existence because we hold the belief that everything that God does has a purpose. For that reason, even death is good because not only does it have a purpose, but a divine one. What would be the purpose or end result of eternal punishment? Although the parable of "Divies and Lazarus" depicts heaven and hell, the message Jesus intended was that we should care for the needy and also prepare ourselves to live a holistic life here on earth and in the hereafter. So, rather than exclusively futurize the meaning of the parable, the emphasis should be on the present awareness of a life of caring.

Understandably early Christians were interested in this single parable because it served to "drive" people to church. It frightened people who tended to ignore the will of God. Our question is, why is it that the same Christians did not have similar interest in the parable of the "Laborers in the Vineyard" which challenges the Christians who demand more than what God has promised everyone because they have been in the Church the longest time? Apparently, God does not recognize seniority in service. From this parable we learn that all depends on the Master's gracious decision to do what he wants with his own. In fact, this parable challenges those who think that they have priority in heaven. Rather than serve to demonstrate how unfair or unjust God is, the parable teaches that it is not for us to weigh and distribute God's abundant grace. No wonder this theme of God's abundant grace and surprising forgiveness fills much of the New Testament pages. God, through Christ, teaches us how merciful, gracious, forgiving God is although we fail to take advantage of this.

If we think of Lazarus, who was dead for four days, and Jesus brought his spirit back to re-unite with the physical body, we have to conclude that the spirit of the dead does not "return" to God right away as such. Rather it lingers on for some time. We cannot say for how long. The Jews gave it about five days! This closely relates to the idea of kurova guva. For instance there is a dialogue between the living (Jesus) and the living-dead (Lazarus). Jesus talked to Lazarus who was dead and Lazarus responded because he was not dead spiritually. For most Shonas, a period of about twelve months is sufficient time before the ritual of kurova guva is done. Extending beyond this period is generally regarded as neglecting the wandering spirit of the deceased.

Theologically speaking, on the one hand, the practice of kurova guva seems to imply that the spirit of the living-dead does not immediately go back to God. Rather it continues to function in its capacity as a created being with some superhuman powers or more access to God. On the other hand, the spirit qua spirit seems to be closer to God. It is like God in that it is spiritual and not physical. We noted earlier that some people can argue that the spirit of the dead, in the African traditional practice, returns to God who gave it. If this is the case, it makes sense theologically to think of the spirit of the dead as superhuman, though it will never be deity. It is God alone who chooses to exalt the human spirit after physical death. This is the example God set in Jesus Christ, the first born of heaven, as we have pointed out earlier in this discussion. So, as we talk of Jesus being at the right hand of God, as well as being with us, so we can think of our living-dead as being with God and the whole communion of saints, as well as being at our service.

The practice of kurova guva seems to contradict Christ's words that we have rooms prepared for each of us where God is (John 14:2-3). First we have to attempt to establish where the "omnipresent" God is. Wherever God is, the spirit goes to be with God. Therefore, when the traditionalists bring the spirit back home, they simultaneously and ritually prepare the spirit to communion with Immanuel, (God with us), since God is with us and everywhere. It could be argued that this is the first resurrection (restoration) of the "dead."

If then the spirit of the living-dead is with God, and God is with us, can God not use the spirit as one more medium through which God channels answers to the prayers of the living members of a family? Also, since the living-dead are with God, who is with us, it clearly implies that the living-dead are also with us. There is no apparent hindrance to that possibility in African spirituality. The only "problem" seems to arise from our lack of understanding of what Jesus meant in John 14:6-7 when he said: "No one comes to the father but through me." We must think critically what Christ meant by those words.

One clue in the gospel of John could help us. Christ says, "I and the Father are one..." It is evident that it is not possible to be with God without being with Christ simultaneously, because both "the Father and the son" are one. Furthermore, we should not think of the oneness of the Father and the Son as a duality, or a numerical unity. We have to think of their unity as basically a singleness of mind and purpose because God is one. In light of what we have said here, it makes no difference whether one is Christian or a Moslem, or an African traditionalist or any other religion. Christ is the way, not a hindrance, to God. Consequently, whatever is the door to God in any religion serves the FUNCTION OF CHRIST - the way. In this regard, to say Christ is the way need not be interpreted in an exclusive sense because Christ is inclusive. Incidentally, most eastern religions (Taoism, Buddhism, etc.) are thought of as "the way". Thus, any religion can be regarded as "the way" to achieving the immortality of the soul.

So, if the most constant need for an African is socio-spiritual welfare and survival, God the Creator would utilize the simultaneous participation of the Son. We have already pointed out that to say Christ is the way does not mean that Christ puts a restriction. Rather, he opens the possibility - the Bible says: "whosoever believes in me..." and "me" here could be used synonymously with "the way." It is in this sense that Christ says "no-one can come to the Father except through" him. Although scripture has been interpreted by some to mean that Christianity is a superior religion, we argue that Christ meant oneness of purpose within the Godhead. Having clarified the meaning of the unity of the Godhead, we can now return to the theological implication of the practice of <u>kurova guva</u>.

Many African theologians infer that since God often works through creatures and creation, it is conceivable that God alone uses the living-dead to protect their survivors. There is an interesting parallel between Christ who died, resurrected and ascended to heaven to be with "the Father" and is now our protector though He is God, <u>and</u> the spirit of one's dead father, whose responsibility is to protect the living members of the family. There is also a parallel in the sense that one who once served mankind in physical form, continues to serve the living in one's spiritual form. Traditional spirituality believes that the living-dead "protects" the living, since this is a God-sent function in the supernatural world.

To say that God can use the living-dead to protect us, is by no means an attempt to be-little Christ who is very God. To the contrary, God is the soul of our spirituality. As such the Divine can use finite methods and means as a way for us to understand God. This was the whole point of the incarnation-God using a familiar and intelligible medium in order to communicate a message to us. In other words, God may reveal Godself to a non-Christian people through religio-cultural media, such as the spirit of the living-dead, special prophets, dreams, or every day reason, revelation or experience.

It is poor theology to argue as some scholars have that God can only reveal Godself, or can only work in history through God's Son. Let God be God. In God's godliness, the Supreme Being has various means of granting creatures what they need; for example, food and protection, to mention only two. We subscribe to the theology that God does not change. Rather, it is our human perceptions that change as we acquire new insights in history. The God of father Abraham is the same as the God of St. Peter and that of Reverend Kenneth Choto of Mukurazhizha. What changed was the perspective of these men of faith, depending on socio-cultural context as well as experience.

In fact, this argument over who really protects us is very interesting because the fact is that people do enjoy protection sometimes. But other times, they do not get it, so they think, hence there are accidents, diseases, deaths and so on. Such occurances are also divine protection although we regard them as catastrophes, deaths and misery. An example of what we may regard as loss when, in God's eyes it may not be, is when a fig tree sheds it leaves. Is it losing or gaining? When a farmer plucks tomatoes in the garden to sell in the city, is that plant losing? When our children grow up, get married, have their own homes, is the "empty nest" losing? Perspective is very decisive. If it is the Almighty God who protects, why do accidents occur? If it is the spirits with supernatural power that protect, still the question is why do accidents occur? Can either one of the two powers stop death from happening? An affirmative answer to these questions has not been our experience.

In pursuit of a sound theology, one has to view death as part of life, and life as part of death in the context of our spirituality that has God not only as the soul but the goal or eternal destination. To argue that fatal accidents occur because God permits them to happen is a rather unpopular theology these days. We can only challenge our finite understanding of protection, not God's power to protect because God is omnipotent. We are aware that even this attribute is being challenged by some theologians, but that is because they are still wrestling to understand who God is. Note that both God and the ancestors utilize death. For instance, Jesus Christ had to die in order that the sinful humanity may be saved. As for ancestors, death is, one may say, their birth; i.e. the ancestors can only come into being "from death." It follows that death ought to be understood not just in finite terms but in divine terms. Death, therefore, is not an instance of lack of protection. If it were a result of lack of protection, many members of the royal family would not experience deaths in their families since they enjoy more than adequate protection. Death is ultimate life, protection and power.

A HOLISTIC UNDERSTANDING OF GOD'S PROTECTION

What does African spirituality understand about God's protection? What is it that God protects us from? And how? Most African Christians seem to believe that before God revealed Godself through the Son (Jesus Christ), God used to work through nature as well as the ancestor spirits. But after Christ had come, God could no longer do what God used to do. This strikes us as crude theological thinking. It limits God. The book of Hebrews (1:1-4) has been grossly misinterpreted by many. African spirituality maintains that the God who has always been, still is. That is the God who provides humanity with protection. Put differently, this is the God who facilitates human survival.

Another aspect of the discussion that needs some attention has to do with our human meaning of protection. For most people, protection seems to mean God does what we expect God to do in order that human beings may accomplish their own goals in history. Unfortunately, what we mean by protection portrays our very human egocentric tendency. One definition of protection is "my physical safety..." It is hard to fully understand why Christians value physical safety so much when they believe that heavenly life is best, and this is only achieved through death. It is not clear why we hold a negative attitude toward anything that threatens to take us away from this earthy life. Indeed, there is truth in the song entitled "Everybody wants to go to heaven, but nobody wants to die."

What is clear is that by protection, we generally indicate our self-interest. Spiritual communion with God seems to threaten us because it implies we must give up our earthly desires. God is expected to be supportive of our finite plan in temporal life even though we believe and admit that God's knowledge is omniscient but ours is finite. When we say in the Lord's prayer: "Thy Kingdom come" what do we really mean? Do we genuinely invite and welcome God's reign? My intuition is that we say this prayer with a grain of salt. Why do we not perceive God's protection even when a young couple crashes in a fatal auto accident, leaving a four-year and a two-year old at the mercy of the extended family or the community as a whole? Our self-centeredness plays a major role in our theological myopia. And, the gospel teaches us not to be overly anxious because we cannot make even a single hair grow on our heads.

If death is the only official way to undergo the ontological metamorphosis culminating in being with God, why do we hold such a negative attitude toward it? If pain becomes unbearable, is death not one of the best ways to bring it all to a permanent end? Even healing is less permanent than death because after healing, one may suffer pain again in the future. When death comes, there is no more pain, mourning, crying or sorrow, "for the former things have passed away."

Not many people will accept death as a mode of positive protection. Although it is a protective measure, not many people can deal with it. We find it difficult to accept the fact that death is God's means of protecting us eternally. Only African spirituality teaches life-in-death and that death is part of life as exemplified in the communion between the living and the living-dead. Christians ought to be the first to understand the positive meaning of death because there could not be Easter without the death of Jesus Christ. There could not be the Resurrection of Jesus Christ without his death. Yet, as we have pointed out earlier, death is the birth of the ancestral spirits. A spirituality that perceives death as part of life prepares our minds to understand the fullness of life. Only African spirituality prepares us to receive death as we welcome life, and puts us on the path to eternal living under permanent protection.

DEATH IS ULTIMATE PROTECTION

God and our ancestor spirits (assuming they have a part to play in our protection) have ordained death for everyone of us because it has a noble purpose. So, if we seek protection against death, we are fighting against logic, reason and the divine method of spiritual progression. Death is guaranteed for everybody: the rich and the poor, the young and the aging, the wise and the foolish. Death is one thing everybody would expect to receive, if it was a gift. This being the case, we can perceive the folly of seeking protection against receiving our gift. Since death is not something we ought to actively seek, but which will come anyhow, it is prudent to respond to God in whom we find eternal life albeit through DEATH.

Death is God-ordained but it is not caused by God. The ancestors, with their semi-supernatural wisdom, co-operate with God in that they too do not cause death. We have heard many relatives who talk of their ancestors "beyond the river," who either beckon to join them, or order the living to stay on the other side of the "big river." Although God is in the midst of all this, we human beings tend to identify only our forefathers "beyond the river." Christians are rather embarrassed to talk about this crucial moment because they choose to blame God. In fact, many Christians "blame God" for causing death although they say it euphemistically in popular phrases: "God knows." "God has taken God's own." This is an unfair allegation! African spirituality recognizes that when God wishes to communicate with us, God uses familiar beings such as our ancestors. So, it is God who either beckons us to cross the river or orders us to remain on the other side of the river but it is only across the river within God's spiritual continuum.

We reiterate, it is not God who causes death because God is our greatest Protector and Provider: "the Lord is my Shepherd." A case can be made for possible protection by one's ancestral spirits, with such power coming only from God, the creator and our refuge. That the ancestral spirit seeks appreciation and even appeasement is only "human" like the pastor we referred to earlier, only proving that these are creatures, not God.

In the world of technology, it is important for us to recognize what God is doing through, and in spite of humanity's ingenuity (which itself is also a gift from God). For instance, one who believes in God as creator, must also believe that it is God who makes an airplane fly. It is God who makes it rain whether a white farmer in tropical Africa has sent a plane to "seed" the clouds or not.

It is God who heals the sick whether the best doctor in town is contacted or not. It is God who makes conception possible whether the woman is beyond child-bearing age or not. This is the meaning of faith in God. The African believes that the protection which he/she has enjoyed hitherto ultimately comes from God who uses whatever God chooses to work for God.

A TRADITIONALIST SPIRITUALITY OF DEATH

We have stated earlier that the traditionalist who believes that he/she is protected by ancestor spirits is aware that such a protector is creaturely, not divine. However, if we listen carefully to our Christian believers, sometimes we hear them saying "your spirits and your God will protect you." In the event of death, sometimes we hear them saying: "the ancestors have fought hard to protect you, but they have been defeated." Again, this comes from the school of thought which regards death as a loss. Otherwise, it is my view that ancestors do not work against God's will. Rather, they work for God.

So, if misfortune comes, the traditionalist does not think that God has put one to temptation, or worse still that God has failed. African spirituality brings a positive attitude that maintains that the ancestor spirit has willed in its creaturely nature, that such be the case. Or, the ancestors have sanctioned the end of this life. This belief that all is in in our best interest, comforts the bereaved in the traditional set up. The traditionalist may even hold the view that one's guardian spirit has been over-powered by other forces, so this death could not be helped. In each case, they think in terms of creaturely powers "failing" to do their work. African spirituality does not conceive of God failing. Neither does it think of God being ungracious. In traditional theology, God is always ABLE, and has foreknowledge and wisdom.

This understanding brings serenity in mind of the traditionalist when disease, calamity or even death occurs in spite of the expected protection from the spiritual earthly agent. But when disaster hits, Christian believers are forced to think that God let them down. In Zimbabwe, the Shona who say: (Matenga atiseka), paint a wrong picture of God by saying "God has neglected us." Many Christians become puzzled or even lose their faith in God when evil seems to prevail in spite of the mighty hand of God that promises them protection always. Based on this distinction between the Christian view and that of the traditionalist, it appears that the traditionalist is better equipped emotionally and theologically to deal with evil (if death is regarded as bad), than the Christian. So, the Church can learn a theology of death which teaches the wholeness of life from African spirituality.

African spirituality helps the practioners to come to terms with "the ways of the Lord." For instance, death which is thought to be the worst enemy of life in many cultures, is given an appropriate place in traditional theology through the practice of kurova guva. Christians, through Easter, ought to know that they have already triumphed over death. In our spirituality, death and birth belong together just as Easter and Christmas are two sides of the same coin. African spirituality's greatest value is that it appropriates mystery into the meaning of life, making life as a whole, a meaningful experience. African spirituality makes life coherent by its dialectic interpretation of both components of life including God, the divinities and other spirits, and the human community.

GOD AND SPIRIT AGENTS

African spirituality provides a way of thinking that accepts supernatural intervention as part of the dynamics of spirituality. For example, there are instances when the traditionalist looks forward to dying at maturity in order to attain the status attributed to the ancestor spirit. Some elderly people may actually call themselves *mudzimu* (ancestor spirit) as they begin to feel a sense of being totally spiritualized. Christians generally do not seem to look forward to dying although they claim that "this world is not my home, I am just a Passing by.." as the Negro Spiritual goes "and I can't feel at home in this world anymore. For the Christian African slaves, death was retirement whereas for the traditionalist it meant work and responsibilities continuing beyond this life.

To summarize kurova guva is a guarantee that the sprit does not wander in the wild; it comes home to be with its people as well as being in harmony in the spirit world as a whole. When the Christians sing: "Ndofamba, ndofamba, kunyika ya Tenzi...madzinza ariyo," it seems they share with traditionalists this sense of belonging to one's dzinza (clan) eternally. The Christian teaching is that in God's Kingdom all are one family under the "fatherhood of God" (sic); of course, one can belong to one's dzinza and all madzinza (clans) constitute God's family. The practice of kurova guva does not prevent the spirit of the living-dead from being directly under God's charge. What the practice does is to install the ancestor, making it known that those who have gone before us are continuing their responsibility of seeing to the welfare of the family.

We have discussed at length that God provides ultimate protection which cannot exclude God's involvement in history. This practice of kurova guva is a reminder that the spiritual world is mindful of the material world. We have stated that one of the functions of the spirit is to protect the family and that this protection is to be understood as ultimately coming from God. Protection,whether in death or in life, is one of these benefits, just as good health or good fortune may be considered a gift from God by those who believe. We have noted that in the Old Testament, God could empower the spirit of "your grandfather" to protect you. God, who spoke through a burning bush, can speak through a human spirit as well. God can and has done that many times (recorded in the Bible.)

As a major source of theology, African spirituality occupies a prominent place in the minds of most theological scholars. In fact, medical doctors, education specialists and agricultural scientists all take African spirituality very seriously in interpreting socio-politico-economic dynamics in most African communities. Similarly, priests and bishops who utilize African spirituality have succeeded in touching the hearts and spirits of their followers. Thus, spirituality is the most comprehensive matrix within which African theology is being developed.

Finally for the reader to better understand African concepts of God, one must have a deep appreciation and some understanding of the sources which we have discussed here. As one cannot understand the depth of Christian theology without appreciating Christ's birth, life, death and resurrection, one cannot comprehend African theology unless one understands the African spiritual world view. African spirituality begins with God and ends with God, via the human community.

Chapter Four

God: The Web of Our Identity (African and Black Theologies)

All African American and African scholars agree that they have a common ancestry rooted in the mother continent of Africa. Several centuries ago the present African Americans were captured in Africa and shipped to North America under extremely brutal and dehumanizing conditions, and auctioned off on the shores of the U.S.A. Consequently they were stripped of their culture and human dignity, cut off from any possible ties with their community and were sold without consideration of kinship ties. Some were re-sold as the conscienceless white American slave-holders saw fit. Such was the inception and historical dawning of the African American experience which has since given rise to the African American religion and consequently African American theology. However, that saga did not sever the African slaves from their God - the Great Spirit God. This God and the ancestors were the last hope the African slave community had. God remembered them!

Many historical records agree that the African American people were stripped of everything including, sometimes, their very life. But it was in that extreme suffering that the seeds for African American liberation were sown, maybe by mistake. In retrospect we can say God had a plan to save the African Americans, just as God redeemed the people of Israel from Egypt. When the African slaves heard the Gospel they took interest in it, but when they were able to tell the story of the Exodus, one to another, and sing the spirituals, the message for their liberation was loud and clear!

In fact, it is reported that some slave owners refused to have their slaves preached to because the Gospel had overtones of freedom. How were the slaves to understand Exodus Chapter 3. where God says. "...I am concerned about their suffering, so I have come down to rescue them from the hand of the Egyptians..." or the statement in Galatians: "in Christ there is no male or female, no Greek or Gentile, no slave or free"? However, others argued that if a slave was Christian, he or she would become more obedient to the master. Julius Lester, in his book: *To Be A Slave*, points out that another instrument used to control the minds of the slaves was religion.   No slave owner allowed his slaves to attend church by themselves, fearing that they would use the opportunity to plan an insurrection rather than thank God that they had such 'good' masters. According to some scholars, the slaves were required to sit in the balcony in church (with their masters, yet out of their sight!) so that they could hear the Christian message and be good slaves.

Another view predominated, namely that if slaves were baptized they would become "truly obedient." They became obedient but not to the master, rather to the Master who actually died on the cross for their true freedom! That was the "tragic flaw" in the history of white racism and oppression in the U.S. because indeed the slaves obeyed their Master - Jesus Christ whom they heard saying,

> the spirit of the Lord is upon me because he has anointed me to preach good news to the poor. He has sent me to proclaim release to the captives, and recovering of sight to the blind, to set at liberty those who are oppressed, to proclaim the acceptable year of the Lord (Luke 4:18-19).

Through "Negro Spirituals," gospel music and hymnals, not to mention the sermons given by the African American preachers, the slaves opted to obey the Master. It seems their faith was all the more deeply rooted in Christ because of, and in spite of the extreme oppressive conditions that they experienced. Without letting their African religiosity go, they became more committed believers in God. Their faith was not in vain because liberation did come, at least legally. After Emancipation and the Reconstruction, it could be said that the blacks were free in principle. In fact, there are records of "Back-to-Africa" movements reviewed in Gayraud Wilmore's book *Black Religion and Black Radicalism*, which substantiate this view. Still obeying their Master's voice, and because of that, African-Americans today are proclaiming the good news that Jesus Christ is the Liberator. That is why James Cone says:

Jesus Christ, therefore, in his humanity and divinity, is the point of departure for a black theologian's analysis of the meaning of liberation. There is no liberation independent of Jesus' past, present, and future coming

So, African American people have to fight for freedom and justice, precisely because Jesus Christ, their future, is the very springboard of their struggle for liberation and humanity today.

A KITH AND KIN DIALOGUE

Earlier, we have pointed out that in the history of African slavery one can detect evidence of God at work. Some people say God's plan began to unfold and manifested itself in the "back-to-Africa" movement which was intended to spread the good news brought by fellow Africans. People realized that Africa should receive the Gospel from her own sons and daughters. The African Methodist Episcopal church (A.M.E.) was one of the groups which prepared to take the gospel back to the mother continent. In their General Conference Minutes of 1892, they resolved to spread the Word:

> ...then pursuing our onward march for the dark continent, we will speak to more than 200 million of men and women, bone of our bone, and flesh of our flesh, and say to them, 'Arise and shine, for the light of civilization is waiting for thee'.

It is this spirit in which I have undertaken to write this chapter - a dialogue between Black theology and African theology - highlighting the main differences and similarities between the two theologies. Gayraud Wilmore, in his book, makes a more contemporary statement, yet he presses the same issue of dialogue between African and African Americans. He says, "the theological programme of African scholars for the Africanization of Christianity in modern Africa has much to say to Black theology's "ghettoization" of the Christian faith in the United States."

In the same spirit, Professor Mbiti from the Continent says, in the conclusion of his article, "An African views American Black theology":

> We (I) wish only for dialogue, fellowship, sharing of ideas and insights, and learning from one another as equal partners in the universal Body of Christ, even if we Africans may still speak the theological language of Christianity with a stammering voice since most of us are so new to

it (Wilmore & Cone 1979, 482).

Mbiti is correct to admit that African theologians are still relatively new, or rather inexperienced and unestablished at the level that Black theologians now are. This fact is also made note of by Gayraud Wilmore in his book cited above, although Wilmore gets beyond Mbiti in terms of vision when he says,

> Only by a sympathetic and intensive dialogue between the younger theologians of Africa and Black theologians in the United States and the Caribbean's will it be possible to uncover the harmonies and disharmonies in Black religion and forge the theological and ideological links which can bind modern Africa and black America together for the unimaginable possibilities of the future (Wilmore 1973).

Why should we encourage a dialogue between African American theology and African theology? Part of the answer must be inferred from the common view that the chief sources for African American theology are the same as those of African theology, namely scriptures, experience of African slavery and African culture. The former and the latter are major sources for African theology as well. Also, while the African Americans were enslaved, the Africans were colonized and subdued to servitude on an international scale. However, Africans went through a psychological and physical enslavement to the point of being dehumanized. Consequently, though to differing degrees, both need to regain their human dignity and a sense of human worth, although admittedly there is a vast difference between the two. Regarding commonalties there is much literature that points to the presence of Africanisms apparent in the African American culture even today. In his book, Lawrence Levine points out on numerous occasions that much of African Americanisms are the legacies of their African culture. He cites several examples to demonstrate this point. He has said:

> Gospel song was a musical and structural return to African and slave music away from Western hymnody, even while its sacred universe of the African and slave past and an adjustment to modern religious consciousness...
> ...blues with its emphasis upon improvisation, its retention of the call and response pattern, its polyrhythmic efforts and its methods of vocal production which includes slides , slurs, vocal leaps, and the use of falsetto, was a definite assertion of central elements of the African traditional communal musical style (Levine 1977, 223).

Since both African and African American theologies are Christian, it goes without saying that both share the use of scriptures as a major source of theology. However, Professor James Cone has a rather more exhaustive list of sources which supersedes the few mentioned above. Cone realizes that there could be more sources; that is why he says "it is too early to define all of the sources which are participating in its (Black Theology) creation." But he itemizes African American experience, history, culture, and revelation as well as scripture and tradition. African theology can also claim all these sources from an African context. In fact, context makes the whole difference.

With regard to traces of similarities, Mbiti erroneously refutes such possibilities categorically when he says, "black theology and African theology merge from quite a different historical and contemporary situations. They are wholly different" (Wilmore & Cone 1979, 481). Mbiti argues further and explains, "of course there is no reason why Black theology should have meaning for Africa." This view, however, is violently and rightfully attacked specifically by a South African theologian, Allan Boesak in his book *Farewell to Innocence*. Boesak declares that "it must be abundantly clear that Black theology cannot be divorced from African theology." In an interview on "African theology and Black theology" (AACC Bulletin 1975), Tutu agrees with Boesak when he says, "black theology is an aspect of African theology. That is to say not all African theology is black theology, but the converse: that all Black theology...is African theology." This is true when we talk of African people as belonging to the African race. Incidentally, African American theology and South African liberation theology share even theological jargon, although each has its own idiosyncrasies. In South Africa, Basil Moore tells us that Black theology has emerged as a consequence of a growing mood among Blacks against multi-racialism. Out of political and racial conflicts emerged a tide of church-based opposition. Attempts at reconciliation failed since such an attempt had only taken into consideration the elite, forgetting the masses - the people!

Black theology in South Africa begins with the people in a specific situation, with specific problems to face. Moore wrote when the Blacks in South Africa were facing the strangling problems of oppression, fear, hunger, insults and dehumanization due to apartheid policy. Black theology sought to understand who these people were, what their life experiences were, the nature and the cause of their suffering. To attempt to answer some of the questions above being raised in South Africa, Black theology turned to scripture, experience, tradition and reason.

Black theology also sought the judgement of the scripture, experience and tradition on the rich people who oppress and exploit the poor. Because some Black theologians hold that the gospel declares that the God of the oppressed came down to identify and suffer with the oppressed and the poor, they assert that this God must be Black "like us!" This statement makes a lot of sense when it is juxtaposed to, or understood in light of, what professor James Cone has said in *A Black Theology and Liberation*, that "Blackness, then, stands for all victims of oppression who realize that their humanity is inseparable from man's liberation from whiteness."

Earlier in *Black Theology and Black Power* Cone had stated the matter of color rather mildly in some people's judgement when he said,

> Being black in America has very little to do with skin color. To be black means that your heart, your soul, your mind, and your body are where the dispossessed are...it essentially depends on the color of your heart, soul and mind (Cone, 1970).

Wilmore challenged that statement as a "half truth." In his book *Black Religion and Black Radicalism* he says with a vehement tone, "to say that being black in America has little to do with skin color is, at best only half true...being black or identifiably 'Negroid,' is a unique experience and has produced a unique religion, closely related to...Christian tradition." Thus the most important point here is the matter of being black; to what extent theologians may hold varying views. In his poem, Mokgethi Motlhabi, a South African theologian who was Vice President of the World Methodist Council, writes,

> they call me African.
> African indeed I am:
> Rugged son of the soil of Africa,
> Black as my father, and his before him;
> As my mother and sister and brothers, living
> and gone from this world. (Motlhabi, 1972).

Note that this African poet uses "African" and "Black" interchangeably or synonymously.

However, there are some African theologians who have a different opinion. Other African theologians argue that it may be true that African theology does not emphasize "blackness," but it is also true that it emphasizes what can be considered the counterpart of "blackness." According to E. E. Mshana, "African theology wants to create something which is uniquely African." Indeed, it is the business of theology to clarify issues, especially matters related to religious faith, our identity and ontology.

Desmond Tutu says essentially what Moore has said but at a more "gut level feeling." In <u>Frontier</u> he says, Black theology is a "gut level theology" relating to issues of "life and death" for the Black people. For Tutu, "blackness" represents the oppressed, whose concrete examples are found in South Africa and the United States of America. Tutu says black theology seeks to make sense out of Black suffering at the hands of white racism. Manas Buthelezi, another Black theologian from South Africa, shares this view in his article "Daring to live for Christ." He says: "the Black people are not regarding their suffering as a step towards liberation instead of a pool of fate and self-pity. Right in the midst of the experiencing of suffering the Black people have made themselves believe that they can do something about their own liberation."

In attempting to interpret Black suffering everywhere, Professor Cone, in *God of the Oppressed*, agrees with the South Africans' point of view and adds: "suffering that arises in the context of the struggle for freedom is liberating. It is liberating because it is a sign of Jesus' presence in our midst." Cone proceeds to the logical conclusion that a Black people is therefore "God's suffering servant," chosen to suffer for and with God in the struggle to liberate humanity.

Tutu thinks that God can be thought of as partial - sympathizing with the oppressed. He calls the oppressed community everywhere to align with the God of the Exodus, the Liberator who leads the people out of all kinds of bondage. This is the God Mshana refers to when he says, "the Christian gospel is the good news of liberation. This liberation is the liberation of the oppressed wherever they may be..." These people, say Mshana, are liberated to be the new people. For Tutu, Black theology is one of oppression and liberation and the God conceived in Black theology is one who can, and does upset the status quo: one in whom "life" is in "death" and through Christ's death, we are liberated from sin. Manas Buthelezi's definition of Black theology is slightly different from others although they are essentially saying the same thing. For Buthelezi Black theology should be conceived of as a semantic term which implies the presence of God as experienced in the Black community. For him, the difference between Black theology and African theology, is that the latter is a more established term than Black theology since it is understood that

Black theology has above it the dominant American theology. Note, that while some people think Black theology as an independent minority people's movement, apparently Buthelezi regards it as comparable to the dominant American theology.

Since African theology seeks to copy all that the Christian tradition has to offer but Black theology claims for immediate application only those issues which relate to the Black people's condition, it would seem at least structurally, that African theology is more established. But such is not the case because, in terms of literature, impact and specificity, more has been written on Black theology than African.

For Buthelezi, theologically, Blackness means the circumstances of the Black people's growth from childhood, and chances open to them in life if there are any. It determines where they live and worship and who their associates can be. Buthelezi believes that a genuine theology grows out the dynamic forces in life, forces which are decisive for the shaping of everyday life. That is why in his entry in *The Challenge of Black Theology in South Africa* Buthelezi says:

> As far as I can judge, Black theology is nothing but a methodological formula whose genius consists in paying tribute to the fact that theological honesty cannot but recognize the peculiarity of the Black man's situation (Moore 1974, 34).

In concluding his article, Buthelezi asserts what can not be said of African theology, that Black theology challenges established Christianity to engage in dialogue with the Black people who feel that somehow theology has not spoken for them to their point of need.

An American scholar, J. Deotis Roberts author of *Liberation and Reconciliation* and numerous other important and instructive works, sums up Black experience whether secular or religious, with the term "soul." Then he indicates where he stands in the world of Black theology and politics by making a definitive statement that "soul theology is black theology." Because he believes that the Africanisms evident in the African American life are important, he also talks in terms of "Afro-American," equating it with "Blackness." As the title of the book indicates, J. Deotis Roberts asserts that reconciliation is "the message" - everything must give way to it. Separatism must give way to reconciliation, liberation is only good and useful as it leads to reconciliation because the Gospel, for Roberts, is reconciling. J. Deotis Roberts answers the question or criticism leveled at Liberation theology's future after liberation. Liberation leads to reconciliation.

Of course, the reconciliation is between Black and White and this reconciliation will depend on what both sides will do! Roberts' prescription is that equality is the only principle of Black-White reconciliation. This position places Roberts, as he says himself, between Black militants and integrationist. Although both James Cone and Roberts believe that the means justifies the end, the former holds the view stated in *Black Theology and Black Power* that whatever means necessary to effect liberation and to perpetuate Black power should be employed in the struggle. Now the latter's "means" is much less militant. However, J. Cone's statement: "whatever means necessary" is to be taken in context. The statement was made in a desperate context for urgent need for liberation. J. Cone did not advocate reparation but liberation. As a believer in God's power to deliver, his statement reflects an open mind, a mind guided by faith.

THE MISSION OF BLACK THEOLOGY

On the matter of mission of Black theology, another vocal African American theologian, Major Jones' *Black Awareness: A Theology of Hope*, holds a somewhat different view. He states that:

> Under the mandate of hope, black awareness literature has a strong sense of Messianic Mission. Whether it is theological or non-theological in nature, there is a sense in which black men think they are called of God to deliver black America from bondage and white America from its lethal folly (Jones 1971).

But for Albert B. Cleage, Jr., Black theology involves Black Christ-ology in which Christ is Black and "His mission is liberation - political, social, economic and religious." Most African American theologians agree that the problem of God for African Americans is not whether God is, or not, but what God's character is. All African theologians concur with this African American perspective. Mshana speaks for all people of African descent when he says, "to know him is to know what he is doing in the historical events as they relate to the liberation of the oppressed" (Mshana, 1972).

Roberts raises questions on James Cone's scope of African American theology. In fact, he indicates that this African American theologian is too narrow and must be rejected for the sake of African American theology itself. This view is also supported by a few African theologians such as Kwesi Dickson and John Mbiti, who accuse Cone and his school of thought on liberation that it does not consider issues in life such as salvation, grace, trinity, and the like. Such criticism however comes from lack of awareness of J. Cone's own words, that

> There was, therefore, an ontological basis for white racism in America and a corresponding ontological ground for Black pride and the Black man's struggle against a latent but frighteningly real possibility of genocide. This is why it is correct to say that the Black American's struggle is against the threat of nonbeing, the ever present possibility of the inability to affirm one's own existence (Wilmore & Cone 1979, 466).

Another argument is, since Cone does not invite white racists in America to participate in the work of God in the Black communities and since Cone excludes the whites for they do not - rather cannot - feel the way the Blacks do, he simply does not intend his theology to "talk" to them, not directly anyhow. On the other hand, Roberts, whose ultimate goal is reconciliation which happens between two or more parties, inevitably addresses both whites and Blacks - hoping that, having convinced both sides, the same would form a single RECONCILED community. In a word, Roberts rejects aspects of Cone's theology of liberation because, after liberation and confrontation, Cone's theology does not seem to proceed to work toward reconciliation. Apparently, hindsight indicates that J. Deotis Roberts was wrong because Black theology in South Africa led to national reconciliation.

In agreement with Roberts, Mbiti argues, "when the immediate concerns of liberation are realized, it is not all clear where Black theology is supposed to go." Mbiti has teamed up with J. Deotis Roberts in error. Again J. Deotis Roberts differs with South African Black theologians like Tutu, who maintains that one has to be Black - and "Black" is used symbolically - to understand and participate in the black experience and liberation of the oppressed. Deotis Roberts argues that one does not have to be Black to understand "Black oppression" in America. For J. Deotis, it is possible to understand a faith claim from "outside." He believes that if a member of the community attempts to study his own faith, there is a greater tendency to be subjective, not objective.

On this matter of experiential distance, J. Deotis Roberts and Cone agree. Roberts expects reconciliation between equal groups both of whom are authentic. So he says, for authentic life for the whites, they must move through humanness to reconciliation; while African Americans move through liberation to reconciliation. Liberation and reconciliation are the two maniples of Black theology for Roberts.

WHAT COLOR IS THE AFRICAN AMERICAN GREAT SPIRIT GOD?

Major Jones and Roberts share some interesting concepts of God from the African American community's vantage point. Roberts says that in Christian faith, God is a "revealer-God." However, what he has to say to the comfortable white oppressor has to be different from the message to the African American oppressed victim of racism in white America because the African American people are concerned with existential concerns of "liberation and even survival." Major Jones asserts that the African American folk have the right to appropriate their God in their own color (Christ is Black!) And to express this in literature. Jones endorses this as a sign of theological maturity. In his words:

When the oppressed no longer is satisfied to accept or adopt the God of the oppressor, especially his explicit colour as it is expressed in art and literature, then the process of liberation has already begun (Jones 1971).

Jones warns against claims on God which will "make our God too small," however. The God advocated in Black theology has to be omnipotent, and this is a very crucial element since the African American community is seeking what Cecil Cone would call the "Almighty Sovereign God" to liberate them from the white power structures. Black people need the intervention of the omnipotent God to deal with the white power in America. Roberts agrees with the foregoing statement and undergirds it with strong affirmation of faith in the God of Moses, the God of the Exodus, (who) has been real to the African American people. This God is one of deliverance from bondage. Thus the God of the Exodus is the Black man's God. When the Great Spirit says: "I have heard the cry of my people" kinship is clearly indicated. God is the color of God's own people. Again Major Jones reminds us that no Gospel of the African American should ignore all the tenets of the Judeo-Christian faith, lest it fails the test of history. In his book, Major Jones points out that a more mature concept of God would reveal a more mature human being who is harder to subject to any status less than equal.

So, like any mature Christian, the African American believers have an adequate faith in the future rooted only in a secure selfhood conceived to be authentic under God. Hope - Christian hope under God - is another aspect of Black theology of liberation. Major Jones argues that

God, for the African American community, must be at work in a visible sort of way. God must be God for all.

This view is expressed by James Cone also although for Cone there are other dimensions to it. Cone says Black theology insists that genuine biblical faith relates eschatology to those historical events which demonstrate what God did yesterday, is doing at the present moment and will perform for his people. It is these acts and manifestations of God which enable the African American people to talk about the future - to hope for the future based on the Divine promises and the activities of today. This African American thinking is in line with the Africans who contend that, "to know God is to know what God is doing in the historical events as they relate to the liberation of the oppressed," as Mshana said.

In *Black Theology and Black Power*, Professor Cone spells out that the task of African American theology is to analyze the African's condition in the light of God's revelation in Jesus Christ with the purpose of creating a new understanding of Black dignity among the African American people, and providing the necessary soul in that people to destroy white racism.

So, Cone sees Black theology as primarily a theology of and for the African American people who stand in firm solidarity and share the common belief that "enough is enough." Consequently for Cone Black theology is a theology for the oppressed African American people aimed at the destruction of racism in the society. This being the task of theology, James Cone would then necessarily agree with those African theologians who believe that the indigenization and contextualization of African theology has to be done by the members of the community, not by outsiders.

Professor Cone also firmly believes that if the African American people are to be liberated, it would have to be the African Americans themselves who will need to do the liberating, not the white racists.

In the same grain, Mkgethi Motlhabi of South Africa records the resolution of the Transvaal Regional Seminar on Black theology held at Hammanskraal in 1971 in these words, "We understand Christ's liberation not only from circumstances of external bondage but also a liberation from circumstances of internal enslavement" (Motlhabi 1971).

Similar to this South African view of Black theology, Cone speaks for many when he says Black theology in America is a theology of liberation with Christ as the liberator. In Christ, God enters human affairs and takes side with the suffering; their suffering become his; he transforms their despair. In harmony with the South African theologians, Cone says that Christianity is Black power since these two serve the same purpose - namely seeking to transform the ghetto situation.

Because Cone's starting point of doing theology is Black experience, he concludes that theology is none other than a Christian theology since most of these blacks are Christian. *Farewell to Innocence* also carries the same message in the statement:

> Any theology which does not take God's liberation of the poor and the oppressed as its central point of departure thereby excludes itself effectively from being a witness to the divine presence in the world. The point is, therefore, not whether theology is determined by interest, but whether it is being determined by the interest of the poor and the oppressed or by those of the oppressor. (Boesak 1977).

At this Cecil Cone sharply disagrees with both Allen Boesak and his own brother James Cone because the latter has used as his point of departure, Black experience - almost identified with Black power - rather than Black religion as an "ecclesiastical entity." In fact, in his book, *The Identity Crisis of Black Theology*, Cecil Cone's major critique of contemporary theology has to do with the point of departure one uses. He argues: "Black theology, accordingly, is rooted in the black religious experiences; it is an analysis of black religion. Black religion is therefore its only appropriate point of departure." Further, Cecil Cone joins hands with Manas Buthelezi in rejecting Black power or its counterpart in South Africa, as the appropriate point of departure in Black theology. So we hear Buthelezi rejecting unconditionally any interpretation which connects Black theology to such secular movements as Black Power and the Black consciousness movement. He says, "the indiscriminate alignment of Christian black awareness with an emotionally-charged political concept is wrong." Cecil Cone says in his book, "the tension in Cone's Black Theology, therefore, is located in its identification with Black Power movement." Appreciating the task of Black theology, Cecil Cone regrets to point out that a more particular handicap on the part of the Black theologians is the use of the historical critical methods in the Black theology. Characteristic of the work within white seminaries, this method has contributed to the identity crisis in Black theology. Such tools of critical inquiry are limited in what they discover.

Having said this, it is strange that Cecil Cone should assert that Black theology must use the historical approach to make Black theology authentic. But appreciating the problem, Cecil Cone goes further to say (as if White are the norm!), "even White theologians,...are beginning to recognize the futility and the dangers of the historical method."

James Cone's view that Black theology is nationalistic and attempts to provide the African American people with a sense of nationhood, is in harmony with some African theological voices which reject leaders who merely imitate the values and standards of white racist imperialist society. One African theologian says, "a truly African theology cannot escape the requirement of helping the indigenous churches to become relevant to the spiritual, social and political ills of Africa." In this regard, Black theology speaks with a precise vocabulary for African theology's social contexts. Both theologies start with where the people are - from below to above! But James Cone says the purpose of analyzing the African American people's condition is so Black theology may "create a new understanding." This contrasts with Mbiti's view which, rather than "creating a new understanding," seeks to "interpret" the faith. It is not clear to me whether these two major theologians mean the same thing or not; but it is plausible that they are both pointing at the same "objective." Albeit, both theologians seek to reflect and understand the faith. Cecil Cone is likely to sanction Mbiti's view because the latter seeks to "interpret" not "create." The main point here is that one has to be careful when reading Professor James Cone because (from his lectures at Union) evidently he considers both secular and religious communities when he deals with theological analysis of the African American folk. Hence the allegation by his brother Cecil that he is influenced by both Black Power motif and religious value. Cecil refuses to allow theologians who use the secular as "point of departure." He agrees that the secular can be part of, but not "the" point of departure.

Mbiti argues that one can only interpret what one can understand to support himself. For Mbiti, the Christian faith is the substance of the interpretative work of theology and the Africans are the recipients and agents of the interpretation of the Christian faith. Mbiti and J. Cone seem to hold the same view that their respective theologies should be first and foremost exclusive because they are intended for their particular respective communities. While Mbiti seems to close the doors to non-Africans, J. Cone seems to welcome and encourage all oppressed people of African descent. On the other hand, leaders in other African nations have accused the Church of lacking the Africanness desired and required in independent Africa. In his article 'African theology: What is it' J.K. Agbeti says,

> I have mentioned this...to emphasize the point that politically, there had been the feeling, among some politicians during the first Republic of Ghana, that the church was foreign in its attitude to national aspirations.

(Agbeti 1972).

In this case, it seems the politicians have gone ahead of the theologians in matters of building African nationalism and personhood. However, it should be said that in general, unlike Black theologians, many African theologians do not seem to be sufficiently politically motivated (except for those in Southern African!) to deal with theological aspects of African nationalism. (One hopes that with the Third World Theological Conferences now held annually there maybe more active participation and efficacious awareness.) It is very possible that most of these African theologians prefer to remain silent because of fear - fear of being victimized by their national government. Although they pretend that they are free nations, the truth of the matter is that they are free from white rule, but there is worse oppression from the new masters in some instances. Mbiti's focal point in African theology is the theological perceptions of God by African Christians. He says African Christian believers are called to an understanding of the faith, that is, understanding it in their own terms, according to their own insights and in ways that are meaningful to their own time and situation. Mbiti also says this understanding is automatically colored by the African heritage and the contemporary situation of their living. This idea is parallel to Black theology in the United States, which is colored by the African American experience and the oppressive situation in which the Africans in Diaspora find themselves in the racist America as we have seen. For Mbiti, the task of African theology is, first and foremost, to understand, then interpret the faith. On this matter there is a fine variation between African American and African theologies, a difference necessitated by respective contexts. J. Deotis Roberts would keep his doors "wide open" even to the oppressor, hoping for a reconciliation eventually. However, J. Cone and Mbiti, are apprehensive. Their valid reason is that these "outsiders" can not obtain that "personal experience" called for.

In Africa, Mbiti says, theology, one's experience and understanding of God, is intimately bound up with one's own understanding of oneself. Mbiti perceives a twofold task in African theology: 1. To help Africans understand themselves; 2. To help illuminate God for them in the Christian context.

Mbiti argues that African theology is African only due to some peculiar ways, otherwise it is, first and foremost just a Christian theology which is neutral. In his own words,

"African theology is not so restricted in its concerns, nor does it have an ideology to propagate...As an African one has an academic interest in black Theology, just as one is interested in the 'water Buffalo theology' of Southeast Asia..." (Wilmore & Cone 1979).

Apparently, Mbiti does not even conceptualize the kinship between the African Americans in Diaspora and the African on the continent. Mbiti wants to add African theology to the classical theology which had no interest in the gospel of liberation which is central in the scriptures. There have been theologies - German theology, Lutheran theology, Protestant theology and so forth, but these never did speak to the condition of the African slaves who brought tea or coffee to the masters who were writing theology. It is also very possible that being the oppressors - nanzi Germans, American colonist and imperialists in Africa, white theologians dared not articulate who they were. It was in their interest to keep their theology general, not specific. African theology has a specificity which SPEAKS to the African people both on the continent and in Diaspora.

The problem is that Mbiti argues that while African American theology is pivoted on racial identity, African theology is not. The question that needs to be asked is: should African theology not serve to identify the Africans and clarify their identity as a particular Christian community after many decades of being a disoriented colonized people? Christ himself wrestled with his own identity when he asked his disciples who he was. If African theology does not serve to help the Africans to know themselves and their needs, it serves little or no purpose. It will remain "exclusive" as Mbiti characterizes it. We could not say African theologies already know their identity since some leading theologians themselves say: "we cannot define," because it is too broad and rather slippery. Mbiti also comments that African theology's contents are too many to be determined.

If African theology is that broad, elusive and slippery, it can not and should not claim to stand at par with the African American theology, with regard to specificity.

However, other African theologians have given tentative definitions in spite of what Mbiti says. J. Kurewa once said:

We could tentatively define African theology as that study that seeks to reflect upon and express the Christian faith in African thought-forms and idiom as it is experienced in African Christian communities, and always in dialogue with the rest of Christendom (Kurewa 1975).

Agbeti's definition of African theology seems to be at a completely different frequency as it seems to be divorced from the Christian church in Africa. He says, "when we talk about African theology we should mean the interpretation of the pre-Christian and pre-Moslem African peoples' experience of their god." But Dr. Agbeti's definition needs to keep pace with the times. What is African theology today? Prof. Harry Sawyer's definition shares much relevance with Kurewa's because it states "theology is not primarily what man thinks about God in an abstract way, but rather what God has done and is doing for man."

The exponents of African American theology, Professor J. Cone for example, would probably say a secular political movement such as Black Power is the counterpart of the Black theology movement. The former focuses on the political, social and economic condition of the African American people while the latter discusses African American identity also in the political and economic context but from a theological point of view. The result and effect of these two "working hand in hand" show that Black Power is the Gospel of Christ just as Black theology is. Writing in the Christian Century, Professor J. Cone asserts that "the significance of black theology then is found in the conviction that the content of the Christian Gospel is liberation," a statement which the Black Power movement would endorse without hesitation. The exponents of African theology would advance the Organization of African Unity (O.A.U.) a secular movement which is parallel to Black Power. But in general, African theologians did not take their political counterpart as seriously as black theologians took black Power in doing black theology. The O.A.U. is organized and run by African heads of state who are more concerned about preserving their political offices than working for freedom for the greatest number. This is different from a movement such as the Black Power movement. However, one African theologian is correct to say that this new quest for a more distinctive African Christianity could be seen as one of the by-products of political independence. Agbeti has also said that the growth of nationalism did not issue only in political independence, but with political independence came the need for religious independence also. This may indicate that African nationalism might have given birth to several aspects of freedom, which include the necessity and rise of African theology. Certainly, during colonial rule, there was no mention of African technology because the church leadership was clouded with a colonial mentality. Furthermore, theological colleges and seminaries on the continent were run by expatriates who designed syllabi which reflected their home institutions in

Europe and America. Literature was predominantly "irrelevant" to African needs. There is no doubt that in Africa South of the Sahara, political movement which Harold Macmillian poignantly described as "the wind of change in colonial Africa" spearheaded Africa's path to liberation. By contrast, in the U.S.A. largely churchmen provided leadership both on secular and religious fronts (Wilmore &Cone 1979).

In Southern Africa politicians (A.N.C.) led the way. Basil Moore says out of political or racial conflicts emerged a tide of church-based opposition. Moore also points out that "in South Africa black theology has emerged as a consequence of the fact that more and more there has been a growing mood among blacks against multi-racialism." The Black consciousness movement in South Africa was comparable to Black Power in the U.S.A. Thus, a parallel between Black theology and Black Power; *and* African theology and South African Black theology and the rise of African nationalism worked side-by-side for the freedom of the oppressed. A theology divorced from the people's political yearnings, is at its best useless, and at its worst harmful. There must be political solidarity in order to attain liberation. Roger Cornish correctly observes that "at a deeper level, however, African theology and Black theology are contending against the same principalities and power, from which Christ came to liberate all men (sic)." Cornish is not saying Black and African theologies should sound the same. He observes that there is a distinction between African and Black theologies, owing to the ever different social context of the two. Another difference which Cornish notes between the two theologies is that while African theology, after European theological overlaps are removed, has about it a refined gentleness and meditative spirituality, Black theology assumes a hard-nosed militant posture. Although these differences between black and African theologies were there, they did not make the two groups antagonistic because their target was the same-white oppression.

Professor Gelzer has really noted several differences between African American theology and African theology. In <u>Christian Century</u> his article entitled "Random Notes on Black Theology and African Theology" tabulated what African theology is not, thereby characterizing what Black theology is. He says that African theology was not a product of slavery as is the case with the African American theology. While African theology deals with issues of life and death, it is not for dehumanized, despised and degraded people who are struggling with survival concerns. The issue of racism, as a point of departure is completely irrelevant in African theology. Maybe Gelzer does not realize that probably racism in Africa has been disguised by colonialism which sets master against servant, upper class against lower class, light skin against dark skin people, the Asiatic, whites and blacks. Gelzer suggests that another difference is that African theology is not "closed" to whites.

Although Africans have been colonized, subdued to servitude by white imperialists, African theology is not concerned with reparations, according to Gelzer. In fact, the property owned by the former mission society has been, generally speaking, turned over to the autonomous churches. Gelzer makes a tragic observation that African theology is not concerned with the dignity of African humanity! With the exception of Southern African, it is correct to argue that African theology is not aimed against white oppression. Of course not all African theologians would agree with Gelzer's observations. These differences are not as clear as they may sound or appear on paper. There are shades of grey here and there.

Another interesting comment made in the Christian Century is that African American theologians have incorporated the meaning of the colonial and slave experience of the past several centuries into their theology. This has been a very serious deficiency but thank God something is being done now [the author refers here to the Third World Conferences of Theologians which have met, for example in Accra, Ghana in December 1977.]

A year before that (1976), such a conference, had met in Dar es Salaam at which Professor Cone and Gayraud Wilmore expressed ideas which really demonstrated that African theology and African American theology will need to pull their resources together - without destroying each other's dignity and identity, or ignoring their respective agendas, or fostering a marriage of convenience. Although they have major cultural, political and social differences, each will benefit from the theological contribution made by the other. Cone and Wilmore summed up their paper with a statement, as reported in the Christian Century:

> African theology is concerned with Africanization. Black theology is concerned with liberation. But Africanization must also involve liberation from centuries of poverty, humiliation, exploitation (Christian Century 1978).

But it is precisely on this matter of liberation that some African theologians prefer to draw a line of demarcation between Black theology and theirs. In *World view*, Mbiti asserts that "African theology has no interest in reading liberation into every text, no interest in telling people to think or act 'black'."

It may be pointed out that here Mbiti seems to forget that since the dawning of Pan-Africanisms, the stress has been to be *African*, not to imitate Europeans or Americans. In fact, there has been crush programs of "decolonization" in independent Africa - "I am the son/child of the African soil" was the theme. As a matter of fact, this is the "fever" which has lately attacked the Church, hence the steps being taken toward theological contextualization and indigenization. When Black theology advocates liberation even in Africa, most African theologians appreciate the concern, and adopt that gospel because that is precisely what is needed! This is because liberation is an on-going process, culminating in a sort of politico-economic equilibrium.

There is need for the Church in Africa to be liberated. (It seems some African theologians do not correctly represent the need of the Church whose activities they claim to reflect upon.) For instance the All African Conference of Churches which met in Alexandria, Egypt, in February 1976 actually called for a more comprehensive understanding of liberation in independent African states. This was in addition to the Lusaka declaration. For the next two decades, were the concerns with economic justice and human liberation. The churhces also jointly said:

> We accept the political liberation in Africa, and the Middle East, is a part of this liberation. But the enslaving forces and the abuse of human rights in independent Africa point to the need of a more comprehensive understanding of liberation. Liberation is therefore a continuous struggle (Lusaka 1974).

In the light of this statement and concern, African theologians are coming to grips with the African American's fundamental theological position. J. Cone has repeatedly stated in his works like *A Black Theology of Liberation*:

> It is my contention that Christianity is essentially a religion of liberation. The function of theology is that of analyzing the meaning of that liberation for the oppressed community so they can know that their struggle for political, social and economic justice is consistent with the gospel of Jesus Christ (Cone 1986).

Hailing from South Africa, Boesak asserts the same idea more bluntly when he says "liberation is not merely a part of the Gospel...it is the content and framework of the whole biblical message." While Cone is not likely to ever demand that African theology succumb to the African American theology, he has left enough room open for "any oppressed people" to utilize Black theology of liberation according to their need. He correctly says in the same book, "...I am convinced that the patterns of meaning centered in the idea of Black theology are by no means restricted to the American scene, since blackness symbolizes oppression and liberation in any society." In these concluding remarks, it is vital to be aware of the sad fact that while some African theologians are reluctant to not only welcome but utilize Black theology of liberation, there are African communities which are suffering oppression at the hands of African governments in the heart of independent Africa.

Political independence in Africa has not guaranteed human rights or human freedom. Africa needs to adopt relevant phases of liberation theology in order to liberate her people from a colonial mentality, poverty, hunger and several phases of oppressive mentalities which Africans acquired before their political independence. Every nation that became independent in Africa won the Flag and lost the value of its currency because economically, African states are far from being truly independent. At the same time, on the American side of the Atlantic, by the time the African American slaves got their "freedom," at least political emancipation, they had started to lose their sense of identity to the point where some of them even hate their African ancestry! They too have lost their "identity currency." All that remains is to be racially devalued. Fortunately the African American theologians are summoning all people of African descent to unite in kinship solidarity.

Black Americans in their search for human and personal identity can get substantially effective results by forming a solidarity with their fellow Africans on the main continent. It is great to know that Black people everywhere are the founders of the earth as anthropological research in Central Africa has shown. There is no doubt that the white people have failed in their attempt to run the world because of their racism, bigotry, greed and inhuman treatment of other human beings. So now we hear the young voices of the Black community who are saying through the late Steven BKilo, "we are looking forward to a nonracial, just and egalitarian society in which colour, creed and race shall form no point of reference," a world free from all forms of injustice, and a life-style based on humanity and equality.

Chapter Five

The Great Spiritual Being: God Here, God There, God Everywhere

Our belief in God is reflected in the characteristic African spirituality. Professor John Mbiti has correctly noted in his book: *The Prayers of African Religion* (1975) that Africans are extremely spiritual because the prayers, more than any other aspect of religion, contain the most intense expression in African traditional spirituality. A study of these prayers takes us to the core of African spirituality, and adds a valuable dimension to our understanding of African religion.

Dr. John Parratt, one time chair of the Religion Department at the University of Botswana says, "African Independent Churches are becoming more and more accepted as legitimate examples of African Christian spirituality." This actually implies that these independent churches were despised by the "mainline" or "missionary churches," because their spirituality and worship behavior did not comply with and conform to Western doctrine. It is interesting to observe that these days the so-called "mainline" churches actually envy the spirituality of the independent churches which have liberated themselves to incorporate traditional spirituality in their liturgy. Now many churches are expressing faith in God through traditional concepts of God with an added knowledge about God which is found in the Bible, which is a primary source. The gospel is preached in context, making the word of God resonate with indigenous God-consciousness. In this discussion of God, we examine God-concepts as expressed regionally.

REGIONAL TRADITIONAL PERSPECTIVES OF GOD

In many African communities, God is known regionally because there is no literature or other media. Our faith necessarily takes on local color and is more eloquent in our articulation. According to African religious concepts, our closeness to God is largely due to our sense of total dependence on God. Because God is Spirit, it is through African spirituality that concepts of the Godness of God are revealed. The worship of God in Africa is very lively because the Church's basic message of the sovereignty of God is well received. This is overwhelming because God is known on the basis of what God has done lately, or according to tradition. Since our religious heritage is one of the major sources of theology in Africa, it is important to highlight some traditional perceptions of God which have been passed down orally from generation to generation. This method is crucial because it leads to a theology built on an authentic African sense of the divine. Particular traditional God-concepts furnish the raw material for African theology. A look at some traditional concepts of God by regions gives us an authentic picture of the African theological world view.

THE CREATOR: GOD OF THE LELE

According to W. C. Willoughby's *The Soul of the Bantu* (1928) the Lele of Kasai, East Africa, believe in the Creator God. Their local name for God is <u>Njambi</u> who they believe created "men and animals, rivers and all things." The natives regard Njambi as the power which controls their destiny eternally. They also believe that they are always at Njambi's disposal. Njambi is their protector and sets their community and personal affairs straight. Their God wants to see justice in the community. Injustice is avenged by Njambi. The nature of Njambi is regarded as a mystery no one may tamper with. Their God is not subject to scrutiny. The Lele believe that they have known their God Njambi for generations. Everyone in the community must know how to live well with Njambi who sustains.

The Lele believe that Njambi has given them dominion over all creation, especially the animals and vegetation in the forest. As far as the Lele are concerned, the flora and fauna is their God-given gift which they are entitled to eat in order to survive. Thus, Njambi is the greatest provider they know. However, the Lele do not confuse dominion with destruction. To have dominion is to manage carefully - in such a way that they can account for everything. They tend to "worship" ecological balance! Thus, the Lele see initially, two categories of Njambi's creation: (a) human beings whose lives are sacred and (b) animals and other creatures which are also sacred but at the disposal of human beings. The second category is regarded as inferior to the first since the former is at the mercy of the latter. They value nature because human life depends on the rest of creation.

There is another category of creation besides the human beings and some invisible and occasionally visible, creatures, a community of spirit beings known as *mingehe*, which constitutes the (c) category. It is important to note that these spirit beings are not regarded as "human souls" although they have dealings with both God (to whom they are answerable) and the human communities, who are accountable to them. They are of such a nature that they may be visible at one point and invisible at another, much the same as the Christian concept of angels to which the scriptures make reference several times. Njambi has created *mingehe*, which are under Njambi's power. When the Lele speak of the *mingehe*, they are careful not to use anthropomorphic terms such as "he" or "she" or to talk in terms of *mingehe's* "hand" or "mouth." Because these spirits are believed never to have been human beings, such language would offend them. It is believed that anthropomorphic reference is demeaning to the spirits. Therefore, it would be improper to use it. The Lele inform us that these *mingehe* are rarely seen by human beings since theirs is a spiritual existence. This is further "evidence" that points to the nature of the existence of the *mingehe*.

However, although the Lele are afraid to make any "human" reference to the *mingehe*, they believe that these spirit beings have benevolent powers which they use to benefit or punish humanity. It is not clear whether they have this power in and of themselves, or they serve as agents of Njambi. However, it is most logical that since they are subservient and accountable to Njambi who caused them to come into being, their power and authority originate from Njambi, the source of all authority. (Incidentally, this idea of "created souls" seems to echo Origen's theology that God created all souls at the beginning of time. The birth of a child occurs when a given soul takes up "the body" and becomes human. [See Origen's On First Principles: Book VI.]

The Lele attribute quite a few powers to the *mingehe*: for instance, 1. the *mingehe* are believed to control the fertility of women; 2. they are believed to determine the success or failure of the hunters; 3. it is believed that they can strike a village with sickness, and so forth. As in many African communities, it is generally held that only the diviners can discern the ways of the *mingehe*. Ordinary people cannot.

For example, a woman may have been barren for a long time during her married life until one day when the *mingehe* makes an appearance and a pronouncement. Or the *mingehe* may give a sign that something (undisclosed) good will happen and such will transpire! This openness to "extra-ordinary" happenings is an element of our spirituality which prepares the African people to receive God's "other-worldly dimension."

African spirituality makes us aware that there are always other factors which can turn things around from disaster to success, from hopelessness to hope, from death to life. Therefore, the Lele know that "supernatural events" do occur, and because they are supernatural, only the diviners can explain. When this happens, diviners are consulted since they are the only ones who can interpret the ways to the spirits. This also orients the African people to a lifestyle where certain individuals are endowed with special authority in spiritual matters. However, the Lele are aware that these *mingehe* are creatures (though spiritual), created by Njambi. Therefore, no matter how much they are revered, they are not regarded as Njambi (God). Also, they do not share the same attributes as the Creator God. What we have among the Lele is a hierarchy of Spiritual Beings with a clear chain of command.

The Lele observe a day of rest each week, when it is believed the *mingehe* are free to "roam about in broad daylight," although even then, to see them is sacred and unusual. Therefore, the community does well to get out of the way. In fact, this particular day is regarded as "holy." This is very similar to the concept of the "Sabbath day." No one may till the land. If anyone does, disaster will fall upon his or her family either instantly or in the future. This is only one way of honoring these spirits which need to be pleased at all times, and demand nothing but what is good for the whole community, which triggers the *mingehe's* pleasure. A belief system such as this was taken by foreigners for idol worship, which is obviously wrong! Right through this work, what can never be over emphasized is the spirit-consciousness of the African people.

This belief system can be illustrated this way:

God

↑

Spirits

↑

Humanity (and Ancestors)

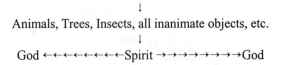

Animals, Trees, Insects, all inanimate objects, etc.

God ←←←←←←←←←Spirit →→→→→→→→→God

Note: This diagram shows that where God is, there are the spirits also. Yet these two are completely separate entities. One may know the spirits in a different way from one's knowledge of God, African spirituality is the matrix within which both are acknowledged and appropriated.

I hope it has become relatively clear that the Lele have a distinct concept of God the Creator which includes attributes of God which are determined not only by what they have experienced but also by what they have not experienced but which they know would be supernatural. Most of their knowledge of Njambi is based on their experience of Njambi's doings for their survival. Their religious beliefs also serve to ensure the sustenance of the community. Thus, the Lele uphold a belief system that ultimately is predictable. They know what to expect from their faith system because it has sustained them for generations. But the Lele are not the only people with specific God-concepts.

THE CREATOR: GOD OF THE SHILLUK

The Shilluk of the upper Nile also believe in Juok, God the Creator. Godfrey Lienhard, author of *Divinity and Experience* says the Shilluk believe that Juok created the world, sustains it, and informs it in its entirety. For them, attributing creation to Juok is an expression that Juok "is that than which nothing greater can be conceived." Not only is Juok (God) the Creator but a Supreme Being who is "the greatest power." Juok is conceived of as that reality upon which "everything else is contingent." They believe that their God is spiritual for Juok exists for them eternally in no single mode, is omnipresent (or multi present), and is invisible yet efficacious. This is more than just an indication of the Trinitarian concept of God, because it expresses what has been labeled in Christian theology as the Trinity without any mention of numbers. I think this describes God more appropriately than does the Trinitarian discourse as we have argued in the next chapter.

We have noted that the Shilluk conceive of Juok as Spirit Being who is relational. Wei, their word for "spirit," describes that Juok is not a physical body. The term Wei comes from the common Nilotic root meaning life or breath, and thus soul or spirit, and distinguishes what is active and alive from what is inert and lifeless, without using image language. John Mbiti notes in *African Religions and Philosophy*:

> As far as it is known, there are no images or physical representations of God by African peoples: ...The fact that He is invisible also leads many to visualize [God] as spiritual rather than physical. To grasp this aspect of God, some societies like the Gra, Langi and Shilluk compare [God] with the wind or air (Mbiti 1970, 44).

Juok is "present" to a greater or lesser degree in all things yet Juok is not a thing! Juok is thought of as the principle that sustains all others and is the ultimate explanation for everything there is. Whatever is beyond the Shilluk's understanding, whatever is mysterious, is Juok for the Shilluk. That is to say what the Shilluk cannot otherwise account for, they account for by this concept. No wonder they attribute the creation of the world to Juok. The mystery of life is also regarded as the work of Juok. Other more or less puzzling events in nature such as birth and death are attributed to Juok as well. Having said this, we have also to bear in mind that it is also taken for granted that all creation, including things we can explain and understand, we have by the power of Juok. Thus, the Shilluk do not live in a world of chance but one created and controlled by Juok whom they consequently worship.

Juok is above all other powers in the Shilluk world view. Juok is also provider, protector, and sustainer. This concept of the divine has led some foreign anthropologists and missionaries to describe this variety of African religion as pantheistic. It seems there was no attempt to discern the possible similarity between the attributes of Juok and those of the Christian God because apparently the Westerners had the preconceived belief that the Shilluk could not know the living God, not realizing that it is God who reveals Godself to any people. We have already discussed this decisive point when we reflected upon the African Christian theological perspective of God. Suffice it to say that this is a crucial concept of God which expresses an authentic African world view that becomes an important framework for the study of theology. There are other African communities that believe in a Creator God.

THE CREATOR: GOD OF THE PEOPLE OF RUANDA

The people of Ruanda, according to a study by J. J. Maguet, believe in Imana, the Creator. Imana describes the God of Jesus Christ.

However, Imana is anthropomorphized to the extreme, compared to other traditions discussed here.

For them, Imana is a Spiritual Being with personality conceived as an intelligence, a will and emotivity. To characterize Imana's might, they believe that if anything is protected by Imana, nothing will ever hurt it. This concept has heavily informed our theology of death as maximum protection. Although this divine power is not material, but spiritual, it is metaphorically said to have very long arms expressing the notion that God does act. Imana's action can influence the whole world, but Ruanda is Imana's base where the Divinity comes back to rest. This compares with the Christian concept of heaven as God's center for operations. Thus, the people of Ruanda claim a close relationship with their God who is also the God of the whole Universe. Naturally they think that they are the center of the world, an idea which compares closely with the claim of the Christians that they, not any other people, are a new nation. When the people of Ruanda invoke Imana, they always say "Imana Ruanda," meaning God of Ruanda, because it is believed that there is a close relationship between the two parties. Much the same as the expression: "God of Israel." However, most people would agree that whenever this expression is used, it is to be understood in terms of a particular but not an exclusive relationship. After all, when either Israel or the people of Ruanda use this possessive concept, they also claim that their God reigns everywhere. So, it seems the purpose of the concept is not to limit God's domain but make it open-ended, yet specific for every people to whom God has self-revealed..

In terms of morality, Imana is believed to be essentially good. The people of Ruanda believe that Imana always gives away without charging any payment because benevolence is Imana's nature. So generous is Imana that the people of Ruanda believe that they do not have to give their creator any offering for it is not needed. Nothing is demanded from the people by Imana except goodness. No wonder there are no cults in Imana's honor in this region of the continent. There are no sacrifices either. The idea of giving to God is strange to them, yet they believe that God is God. This may bring new light to some Christians who have unfortunately reduced faith in God to the idea of just religion, i.e. measuring their faith by how much money they give to the church. "Religion" defined as rituals and acts of worshiping and relating God may be an important expression of our faith but should never replace the faith.

With regard to the creation of humanity, that is, for every new human being, it is necessary that from the time of conception the expectant mother observes a particular custom before she goes to bed to enable a normal formation of a human being. According to this practice, she drinks some water and leaves a little bit in the container so that when the creator comes with clay at night, there is sufficient water needed for the purpose of molding a human being in the mother's womb. This is where the child is endowed with gifts and graces! Thus, Imana is conceived as "the potter" and the people of Ruanda merely play a supportive role. Note that for the people of Ruanda, impregnation of the wife by the husband in itself is not enough to "create a human being" for there is no life without Imana's work being invested in the human formation. Of course, this concept of creation of humanity has to be understood in terms of a metaphor. That is, the actual truth is beyond the myth, but it is there.

However, if the birth results in a miserable, unfortunate, or crippled human being, it is believed that that is not Imana's fault, but an alien power which always produces cursed beings. This power is named <u>Ruremakwaci</u>. We note here that as with many religions, including Christianity, no serious attention at least theologically speaking, is paid to the apparent contradiction between the claim that God has power to influence the whole world which God created for the good, and the Ruremakwaci (the evil one) which can cause adverse effects on creation! A careful study of theodicy with special reference to African theology might help explain why there is what we experience as evil against (as we must assume) the creator's intention. However, the African people are contented with the belief that Ruremakwaci does not have ultimate power. It must be that to talk of the evil one and attributing all evil to the same is a way of exonerating God who is believed to have created everything good.

Ruremakwaci has some power to "create" defective beings and Imana does not seem to have the power to prevent the former from creating such persons. In the meantime, Imana is believed to be always beneficial to human beings. Consequently, only good things come from Imana, who is the source of all creation. Evil is not attributed to Imana, but to Ruremakwaci. However evil is acknowledged in such a way that does not discredit Imana (God). The relation between these two forces is not always clear to us, but it appears that Imana obviously has an upper hand insofar as Imana has ultimate power. All Ruremakwaci can do is interrupt, but not cause anything good to come into being. When a defective child is born, Imana has given the life which the evil power has managed to deform. Apparently, the people of Ruanda have a clear theology relative to creation and the origin of good and that of evil.

THE CREATOR: GOD OF THE MENDE PEOPLE

The Mende religious beliefs are peculiar to, yet consistent with the rest of the continent of Africa. Kenneth Little's overall impression of the Mende people of Sierra Leone is that they have "an essentially practical attitude to life: that is, most of their beliefs seem to be based on "principles of pragmatism." They prefer to concern themselves with the problems of today rather than those of tomorrow.

Most of the Mende beliefs, as is the case with many other African groups, are formulated according to typical African world view, or thought-forms and may be expressed through proverbs as well as other forms of communication. By thought-forms we mean "a man's way of life," (sic) "the way by which he apprehends reality," (sic) to quote Christopher Dawson (Dawson 1952,58). Kwesi Dickson also says that religion informs the African's life in its totality. The Church needs to move away from a 10:30 am faith back to faith all day long and all night! This is the faith of our African fathers and mothers living still. All the four regions we have discussed above practice religion around the clock, as it were. Theirs is a holistic religion.

Translated, a Mende proverb, conveying a philosophy of life says: "If God dishes your rice in a basket, do not wish to eat soup," meaning, if God has made you a poor man, do not desire to be rich. One's lifestyle becomes a simple one and if one realizes this, one is likely to live a more meaningful life of faith. It would be wrong to interpret this as discouragement or fatalism because the saying simply appeals to basic wisdom to discern and utilize the talents and gifts available to one. At a deeper level, the proverb appeals to our awareness of the fact that God is involved in our welfare . God is the creator, sustainer and protector.

Neither is this a deterministic theology, expressing the view that ultimately God is in control of our destiny, but in fact this is more of an analysis than a prescription. The Mende perceive this as Wisdom to seek to understand gifts that God has given them and strive to realize those gifts rather than agonize over them. With reference to gifts, the proverb can also be interpreted to mean that human beings are endowed with a variety of gifts which come from the same source, namely God.

There are numerous other sayings, proverbs and tales among the Mende, but they share on commonality - the notion that God is God "who created the earth and everything in it." Another Mende proverb which indicates that people's religious world view says, "God gives us groundnuts but God does not shell them for us," meaning there are opportunities in life but the individual has to be creative in utilizing them. This proverb actually helps us to understand the one above. Indeed, the Mende are not fatalistic. Life has options. In these two proverbs God is the subject because God plays a central role in our life. The Mende name for God is Ngewo or Leve who is ultimate. The Mende saying that "Ngewo is the Chief or Ruler" indicates that their God sits in a lofty place - way above them (Idowu 1969, 27).

The Mende do not think of Leve (God) as an immanent God. Their belief is more or less deistic: after creating the world, Ngewo withdrew to a quieter realm because people kept bothering the God with requests. This idea of withdrawal is conveyed in tales such as one told here by W. T. Harris. According to one, long ago, after creating the world, God told men and women that they could have anything they wanted as long as they asked God first. So people came to ask too frequently and God did not want to be worn out by their requests, so God moved to a quieter, more remote place, way above people (the sky). There are several myths like this, and all point to the thinking that there is a talking relationship between God the Creator and humanity. This tale explains a deist theology which other cultures have arrived at through other methods-i.e. one of the proofs of the existence of God. The Mende, however, say that no one has ever seen God. God is "the Great Spirit." Mbiti says,

> In the case of God, people might know some of His activities and manifestation, but of His essential nature they know nothing. It is a paradox that they "know" Him, and yet they do not "know" Him; He is not a stranger to them, and yet they are estranged to Him; He knows them, but they do not know Him. So God confronts men as the mysterious and incomprehensible, as indescribable and beyond human vocabulary. This is part of the essential nature of God (Mbiti 1970, 45).

Such is the extent to which the Church may teach who God is. In spite of this, the Mende sometimes make prayers directly to Ngewo who they believe is quite approachable and responsive, even though Ngewo is invisible. Apparently this belief is based on the positive results they have seen in their religion. For example, even the medicine man or woman may have to ask Ngewo to make the medicine more efficacious. Without Ngewo's blessing, their efforts to heal may be in vain. The Mende also believe that everything that was created was made by Ngewo. Even some of the spiritual bodies known as hale (much like the *mingehe* we have discussed above) are believed to be much nearer and closer to the Mende people than Ngewo, who is believed to be very remote. For the Mende, remoteness does not suggest passivity or disinterestedness rather it signifies superiority, respect and honor. Moreover, there are priests who are always available to mediate between the creator and humanity. W. T. Harris agrees with this concept when he says: "the name Leve [God] suggest one who is 'up' or 'high' the 'high up one' (Harris 1950, 279). And yet this does not connote distance or remoteness. It implies omnipresence and omnipotence.

Just from these four regions we have examined, whether it is Njambi, Juok, Imana or Ngewo, it becomes apparent that the Creator is the same as the God of Jesus Christ and this is the identical God traditionalists worshiped though using various names. Names vary but the ESSENCE is the same. The Church in Africa is learning a lot from traditional God concepts which are not alien to the African people. The great danger in the Church today is that the logical diversity leads many Christians to believe that there are as many gods as there are names of God and theologies. I believe that theological diversity representing various perspectives is quite welcome, in fact, healthy. But when this leads to a polytheistic faith, then serious difficulties arise and confront the Church. Furthermore, African spirituality could even accommodate henotheism as long as it was various religions worshiping the same God. Hear ye, hear ye, the God of Africa is one - none other than the Creator of the Universe!

SUMMARY: THE METHODICAL RATIONALE

Throughout the regions we have surveyed, the concept of a spiritual Reality who is Creator with a divine identity, ontology, character and uncaused being is clear. However, God's "personality" is not to be conceived in the same manner that we study "human personality." Most Africans do not seem to concern themselves with metaphysical questions and related abstractions if the subject has no direct relevance to life as they experience it. Obviously, they might have raised some questions at times, but what we have today is a record of only some of the more pertinent and practical issues such as creation, providence, sustenance, and salvation. However we have noticed that there are not written teachings about God apart from discussions and explanations of divine manifestations and happenings. The Church can still enrich its doctrines by adding crucial African concepts of God preserved in traditional proverbs, prayers, myths and so forth. What is significant is that the concepts noted here have been in circulation for the longest time because there is truth in them. The whole debate on the Trinity for instance, is irrelevant unless it focuses on what God does in God's various modes of manifestation. African believers are not preoccupied with, neither are they apprehensive about, the doctrine of the incarnation because there are similar cultural phenomena in their spirituality. If God molds each human being in the woman's womb, as the Imana believe, of course God could cause a virgin to conceive as long as she remembers to keep a glass half full of water next to her bed at night! God may choose to operate in hidden and mysterious ways sometimes. Therefore, the African Christian believers are aware that knowing a person depends not only on what is knowable but what is unknowable as well. African epistemology sometimes acknowledges knowledge of something by admitting how much we do not now about the same. God concepts include mystery and consequently belief, rather than unaided intellectual content, as primary for our faith. Belief is as important and valid as cognitive knowledge, only richer due to its infinite character and expandabilty.

When theologians discuss such topics as the nature of God, the incarnation, salvation, forgiveness and others, and African philosophical "understanding of mystery" or "understanding the ununderstandable," the matrix within which a theology of the eternal beginnings, omnipresence, multiplicity, and the omniscience of God as well as God's immanence and transcendence expresses our perspective which is influenced largely by culture in Sub-Saharan Africa. Most Africans understand God better when decisive aspects which make God God are unquestionably identified as mystery since much of the Godness of God is mystery. What God does that is clearly beyond human conception, anticipation and not to mention capability, defines what we "know" about God. We have noticed that in most regions, all mystery is appropriately attributed to the Great Spirit.

Now, we are not saying that we do not appreciate clear explanations. To the contrary, we do. With reference to God, however, there can be no satisfactory and exhaustive theological language that explains the Incarnation, for instance, or the Trinity without ultimately recognizing the place for divine mystery. For God to have a son who is eternally unbegotten is a mystery and yet such is the language of the faith! Theologians must continue to seek the meaning of God's mystery and immanence in the light of what God has revealed to us through Jesus Christ and other acts. The Church may teach the doctorine of God based on the divine revelation as recorded in the Scriptures because the African people traditionally understood the phenomenon of revelation. In so doing, all we struggle to do is teach the "what" and not the "how" of revelation. Christian theologians who dismiss "mystery" in their theology, border on being atheists. Scholars do well to dwell on issues that speak to our people and use African philosophical categories, thereby creating an appropriate theology. African scholars do not seek to explain away the indigenous understanding of God and replace it with foreign ideas because such ideas have already come to a dead end.

Since theology is attempting to teach the truth about God in a relevant language, the element of DIVINE MYSTERY is inevitable to our understanding of God. Fortunately for us, the unexplainability is "the explanation" of the mystery, and this represents depth in the faith. There are many rich symbols about God among our people, and these do provide us with the conceptual from within which to articulate and develop a meaningful theology for the African Church today, provided that such knowledge does not explain away the Godness of God in the interest of logic. Among the Shona of Zimbabwe there is a "trinitarian" expression of God: *Chidzachepo, Muwanikwa, Mutangakugara*. Each of these names is intended to give the connotation of the original, the uncaused Cause, the first to exist, the prime mover. The undercurrent throughout the terms is mystery - something no one can explain fully really. In light of this, the most comprehensive way to describe God is to say God is God.

Today, we are having to ask theological question which our forefathers and mothers never raised because God is conceived as a dynamic power, and in light of changing times, science and technology, new question do arise. New needs are emerging at the same time that technology is solving some of our old problems. The same technology, however, has also introduced other difficulties which it cannot solve. Methods of communication are more sophisticated and belief systems are influenced not only by our own technology but by other cultures as well. Therefore, questions raised then and today may necessarily differ, yet most of us still find ourselves asking the aged-old question: Why Lord? Why God?

For instance, although problems regarding childlessness are better explained with the help of our modern technology, and deaths (especially sudden death, as it is generally understood as a tragedy) can be explained by the medical doctor without depending on more primitive traditional methods of consulting the diviners and casting lots, many of us still turn to our Almighty God, the Ultimate, and ask for divine intervention when we find ourselves in what my colleague at the United

Theological Seminary (Dayton, Ohio) Dr. James Nelson, calls "limit situations." Put differently, we generally turn to God when our finite existence is threatened because deep in our subliminal self we always recollect, though sometimes vaguely, <u>WHO</u> God is and <u>WHAT</u> only God can do. The mystery, which is part of who God is, is responsible for dealing with our "mystery" situations.

In concluding this short chapter, one notes that there is constant contact, interaction and awareness of the divine presence among the Lele, the Shilluk, the People of Ruanda and the Mende.Thus, any of peoples can concur with the biblical declaration: "God is with us" which explains why Africans are "notoriously religious." For the African, life is because God, the creator is.

Chapter Six

Is It The Trinity, or The Treeness of The Great Spirit Being?

One of the most cumbersome God concepts is the Trinity. The majority of theologians would agree that a discussion on God is not complete until we discuss the nature of God, traditionally done under one of the most controversial topics: the Trinity. Our thesis here is that the being of God can only be better comprehended as the *TREENESS OF THE GREAT SPIRIT BEING*. The author contends that to talk of the "Threeness" of God in God's Oneness is attempting to employ mathematical philosophy to interpret the nature of God by utilizing abstruse metaphysics which itself however is inadequate.

DIVINE REVELATION

Professor Brian Gaybba, an African systematician, speaks for many in these words: "The doctrine of the Trinity, which puts the Christian view of God in a brief formula, can lay claim to being the most important of all Christian beliefs" (De Gruchy & Villa-Vicencio 1994, 77). Our task in this chapter is to ascertain if this formula serves the intended purpose by examining what select western theologians have said, then juxtaposing their thinking with an African view based on the analogy of a tree, which is expected to give us more profound comprehension of the Great Spirit God. Among numerous authors on the subject, I have selected Robert Grant, Cyril Richardson, Claude Welsh, Walfang Pannenberg and Jurgen Moltmann, to weigh their thoughts against an African theological balance. The author will attempt a constructive statement on this doctrine as not only a response but a contribution to our understanding of this major God-concept. It is this author's view that the subject of DIVINE nature has not presented a problem to African thinkers since God is conceived as for example *MWARI: The Great Spirit God*, according to the Shona People of Zimbabwe. There is a general consensus among most theologians I have read in the libraries that the Holy Spirit is the third and last of the three revealed persons constituting the Godhead. Therefore not only is the history of the doctrine of pneumatology relatively short compared to that of "God the Father and God the Son" but the appearance of the third person further complicates the belief in monotheism. Be that as it may for serious Christian believers, the Holy Spirit like the other persons, is an important component of the Godhead. its conception, the doctrine has been a mathematical or philosophical conudrum, and not about the ontological quality of the Revelation. It cannot be denied that the debate on the subject arose as a defense of monotheism rather than a presentation of the nature and person of God.

THE ORIGINS

Regarding the origin of the doctrine, Bernard Lohse observes that:

> "It is important to note that the doctrine of the Trinity does not go back to non-Christian sources...there has been no lack of attempts to find the initial form of the doctrine of the Trinity in Plato, or in Hinduism, or in Parsiism. All such attempts may be regarded today as having floundered " (Lohse 1958, 37).

Pointing to Plato or Hinduism sets a philosophical rather than a revelational agenda. As a matter of fact, the doctrine of the Trinity in its developed stages is not found even in the scriptures, the most extensive existing record of the revelation. It was constructed by the Church. Gaybba is correct to say, "Scripture does not talk about three persons in one God. But it does talk about Father, Son and Spirit in such a way that the development of some sort of Trinitarian view of God was inevitable" (De Gruchy &Villa-Vicencio 1994, 77). Yet it did not have to be mathematical or philosophical. Consistent with God, should it not have been revelation? The result is a debate -- really a debate between philosophy and the Revelation. Instead, the debate arose from the church's doctrines of God and Christology as a numerical quandry. Admittedly much insight is drawn from the contemporary Greek philosophy since in Greek spirituality, there is a concept of multiple gods which can be counted numerically. According to the Greek, a religious person is one who knew and worshiped gods and attributed each god with the appropriate powers and glory. Quantity signified sanctity and holiness.

Plato's Timaeus, for instance, could shed some light on the trinity although it is not about the Trinity per se. The concept is enlightening. However, it needs to be made clear that from our point of view here, philosophy is not theology, although there are numerous instances when the former provided the latter with thought-forms and useful linguistic expressions. Yet, we must remind ourselves that "thought form" and "thought-frame' are different. The one is content, the other is language.

Although this chapter is intended primarily to deal with the contemporary views on the Trinity, constant excursions back to the Second or even First Century are not unwarranted here. Robert Grant, for instance, spends a considerable length of time discussing the Trinitarian roots and implications in the Second Century in *The Early Christian Doctrine of God* (1966). Cyril Richardson's utilitarian point of view makes it possible to discuss the Trinity critically and with fresh insights. His book *The Doctrine of the Trinity* (1958) is worth thorough study. Claude Welch's book *In His Name: The Doctrine of the Trinity in Contemporary Theology* (1952) also makes an extensive survey of the Nineteenth Century affirmations as well as objections to the doctrine of the Trinity. Walfang Pannenberg and Jurgen Moltmann give the subject a twentieth century treatment that ought to spill over into the twenty-first century. Earlier theologians such as Tertullian and Origen, as well as recent thinkers like Karl Rahner and Karl Barth come in as resource theologians on the theme under scrutiny. I will cite my South African colleagues who authored *Doing Theology in Context*, (1994) a source which brings the Trinity into our community and invites the community to participate in holy communion. For instance, Gaybba believes that one way to understand the nature of God is to conceptualize what it means to say:

> God became part of humanity's world so that we can become part of God's world. In so doing humanity intermingled with the Person of the Trinity. Thus the Trinity is a doctrine that God is in community...God's plan is not that the two communities (humanity and the Godhead) should each have their own group area but rather that they should be fully integrated. That is why the Word became flesh and the DIVINE spirit of love was poured out on all at Pentecost (De Gruchy & Villa-Vicencio 1994, 84).

Ideally Christian theology should be consistent with the perspective of this book that God the Great Spirit, is to be conceived as One without any numerical implications beyond the ONE (Deuteronomy 6:4). This perspective, once accepted, helps us to enter the arena of the mystery and thereby appreciate it better; or could at least facilitate our reception of the mystery. When the believer becomes part of the 'mystery', the conudrum dissipates.

Beginning with Robert Grant, we shall not bring the five scholars into a theological debating arena but simply try to follow their representations and points of view which, hopefully, should bring us to some understanding of the mystery of the Trinity. Ultimately we desire to establish a dialogue between these thinkers *and* the African perspective of the Great Spirit God.

ROBERT GRANT: IDENTIFYING THE ORIGINS OF THE DOCTRINE

Robert Grant observes that there was a distinction between "God the Father <u>and</u> God the Son" in the early Second Century theological thinking. He notes that:

> according to the New Testament writing and Second Century theological thinking, God is the one who is eternal, invisible, intangible and impassable. According to the apostolic tradition, Jesus was in time, visible, tangible, passable (Grant 1966, 10).

But it seems this sheds more light on the incarnation, making it a lot more meaningful and significant than it does on the trinity, especially since we have only two Persons: God the Father and the Son. With the Holy Spirit not yet in the picture, Jesus was the sole Revelation of God. Also, all tendencies toward Christian docetism are dismissed if Jesus was "visible, tangible and passable". In *The Early Christian Doctrine* (1966), Grant informs us that from the apocryphal preaching of Peter, we first encounter a specifically philosophical discussion of the one God. There we learn there is one God, who made the beginning of all things and has control over their end" (Grant 1966, 20). It is Grant's view that, evidenced by examples of such occurrences as Justin's conversion, philosophy played a rather important role in the Christianization and theologization of the Second Century theology. Of course philosophy alone (or reason alone) did not lead one to the Christian faith. The revelation of God always makes a significant contribution to religious-philosophical inquiries if there is such accommodation in the mind of the scholar. Revelation is the content. Philosophy merely formulates an argument. It may even provide "some logical conclusions" but reason without faith does not make one a believer. We must however briefly explore the role of philosophy vis-a-vis the Trinity. How much has philosophy helped our understanding of the trinity? Can philosophy "uncover", or "unveil" the content of the REVELATION? It is best to leave this as a rhetorical question.

According to the Second Century philosophy, God could be reached in three ways only; 1. by abstraction, 2. by analogy and, or 3. by gradual ascension. It is interesting to note that these categories were also advocated by the anti-Christian writers such as Celsus, (Grant 1966, 28) since they are devoid of the content of revelation. Grant says that the Platonists were in general agreement with the Stoics on the question of the nature of God, but did not agree on everything. For instance, for the Stoics, God was not a "He" or "She" but "It".

With reference to the Stoics Grant says: "their God was not so much ineffable as impersonal..." Of course the Christians of his day would not accept this view. For them God is "the Father" who is personal. Perhaps the Stoics believed God's gender was neuter since their philosophy (ZANO) teaches that the highest virtue is without passions like most men. So God had to be above the "he" and the "she" of the world. However, Grant notes that although Christian theology utilized philosophy and was in harmony with the same, it "transcends" the teachings of these various schools of philosophy because its subject, God, is by nature "transcendent". Christian theology may begin with human questions about what God has done but it must ultimately end with God the creator of all. Theology is Christian when the discourse points us to the God Christ revealed to humanity in his teachings, life, death and resurrection.

Clement of Alexandria sets more fully philosophical theology as he makes considerable use of Philo. Grant observes that Clement insisted upon the monadic unity of God and describes him as ineffable and invisible. However, Clement supersedes Philo insofar as he (Clement) argues that: "since God is the cause prior to the origination and existence of all other beings, it must be held that he cannot be assigned genus, differential, accident, or substance. He has not parts because the one is invisible" (Grant 1966, 30).

We agree with Grant that the categories which Clement is using are Aristotelian mediated by Middle Platonism. It is also important to bear in mind that although there are similarities between Clement's theology and Gnosticism as portrayed by Basilides, the latter is very distinct from the former. "The Gnostic Basilides knows Clement, though he values knowledge highly, believes -- in God" (Grant 1966, 31). To know is different from "to believe". Belief in this instance has greater depth than knowledge which often has limitations. Origen, generally recognized as "the greatest of the Alexandrian theologians" - followed the path paved by the apologists and Clement but he superseded them. Origen defines God as, "a unified intellectual being (Natural), permitting of absolutely no addition in himself, so that it may not be believed that he is either anything greater or anything lesser in himself, but that he is in every way a monad and, so to speak, a henad" (Grant 1966, 74). Although Origen initially maintained that God does not have passion or emotions, he eventually talked of God in Christ as being "actually moved by man's petitions. Indeed the whole story of the Incarnation is a proof of this. First the Saviour was moved by compassion, then he descended and appeared among men. He experienced the passion or emotion of love" (Grant 1966, 74). To this, Stoicism might respond in a manner that differentiates God's emotion and compassion from that of humanity since God is the highest Good.

However, the greatness of Origen lies in the fact that he has placed more weight on the revelation of God in Christ "than to the negative conceptions provided by philosophical theology". As we do, Grant sees in Origen: "an authentically Christian insight" appearing. This would have great influence and consequences later in the Christian tradition. Grant notes a single phenomenon for sure: "a healthy recognition of the limits of philosophical theology and a firm insistence upon the absolute transcendence of God" (Grant 1966, 32). In the thought of the early Second Century Christian writers including Origen himself, philosophy alone could not explain the fullness of God. Philosophy provided the thought frame but could not furnish the content. Reason stood in need of the aid of revelation. Origen leaves us on a good note: philosophy is unable to achieve what Revelation does.

THE HOLY SPIRIT WITHIN THE GREAT SPIRIT GOD

For Grant, while the WORD was God, "God in his fullness was not the word". Similarly, while the Spirit is God, "God in his fullness is not "just" the Spirit. The Spirit is the Spirit of God" (Grant 1966, 74). Thus, the Holy Spirit is a necessary component within the Godhead but not one and the same entity. However, according to the bible, there is identity of functions among the Spirit, the Lord, and God himself (1 Corinthians 12:3-7).   For St. Paul the work of the Holy Spirit is "co-ordinate" with that of God and that of Christ. By saying "yes", Christ was a real human being but he is no longer, Paul handles the docetic debate very tactfully (2 Corinthians 5:16). As in Pauline letters, the problem of the relationship between Jesus and the Spirit, for instance, does not bother the author of John's Gospel. We agree with Grant that it would be much better and intelligible to simply concede that it is God who reveals himself to our limited apprehension as Father, Son and Spirit. After all, since God is one, the scriptures (Matthew 28:19) points us to the same in what becomes our baptism formula. One is not baptized in the names of three Gods, but only One, named three times. The One has self-revealed three times.

Reference to the Triad is much more frequent at the end of the First Century, according to Grant's observation.   However, since references to the Triad are made "in passing", it implies that there is no developed doctrine of the Trinity. Secondly, the pre-eminence of the Triad is taken for granted. But perhaps more crucial is the fact that it is the same God who repeats own revelation for a purpose. In the scriptures we also find the ingredients of the Trinity in the oath: "as God lives", and "as the Lord Jesus Christ lives," and "the Holy Spirit". Apparently there is no indication that the Triad is problematic. Origen is not the only one who was lukewarm, Justin Martyr and others also presented the Triad in a rather naive tone. Justin was followed by the apologist Athenagoras whose conception of the Trinity is much clearer than that of Justin. But the discourse did not end with these, indicating that the matter was not resolved at all.

Athenagoras' doctrine of DIVINE metaphysics was especially useful and convincing in his response to the pagan charge that Christians were "atheists" because they did not worship the state gods. To this Athenagoras retorted:

> how can anyone say Christians are atheists when they worship the One Uncreated, eternal, invisible, impassable, incomprehensible, uncontainable God; comprehensible only by mind and reason...the Son of God, who is the word of the Father in idea and activity; in relation to him and through him everything came into existence, since the Father and the Son are One...the Holy Spirit, emanated from God, emanating and borne along like a ray of the sun (Grant 1966, 92).

In this response is the concept of the "Three-in-one and One-in-Three".

Since all three persons are mentioned in such a manner that their existence or presence is inextricably one Grant remarks that Athenagoras' doctrine of God is of the highest importance because, although some of the language is philosophical, "the basic structure of his thought is latently biblical and is derived especially from the New Testament". For instance, he points out that "the idea that the world is held together by God through the pre-existent Christ comes from Colossians and Ephesians" (Grant 1966, 92). Language such as "the Son is in the Father, and the Father in the Son" is clearly Johanine (John 14:9-10). Athenagoras' language about the spirit is clearly from the Old Testament Book of Wisdom. However, beyond this if the reader does not find much, if any, Scripture words used, it is because such was the writing of the apologists. Grant's summary of Clement's, Origen's and Athenagoras' philosophical interpretation of the Trinity gives a reasonable basis for the beginnings of the doctrine expressed philosophically. So, Grant can construct his own view based on these. Concluding, we note that his view is patterned after theirs; it too is philosophy, not revelation. The issue is not resolved.

GRANT'S VIEW ON THE TRINITY

Grant reminds us that we should "not imagine that there was a golden age, or that a doctrine of the Trinity such as we have found in Athenagoras writings had always existed in the Christian subconscious" (Grant 1966, 95). Rather, a proper perspective is needed to understand how Trinitarian statements were constructed and formulated. Grant's thesis regarding the doctrine of the trinity is that it represented an attempt to do justice to the unity of God and the diversity of God's dealings with humanity (Grant 1966, 95). The doctrine is Christian in terms of literature, since "the unity of God was based squarely on the testimony of the Old Testament and the new Testament as well" (Grant 1966, 96). Second, it is Christian not because it is philosophically sound but because it is a theologically coherent statement about the revelation, provided that it is articulated in a sound manner. The third factor to keep in mind is, as Grant correctly notes, that although the doctrine of the Trinity was being developed in the world of the Graeco-Roman Philosophy, the metaphysics did not and could not produce the revelation. Rather, the philosophical thought was used as a vehicle with which to convey some of the implications of the religious socio-cultural realities and terminologies (Father, Son, and Holy Spirit) which Christians were already acquainted with.

Thus, while we cannot argue conclusively that the Trinitarian doctrine is a product of philosophy, there is integrity in contending that philosophy was a tool used to formulate, not only this but other doctrines such as Christology, Creation, Incarnation and the like. By implication any philosophy could have been utilized for this purpose. In agreement with Grant, Gaybba also says, "It should be clear by now that the Christian doctrine of the trinity has its roots in scripture and is not, as some have tried to argue, derived from pagan polytheistic or philosophical ideas" (De Gruchy & Villa-Vicencio, 1994, 78-9).

Furthermore, Grant warns us not to speak of the Trinity as if we possess "direct access" to God. This caution is crucial but should not be misconstrued to advocate agnosticism. We could not agree more with Grant in his words,

> To speak over-precisely about the ineffable God, to define too clearly the relations between the Father and the Son, to produce exact analysis of the place and function of the spirit in the Trinity - this is to set ourselves up as judges of God and to forget that his ways are not like ours (Grant 1966, 100-101).

We can only dare talk about the trinity because such is the task of theology - to articulate religious concepts in an intelligible manner in a language that is clear and understandable. Theology does not and cannot create its own truths about God apart from the truth revealed by God in various situations and contexts.

The most important contribution Grant has made in his few but discerning remarks is two-fold. 1. That God's ways are not like ours...in other words, we must let "God be God" and understand Divinity as such; 2. That the trinity is our attempt to name God's diversity in God's dealings with us. The Trinity is a philosophical statement of God's action in diverse situations and circumstances in history. However, Grant had not solved the mathematical language that attempts to describe God. We now turn to another Western theologian to see where his idea of the trinity points us to.

CYRIL RICHARDSON'S PROLEGOMENA

Cyril Richardson approaches the problem of the doctrine of the Trinity in quite a different manner which may actually seem negative. Therefore in the preliminary stages Richardson clarifies certain points so that he is correctly interpreted in discussing this rather delicate issue in which the distinction serves also as the element of cohesion. Richardson's theology is basically Christological. His point of view on this subject of the Trinity is "not unitarian". In one of his major though older works, The Doctrine of the Trinity (1958) he says:

> my purpose is to try to say something which is relevant to those who hold a very strict, orthodox view of the person of Jesus Christ, as to those who have more liberal persuasions. That it was God himself who was taking action in human history in Jesus of Nazareth, and revealing himself in terms of a human person, is not to be questioned (Richardson 1958, 14).

Apparently what is at issue in the Trinity is whether mathematics or philosophy is the proper way of speaking of God as God manifested Godself in history. Along that same trend of thought Richardson questions whether the Trinity adequately deals with these contradictions in God-talk. His opinion is that the language of the Trinity confuses by trying to combine different paradoxes in an artificial three foldedness. Also Richardson feels that the problems that give birth to the Trinitarian controversies are so "real" that he wonders whether they are dealt with adequately in this doctrinal framework. Richardson's intention is "to show that the Trinity does not adequately express them (the real problems involved), and confronts the Christian with a doctrine which engenders bewilderment instead of true faith" (Richardson 1958, 17).

Richardson concedes that the subject of the Trinity is difficult. In attempting to deal with it, theologians have brought into the arguments many things - symbols and scripture passages - which are not pertinent, thereby further complicating the doctrine. In agreement with Grant, Richardson notes that the Trinity is not a doctrine specifically to be found in the New Testament in its present formulation. It is a creation of the Fourth Century Church. However, there were elements which pointed toward the doctrine as early as the First or Second Century as we have already discussed. The Trinity as doctrine is only alluded to in both the Old and the New Testaments.

Many before and after him made the same point. Although the basic problem of the Trinity is how God can be "Three in One and One-in-Three", more fundamental for Richardson is "the difference between the Father and the Son" which he feels has never been dealt with sufficiently. It is Richardson's conviction that "all Trinitarian theology ultimately hangs on this distinction and it has been variously interpreted in Christian history. Why should we posit two terms, *Father* and *Son*, in the Godhead

(Richardson 1958, 21)?   This rhetorical question pin-points the mathematical problem of the DIVINE metaphysics.

Richardson points, for instance, to the Book of John 10;30 where Jesus clearly states: "I and my Father are one." Why use the two terms? He is not satisfied by the traditional explanation that the Son is "begotten" from the Father, rather he wants to establish the meaning of this mysterious "begetting". He notes that the transaction from the early creature, the man Jesus of Nazareth, in relation to his heavenly Father, to a supramundane being in relation to God represents the most fundamental step in the direction of Trinitarian thinking. To say God the Father and God the Son makes reference to two, not one. What is the difference, and should there be ANY difference between God and God? If there is a difference, then we have not one but two Gods, which is contrary to Christian monotheism. If there is one, then why use titles that create in our minds two numerical entities?

THE PARADOXES OF THE TRINITY

For Richardson what is involved here is the basic idea that "God works through his agents" but his Son is more than just an angelic being. The Son is the image of God, through whom and for whom creation comes to be (Colossians 1:16). This way of talking already points to possible distinctions within the Godhead. To say Jesus is the Word, the Logos that becomes incarnate means that the Word or Son is that aspect or 'mode of being' of God through which God comes into relationship with the world, whereby he creates and reveals himself. One distinction is the "paradoxical nature of God: absolutely above and beyond, and yet at the same time near and immanent" (Richardson 1958, 21). Philosophically speaking, one has to regard God as an Absolute of which there can never be more than one. On the other hand, this "Absolute" comes into relationship with that which it creates.

Thus "the remoteness, the self-sufficiency, and the absolute transcendence of God, are overcome in his and being related to his creatures" (Richardson 1958, 22). However, Richardson contends that God does not disclose Godself completely, neither does God create directly, "He creates and reveals not directly, but by his Son or Logos. The Father thus stands for God in his beyondness, the Son for God in his relatedness" (Richardson 1958, 23). In light of this paradox, Richardson asserts that the distinction between the Father and the Son is intended "to guard the absolute character and transcendent glory of God (Richardson

1958, 23). On the other hand, the distinction serves "to affirm...that the created world is his" (Richardson 1958, 23). Richardson states in no uncertain terms that "God is beyond and yet he is related; that is the essence of the distinction between the Father and the Son" (Richardson 1958, 23). It is this mystery which summarizes the whole Trinitarian controversy. One might add that tension between God's relatedness and God's beyondness is maintained by the Holy Spirit who enables us to understand both (teaching). Richardson gets very close to describing the nature of the divine but the moment he draws on mathematical philosophy, he loses the "divine grasp". He notes that there are several Trinitarian doctrines which should be analyzed one by one in order to eradicate unclarity and at the same time acquire more relevant and precise information.

THE SON AS THE MEDIATOR

The "mediation" makes the basic distinction between Father and Son. In essence the idea here is that "the Son is the Logos, by means of which God comes into relation with this world" (Richardson 1958, 56). Going back to Tertullian, Richardson remarks that, according to this renowned African theologian, since God the Father is "absolute", the Son who is "visible", seen, heard and encountered in human history and nature is the mediator - the one who effects man's salvation, thus doing the will of him who sent him.

But Tertullian's interpretation of the Father-Son relationship was unsatisfactory because for him in order to have Father and Son, it is necessary that one comes after another. Thus, "there was a time when the Son was not". The created, temporal Son and the absolute Father can only form an artificial unity or the character of the absolute God is "changing". However, it was this African scholar who coined the term "Trinity" which was adopted in the West in their theological discussion about the Trinity. Arius and Tertullian held more or less the same position, which was rejected by the church because, the Son as God, has always been with God (John 1:1f).

The Athanasian school of thought rejected this theology because it would mean a constant supply of mediators! There had to be a better way - better theology. There was to be a permanent mediator. Hence, the idea of the eternal son - the only begotten son. Origen's theology of the eternal begetting has its own set of problems. For one thing, it would make God secondary to God's essential being. This theology was to be rejected by later thinkers such as John Calvin. The point is, once the one is begotten by the other then neither is any longer "absolute". "The result of deriving God in his visible and encountered nature from God in his invisibility and self- sufficiency is to compromise the later" (Richardson 1958, 59). Both God the Father and God the Son are vital for Christian faith in the divine essence of the One. Nor is the Son nearer to suffering than the Father. The solution lies in the paradox that "God is joy, yet he suffers; and this is one more aspect of the basic paradox of God's beyondness and his relatedness" (Richardson 1958, 64). This tension is what Richardson calls "the very centre of the Christian mystery, that redemptive suffering (which) is the quality of God" (Richardson 1958, 64). This is symbolized in the Christian tradition by the cross.

In light of this Richardson argues that God's character consist in this paradox. "He exists in these two ways, these two modes of being. But neither is derived from the other" (Richardson 1958, 61). Richardson insists that we should refuse the thinking that since Christ is "begotten" therefore he stands nearer to suffering than does God the Father. We should reject "the derivative principles," he argues, because it is misleading. On this point Richardson disagrees with Barth who maintains that the one derives from the other. Christ does not stand nearer to suffering because he is "begotten" but because the paradox of "joy and suffering" is the very character of the One God who does not derive from the other. Furthermore, Christ cannot be nearer than God the Father if the two are one and the one is two.

One more issue that Richardson raises has to do with what it means to say that the Father and the Son are one God but two distinct persons or <u>hypostasis</u>. This question was raised before the age of the social sciences such as psychology therefore, while we, today, would think in terms of self-consciousness, the early Christian thought in terms of "confrontation", not self-consciousness. This means that the <u>persona</u> was he that was speaking or acting presently behind the appropriate "mask" or "face" without necessarily having a different "self-consciousness". Therefore Barth's term - modes of being - expresses what was intended. I think Richardson is correct to conclude from this analysis that

> God is known or inferred, as existing in different modes. As Father he is, as we have seen absolute; as Son he is related to the world. But in both instances he is the same One God. Hence the modes, clearly and even paradoxically distinguished, share an identity of essence. They are both God (Richardson 1958, 63).

Therefore, it should make sense to say God is One, that the Father and the Son are One and the same God. Richardson emphasizes the fact that the early Church Fathers were attempting to distinguish two different forms in which God existed - two different modes of Divinity. To achieve this as we move further in this discourse, we need to focus on the "what," rather than the "who" of God. The "who" seems to run Richardson's argument aground because it becomes necessary to talk of two or three, not just one God. So he moves to the "what."

THE TRINITY OF LOVE: (LOVE EXPRESSING ITSELF THREE TIMES AT ONCE)

Richardson asserts that Trinitarian language which implies distinctions is only "symbolic, not literal". Whenever a happening is attributed to the Father, or Son, or Holy Spirit, Richardson observes "in literal truth it is the WHOLE Trinity doing something, but the omnipotent character of the event makes us think of the Father as the source of all, the final principle of being" (Richardson 1958, 76). It is for this reason that we appropriate any given happening to any one of the Three Persons even though the happening belongs indivisibly to the trinity. For instance, when we think about creation, Richardson argues that although we assign the decree to create to the Father, and the actual execution of the decree to the Son and the act or process of perfecting the creation to the Spirit, "it is not literally this way. All Three Persons are equally involved in all three aspects of creation" (Richardson 1958, 80), as the bible states: "In the beginning God created the heavens and the earth (Genesis 1:1).

According to this Roman doctrine of appropriation, this metaphorical language points to the distinctions 'within' the Godhead or the Trinity, rather than any thing externally based. According to this doctrine, we are not supposed to think that the Son cannot play the role of the Father who is the very source of everything. And, in light of the trinity, we cannot imagine God the Father apart from God the Son and God the Holy Spirit.

There are problems involved here. First, how can we talk about this co-equality, but may not talk in terms of the Father being incarnate just like the Son without running into the danger of patripassianism? Can we refer to the Spirit as incarnate? Also, how can the transcendent and absolute God "suffer under Pontius Pilate" or be raised on the third day? Just what is the nature of the internal relations within the Godhead? Is it necessary to distinguish this "One Reality"?

Richardson suggests that the principle of "God is Love" frees us up from preoccupation with who is Father, Son or Holy Spirit. We are ready to talk about *WHAT LOVE IS*, i.e. what God is. But one more question arises. Does it mean that God would necessarily need creation - i.e. the world - as his object of love? Evidence points to a negative answer to this question. Then what does it mean to say 'God is Love'? Richardson discusses several implications and surfaces paradoxes one after another. For instance, one paradox is to think of God both as the One who loves himself (the *agape* kind of self-loving) and as a society in which persons enjoy the mutuality of love.

Persuasive is Richardson's view that when we talk about the Trinity we do not include Jesus' physical body but "the Christ" in Jesus of Nazareth is definitely part of the Trinity for he is the one who said "Believe me when I say I am in the Father and the Father is in me" (John 14:11a). In this sense we assert that the "God is Love" symbol must mean mutual love in a sense that resembles society, i.e. the spirit of society that works in different modes and ways. To think of God as society makes a plausible picture of the Trinity where neither one of the Three is necessarily greater or lesser than the others. No single portion can be designated "society". Either there is society or it does not exist. Similarly, a co-equality of the Three persons needs to be apparent in order to preserve the integrity of the Trinity. Discussion on the Trinity cannot be deemed complete until all three persons have been incorporated. So far we have discussed how the Father and the Son relate. We now turn to the third component -- the Spirit -- how does this operate in the Trinity in which it is an integral part?

In early Christianity what was understood to be the distinctive work of the spirit was "that of inspiring, hallowing, sanctifying". The spirit was conceived as the internal work of God with in the human heart. In attempting to understand the role of the Three Persons of the Trinity, Origen is known to have designated the Father as "source of existence", the Son as giver of the "gift of reason" (Logos) but from the Spirit, Origen believes that we receive "the grace of holiness". Unfortunately, in the spirit of addressing a particular community Origen confines the Spirit to the Christian converts. In which case one more question arises: shere was the Holy Spirit up until the Christian era? and what was the Spirit doing?

Augustine's concept of the trinity, (according to his <u>On The Trinity</u>) is that the Spirit provides not just "hallowing" but "the bond of union". In Book Six, Augustine that there can only be Three in the Trinity: namely the Father, the Son and their relationship, i.e. love.

Augustine discusses at length the subject of "person of the trinity. But his position is hinted at in his often quoted statement: "we say three persons not that we wish to say it, but that we may not be reduced to silence" (Augustine 6 5.7). Richardson summarizes Augustine's central thinking correctly, I think, by saying, "that all members of Augustine's Trinity are internal relations within the one personal God" (Richardson 198, 96).

Another theologian worthy to listening to is, Claude Welch. His discussion covers the Nineteenth Century views against and for the Trinity. This is by no means conclusive but it is very instructive.

CLAUDE WELCH; 19th CENTURY VIEWS ABOUT THE TRINITY

Schleiermacher and the subsequent so-called "liberal theology" of which he is said to be the father, insisted on questioning the traditional conceptions of revelation. To this Claude Welch says,

> Schleiermacher, Ritschl and liberal theologians generally were profoundly suspicious of the classical Trinitarian conception of God because they did not see how it could be derived from the new understanding of the basis of Christian affirmations (Welch 1952, 125).

However, Welch also observes that although the foregoing trend of thought was against the doctrine of the Trinity "it may be affirmed that in the main stream of contemporary theological development, there is a strong current of thought in the direction of renewed recognition of the necessity and importance of a Christian doctrine of the trinity" (Welch 1952, 126). Welch makes and substantiates his observation on the basis of the appearance of systematic theologians like Karl Barth, Peter Hodgson and others as well as the place accorded the doctrine by several contemporary theological authors like W. N. Pittenger and D. M. Baillie. Also it is pointed out that interest in the Trinitarian doctrine has had to be roused because the Christian community itself is a "response" to the experience which in order to understand, calls for the doctrine of the Trinity. If Christ is "the Revelation", "God with us", there is no way Christian believers can proceed without reckoning with the Trinity of which not only Christ the Son and God the Father are involved, but the Holy Spirit as well - hence the Trinity.

Welch advances an important claim that "the doctrine of the Trinity is not developed simply by piecing together Trinitarian proof-texts, understood as divinely given truths, but is constructed as a consequence of the gospel taken as a whole" (Welch 1952, 126). Indeed, the doctrine of the Trinity should not be understood as a revealed doctrine "per se". Rather it should be regarded as - and it is, doctrine by which we can explicate the meaning of the Incarnation - a doctrine whose subject matter touches the question of the nature of Divinity. Thus we study the Trinity in order to understand the incarnation, which itself is a focal point of divine intensity. But we cannot equally study the Incarnation in order to understand the trinity.

Another important aspect of the doctrine is its "religious significance". The whole Christian faith needs to understand the central elements of the faith. Since the revelation of God in Jesus Christ, the crucifixion, the resurrection and the Pentecost all add to religious significance insofar as God was present through the Holy Spirit in all this, it is absolutely necessary to articulate the nature, "personality" and appropriations of the Trinty. It almost seems that we have to discuss that which makes it necessary for us to consider the doctrine of the Trinity in the realm of Christian faith. The quesiton for Welch is what place does the Trinity occupy in the Christian faith? In what sense is the Trinity the "ultimate and necessary consequence or synthesis of the data of Christian revelation and experience" (Welch 1952, 128)?

Welch maintains that the subject of the Trinity can be approached from a Christological point of view as does Richardson (as we have already seen.) For instance W. N. Pittenger suggests that we approach the Trinity as a presupposition and implication of the incarnation. In fact these two doctrines - the Trinity and the incarnation - can properly be regarded as mutually "interdependent and inseparable". But this assertion immediately presented the Church with three mutually incompatible axioms: 1. how do we reconcile the ideas of monotheism (Holy God), the divine Christ who is Lord and God as Spirit which now must be synthesized into a Trinity? 2. how can these Three be One and 3. how can this One be Three without making the Christian faith tritheistic or a monad? It is hoped that as many theologians wrestle with this "problematic", we will one day "stumbel" in the clues to the explanation. Welch makes a systematic analysis of the Trinity which leads him to remark that:

> there is formal agreement (among various authors he cites) that the doctrine of the trinity is based directly (and solely) on the facts of Christian experience or history, that it is a necessary intellectual implication or consequence of those facts (i.e. that Christianity is a

Trinitarian religion), and that it is the central or all-inclusive doctrine of faith (Welch 1952, 125).

However, disharmony inevitably and invariably arises when theologians attempt to articulate the content and postulate perimeters which necessitate and constitute the doctrine of the Trintiy. But this is not the scope of this chapter.

THE TRINITY AS SYNTHESIS OF ELEMENTS OF REVELATION:

Welch presents us with two general yet distinctive concepts of the role of this doctrine. On the one hand Welch says, "the Trinitarian conception is a necessary combination or synthesis of several fundamental elements of Christian revelation and experience; it is therefore as the ultimate and inclusive implicate, that final safeguard of the faith (Welch 1952, 155-6). On the other hand, Welch suggests that "the doctrine is an immediate implication of the fact, form and content of revelation" (Welch 1952, 156). Welch wants us to realize that in these two "conceptions" of the doctrine is "the heart of the problem" regarding the Trinity in contemporary theology. The problem is none other than one of "the unity of the ground or basis" of the doctrine.

Firstly, the problem is posed by Schleiermacher's systematic position that requires that "all theology be an organic whole", so that everything Christian must necessarily derive from the "immediate utterances" of the Christian consciousness. Schleiermacher rejected the doctrine of the Trinity on the basis of his "subjectivistic understanding of religious experience". Also for Schleiermacher the doctrine is nothing less than a combination of some direct utterances of the Christian consciousness. Schleiermacher argued, therefore, that the Trinity should occupy the "second rank" in our system of the Christian faith, since the doctrine is not part of the primary witness of the Christian faith (Welch 1952, 156). It is synthesis of elements. Since many more theologians went along with Schleiermacher, "the father of liberal theology", Welch sees that thinking as one that dominates the contemporary thought. On the other hand, those who defend the doctrine do not deny that it is "a synthesis or combination of elements of faith", which is a very necessary, logical and valid synthesis. Viewed as synthesis, the Trinity cannot be on a par with God, the Holy Ghost or Jesus Christ. Welch suggests that "it would be better to say that if the doctrine of the Trinity is the Centre of the faith, it ought now to be a source of illumination for all other doctrines"

(Welch 1952, 160).

This is what most Protestant theologians discussed here would like but they are prevented by "the indirect (or synthetic) method of developing the doctrine from its roots in revelations" (Welch 1952, 160). Consequently, the Trinity "cannot be held to be a genuine arch or first principle of Christian thought" (Welch 1952, 160).

THE TRINITY AS AN ANALYSIS OF REVELATION:

There is yet another way of looking at the Trinity - namely an analysis, (not synthesis), an immediate implication of revelation - making the Trinity "essentially identical with the content of the Revelation". This is what Barth did, making the most elaborate and detailed treatise on the Trinity. For Barth, the doctrine of the Trinity is "an implication or an interpretation of the revelation" (Barth 1968, 334). The question for Barth is whether the interpretation is proper. Unlike the school of thought which regards the doctrine as a synthesis, Barth regards the Trinity as what Welch calls "an analytical development of the central fact of revelation" (Welch 1952, 165).

For Barth "the basis or root of the doctrine of the Trinity, if it has one and is thus legitimate dogma - and it does have one and is thus legitimate dogma - lies in revelation" (Barth 1968, 334). Barth holds that the Trinity is not one isolated affirmation about God. It infiltrates every aspect of the Christian faith. God self loves and lives through God's Trinity. One may add that indeed any mention of any of the three ought to carry the weight of the Trinity because there is not a time when the Trinity is not. Welch's summary of this thinking gives us a very concissive statement about Gods. Welch said, "His (God's) freedom consists in the 'inner Trinitarian' life of the father with the son through the spirit" (Welch 1952, 165).

In the doctrine of the Trinity is the possibility of creation as well as a proper view of Divine manifestations. Barth is correct, in my opinion, to say that in trying to analyze the doctrine of the Revelation we inevitably find ourselves dealing with the "Threeness-in-One, and the Oneness-in-Three" i.e. the Trinity becomes the format as well as the content of the discussion. No wonder Barth gives the Trinity priority in his voluminous Church Dogmatics. For Barth the biblical concept of the revelation is itself the root of the doctrine of the Trinity (Barth 1968, 334). Because all Christian theology must have Scripture as one of the major sources, scripture itself whose subject matter is basically theocentric, must provide us with data that indicates and clarifies who God is - a mystery that we can only attempt to appreciate with the help of the Revelation, which itself is an attempt to disclose God the Father, the Son, and the Holy Spirit. This is why Barth argues that the Trinity must be both externally and internally placed at the head of Dogmatics. If one may add, one cannot understand God the Father, God the Son, God the Holy Spirit without comprehending the Holy Trinity.

> It is further argued that the Trinity is the content of the revelation, not of Philosophy. Welch makes a decisive assertion that "Barth attaches a supreme significance to the doctrine of the Trinity because...he really believes it to be an immediate implication of the fact, form and content of revelation; the doctrine is truly descriptive of God as he is in himself and therefore has a 'practical, comprehensive significance' for all the rest of Dogmatics (Welch 1952, 165).

Note that for Barth, the Trinity is an "all-pervasive" importance and influence in the entire body of the Christian doctrine of God as well as all other related Christian doctrines. "Every Christian doctrine which purports to be based in revelation must be understood in terms of a Trinitarian revelation" (and thus the doctrine of the Trinity offers a crucial test for any theology which claims to speak of revelation) (Welch 1952, 165). Like many theologians before him, Barth acknowledged that the doctrine of the Trinity is not stated in the scriptures in its developed form, rather it was developed by the church. Therefore, we can only regard it as an "interpretation".

However, Barth maintains that since Trinity is rooted ONLY in revelation, there cannot be other roots. This eliminates the possibility that it might be rooted in philosophy as well. Welch underscores this rejection most vehemently when he says, "Jesus does not simply give the name Father to a Philosophical Creator-God; he reveals that unfamiliar Father, his Father and thus shows that and what the creator is" (Welch 1952, 180).

Barth enhances Welch's point of view when he argues that the New Testament speaks unquestionably from the beginning to the end of "the unity of God." But unity implies plurality, therefore let us turn to Barth's understanding of the nature of God. Although there had been numerous hypotheses over the centuries, Barth tended to equate the "Lordship of God" with "the Essence of God". In terms of God's personality, again it has to be one, not three personalities. Barth objects to three personalities of God on the basis of the biblical witness to the unity of God's Lordship. For Barth who is always saturated in scripture, the Lordship of God is not tripled.   Rather it is "triply *ONE*" (Deuteronomy 6:4). Put differently, there are not three Lords but one, who is "triply One."

In addition, as there is unity of the Lordship, there is also "equality"of the essence of the Son and the essence of the Father. This is what Barth means when he says "from the identity flows the equality of essence in the Persons" (Barth 19, 503). The theology of this leading Protestant thinker coincides with the Catholic theology on the concept of 'perichoresis' which brings "completion of the dialectic of the unity and Trinity" (Welch 1952, 188). Welch gives Barth's interpretation this meaning:

> that the Father, Son and Holy Spirit are one 'among themselves'. The definite and 'complete participation by each mode of existence in the other modes of existence' follows from the understanding that the one essence of God is truly and indivisibly present in his existence as Father, Son and Spirit (Welch 1952, 188).

It is from this understanding that Barth offers the terms *seins-weisen* rather than the classical Personae. For Barth the 'mode of being' is not understood to be temporary or merely "docetic", neither is it to be understood as an absolutely accurate description of what God is. Welch shares Barth's reverence for God when the former says:

> all of what Barth has to say concerning the designation "modes of being" comes, of course, under the qualification of the inconceivability of God. No term can be adequate and Barth does not claim that his answer to the question "quid tres?" is more than a 'relatively' better answer than is given by the term Person (Welch 1952, 192).

This author's view on Barth's argument is that the concept of "equality of the essence" signify multiplicity, not singularity. This leads to a serious flaw.

WELCH'S VIEW:

Welch's view is influenced by his special definition of "the doctrine of the Trinity" as "the conception of God as in his very being (i.e. ontological or essentially) Triune - one God, the Father, the Son and the Holy Spirit" (Welch 1952, 218). These terms, according to Welch "refer to eternal and co-equal 'distinctions' in the One Being or Essence of God" (Welch 1952, 219). Welch declares that the contemporary theological enterprise "is committed" to the affirmation that indeed God has revealed Divinity in Christ. For Welch, the real question is not whether there is the Trinity but what the nature of the Trinity is and what it signifies relative to our knowledge of the Godhead. Welch's central focus is that we should seek to understand the Trinity so that we can interpret what God is doing in the World for we cannot say what God is doing unless we are familiar with the ways of the Lord.

To respond to those who reject the conception of the Trinity that "goes beyond" God as the revelation, Welch's school of thought expresses the necessity to re-affirm that God cannot be anything else other than God in God's revelation. That is to say "if God is come to us in his Holy Spirit, then it can be no less than God who is so come to us" (Welch 152, 220). This position counters the Medalist and Subordinationist stance. For Welch and his school of thought, "the doctrine that God is in himself three Person or modes of existence is a necessary consequence of the assertion that God has truly revealed himself in Christ" (Welch 1952, 220).

According to what Welch has called the "Monarchian" conception, the terms Father, Son and Holy Spirit ought to be understood to be referring to "distinction in the 'content' of divine activity". This Monarchian conception has a much better appeal because "it permits us to speak of eternal, divine, functions or fundamental aspects of divine activity, thus of a sort of 'essential' Trinity, without being involved in the difficulties of the traditional efforts to define the divine Persons" (Welch 1952, 220). Welch also points out that to merely equate the Three Persons with the functions of sovereignty, redemptive love and Sanctification is really to degrade the Trinity. Welch would rather add to monarchianism a dimension of ontological or essential Trinity.

After this lengthy discourse, Welch admits, "we cannot separate the 'form', and the 'content' of revelation" (Welch 1952, 221). That is, God is One, inseparable, indivisible and eternal.

Walfang Pannenberg is another theologian whose views shed some light for us on the Trinity. Of course Pannenberg takes advantage of the on-going discussion on the doctrine of the Trinity.

WALFANG PANNENBERG'S DISTINCTION BETWEEN THE FATHER AND THE SON

Walfang Pannenberg postulates that if the man Jesus of Nazareth is God's revelation, the Jesus' Person cannot be separated from God's essence. Pannenberg believes that Jesus personally "understood himself as set over against the God who he called Father" (Pannenberg 1977, 158). If we transfer this relationship from history to eternity it seems clear that there is a distinction between Jesus and the Father - a distinction which also belongs to the divinity of God. Pannenberg describes Jesus' relation (as Son) to the Father as Obedience - one which is coherent with the essence of God. The terms "Son" and "Father" are to be conceived as relational. The word "Father" refers to the God of Jesus to whom he channeled his prayers even that decisive Gethsemane prayer. The word "Son", as Pannenberg uses it here refers to "primarily his relations to the "Father", a relation of obedience and 'mission' according to the scriptures (Romans 8:3, Galatians 4:4, John 3:17). "Son" also refers to Jesus' trust in God the Father.

For Pannenberg, God's essence contains within itself the twofoldness as it is revealed in the Christ event, namely the tension and the relation of Son and Father. Because in Jesus of Nazareth, God himself did not appear in human form, there must be a differentiation between the deity of Jesus Christ and divine nature as such. To say the deity of Jesus Christ has undifferentiated identity with God the Father, as the medalists would say, is rejecting the Trinity. For Pannenberg,

> the differentiation of Father and Son in God himself must be maintained, because his differentiation which is characteristic of the relation of the historical Jesus to God, must be characteristic to the essence of God himself, if Jesus as a person is God's revelation (Pannenberg 1977, 160).

The "Logos Christology" had its origin with the Second Century apologists. It prevailed over modalism and its merit is that "it asserted the differentiation of Father and Son within the Godhead" (Pannenberg 1977, 160). This became the official position of the whole patristic theology because it was able to demonstrate how the Son could be conceived of as different. Unlike Ignatius, the Second Century apologist understood the Logos concept primarily cosmologically though in the context of the Hellenistic philosophy. For them Logos was the reason, the natural law holding the cosmos together. This Logos concept understood this way, was best known in Stoicism.

For the Stoics, "the Logos order the world into the unity of a system (systema) by setting matter in motion and giving it form just as the Logos in man established the unity of the soul (Pannenberg 1977, 161). The Platonic understanding that Logos is the guide to true being is very different from the Stoics. Platonism did not conceive the Logos as pantheistically as the Stoics did but "as a middle being between the transcendent God and the world". This is the philosophy held by Philo and the apologists. In fact, the Logos concept for the apologists was a mixture of both Stoic and Platonic elements. The former's influence can be seen insofar as the Logos is believed to have come from God and the Logos' appearance in Jesus, while the latter's influence (Platonic) comes through insofar as the Logos occupies the middle position between the most High God and the world. What we have here is a mixture or cross-pollination of philosophies-which could cause more theological complication. Pannenberg, utilizing this insight from these two schools of thought, and aware of the dangers, asserts: "the relation between God and the Logos was thought through primarily in the context of the philosophical problem of the world's origin, rather than in view of God's historical revelation" (Pannenberg 1977, 162).

Pannenberg sums up this discussion by noting that "the Logos is the prototype of the world, or more precisely, the essence of the prototypes of all things in the world, just as it itself is the image of the Father" (Pannenberg 1977, 163). Philo's view of the Logos is also worth noting at this point. He says essentially that though the Logos appears in human being as rational beings, and the seeds of the Logos are effective in the whole of mankind, it is in Jesus Christ that the whole Logos appeared. With these insights, Pannenberg succeeds in distinguishing the Father from the Son without divorcing them in essence. He maintains that unity of God without dissolving "the two persons." However, what this scholar has done could be used to "undo" what other theologians have worked hard to disprove, namely that there is no difference between the Father and the Son. One way for Pannenberg to escape from the trap he has set for himself is to allow himself to melt his "Father" and "Son" into the African concept of the Great Spirit God which is believed to be unquestionably one.

THE RELATION OF THE HOLY SPIRIT TO JESUS CHRIST

Both in systematics and in history, Pannenberg's beginning point of the doctrine of the Trinity lies in the distinction in the essence of God between the Father and the Son. But to talk of just the Father and the Son would be a Duality, not Trinity. So here let us examine the relation of the Holy Spirit to Jesus Christ. How does the Holy Spirit belong to the Trinity and Divinity of God as an independent and differentiated person without posing as a separate God? After all, the Holy Spirit is the third person of the Trinity.

In the Old Testament the Spirit of God was understood to be "the ground of life" in the most inclusive sense and not primarily a source of supernatural knowledge. For an especially unusual activity to occur, a unique endowment with God's spirit which is creative was necessary. Also, the spirit of God was thought of as the power of life, rather than the "source of knowledge". But, of course it is best to combine the two functions if we are to have a more comprehensive understanding of the Biblical conception of the Spirit. It is this double function that makes the Spirit very crucial in the doctrine of God. Pneumatology ought to occupy the most central position in the entire Judeo-Christian faith.

The spirit guarantees the participation of the believers in the living Jesus Christ. The Christians are 'sons of God' because they are filled with the 'spirit' (Galatians 4:6; Romans 8:14). Because the Spirit is of God self, the same unites with God. It is on the basis of this fact that we can be in community and have communication with God. Pannenberg reiterates this rather profound insight. Through Jesus the Spirit makes Christians the sons and daughters of God, just as Jesus has been designated to be the Son of God through the Spirit. But, of course, our status as "daughters/sons of God" cannot be the same as Jesus' status since not only is he "son" of God but he is God as well. We become sons and daughters "through participation in the Sonship of Jesus" although the latter's Sonship is also "Very God, of Very God." Another distinction between Jesus (as Son of God) and us is that we would have to be sons and daughters by adoption while Jesus is Son *ontologically* and *eternally*. Because the Spirit is present in God, in Jesus and even in us, the same is the Common denominator in the Trinity. Pannenberg says, "this is the most inclusive concept of the Spirit in the revelation of God and thus in his eternal essence as well" (Pannenberg 1977, 176). Put differently, the Holy Spirit unites the Godhead.

THE UNITY IN THE TRINITY

Regarding the numerical quality and quantity of the Divinity, Pannenberg argues, "If Father, Son and Spirit are distinct but coordinate moments in the accomplishment of God's revelation, then they are so in God's eternal essence as well" (Pannenberg 1977, 180). Like most thinkers, the problematic which Pannenberg must address is that of the "Divine conundrum": how the three are one and the one is three! As does Augustine, Pannenberg maintains that "the unity of God is the presupposition of the concept of revelation..." (Pannenberg 1977, 180). If God is synonymous with Trinity the task of the theologians is to elucidate the ONE GOD as THREE-IN-ONE. Pannenberg offers us three possibilities which we now proceed to examine one by one.

a, THE DOCTRINE OF PROCESSION

First, let us consider the doctrine of Procession in the Eastern Church which understands God's unity along the lines of the Logos Christology as a unity of origin. According to this school of thought, God the Father is the SOURCE from which both the Son and the Spirit proceed all in eternal movement. This is what Origen refers to as "eternal begetting." In the background, is the Neoplatonic philosophy of the emanation of the many from the One. This Trinitarian formulation can be traced back to the Cappadocian Fathers of the end of the Fourth Century. Insofar as the Father is regarded as the "SOURCE OF DIVINITY", we can still identify some of the subordinationist tendencies of the Logos Christology. This character makes it distinctly Origenist. We have already noted that the problem here is: either the essence of God changes or the Father is older than the Son. This is the flaw.

b, THE DOCTRINE OF THE RELATIONAL:

On the other hand, the Western Church since Augustine, has maintained the doctrine of the relational. It is exactly because the Father, the Son and the Holy Spirit are mutual and relational that they form the Trinity or else we should be talking about Tritheism! It is because they stand in this unequaled relation that the Three Persons are uniquely One in their Threeness. Pannenberg summarizes it in what I call "the logic of necessity":

> The Father is Father only vis-a-vis the Son; the Son is the Son only vis-a-vis the Father; the Spirit is Spirit only as bond of the community of the Father and Son. No one of the Trinitarian Persons is who he is without the others; each exist only in reference to the others. (Pannenberg 1977, 181).

Following such a clear logic, we readily perceive a problem - "the personal character" and "identity" of each of the Three seems automatically undermined. We cannot think of a "God" whose Divinity is "conditional." This, like the doctrine of Procession, has a major flaw also.

c, GOD IS GOD:

To avoid this inevitable problem, we turn to Karl Barth who suggested that rather than speaking of Three Persons, God is one God - a position which has withstood all theological weather since the inception of the doctrine. This point of view is neither synthetic nor analytical. I want to call it a "theological prostrate" position because we say this with uttermost humility.

God is God, in God's modes of being as "Father, Son and Spirit," because creation, redemption and reconciliation, our whole being and action, in which God wills to be our God, have their basis and prototype in God's own essence in God's own being as God (Barth 1.1. 1968, 383). Now we turn to Jurgen Moltmann's trinity which is focused on the Cross.

JURGEN MOLTMANN'S TRINITARIAN THEOLOGY OF THE CROSS

Moltmann notes that while the cross today has become the sign of the church, in the very early days of Christianity "the doctrine of the Trinity in the concept of God is the doctrine which marked off Christianity from polytheism, pantheism and monotheism" (Moltmann 1974, 241). Thus it was the belief in the doctrine of the Trinity which was the object of passionate polemic from Islamic monotheism. According to Moltmann, "the great Greek theology of the Cappadocian certainly understood all theology as the doctrine of the Trinity" (Moltmann 1974, 247). However, they distinguished between the Trinity in the economy of salvation and the immanent Trinity, which meant some distinction between "the inner being of God" and "salvation history". Unlike the entire Nineteenth Century Protestant theology, Karl Barth took the Cappadocian approach to the doctrine of God which consisted in distinguishing between the immanent Trinity and the economy of the Trinity as we have already pointed out.

On the Catholic side, outstanding theologians like Karl Rahner regard the two distinctions as inappropriate. Rahner formulates a two-point thesis paraphrased by Moltmann in his *The Crucified God*: a) "the Trinity is the nature of God and the nature of God is the Trinity..." and, b) "the economic Trinity is the immanent Trinity, and the Immanent Trinity is the economic Trinity". Moltmann makes some insightful statements towards an understanding of the Trinity which are not just speculative. He asserts that:

> the theological concept for the conception of the crucified Christ is the doctrine of the Trinity. The material principle of the doctrine of the Trinity is the cross of Christ. The formal principle of knowledge of the cross is the doctrine of the Trinity (Moltmann 1974, 241).

Having made this assertion, the question that arises is: "where do the first beginnings lie?" We cannot point to the New Testament per se because, as every author discussed in this chapter has pointed out, the New Testament does not provide us with a well developed doctrine of the Trinity, we can only identify the roots. The doctrine in question developed from the theological controversies of the Early Church with regard to the unity of Jesus Christ with God (the father) and the role of the Holy Spirit. It is true, however, that we get most of the theological material from the Scriptures themselves, while philosophy helps us to formulate the language we may use to express and explain the doctrine.

Moltmann says, "if the cross of Jesus is understood as a divine event, i.e. an event between Jesus and his God and father, it is necessary to speak in Trinitarian terms of the Son and the Father and the Spirit" (Moltmann 1974, 581). This author agrees with Moltmann that in order for the doctrine of the Trinity not to be made a mere theological speculation, which it should not be, we have to perceive the Cross as a Trinitarian event because the Jesus who was "conceived by the Holy Spirit" and is the "only begotten Son" of the Father, *IS* the One who was "crucified", and, before he died, he commended his spirit into his Father's hands (God). Then he was raised from the dead by God the Father. All Three Persons are involved in what happened to Jesus Christ from birth to death, and also in what the Father did from "creation to redemption". In this discussion, Moltmann correctly says "the content of the doctrine of the Trinity is the real cross of Christ himself. The form of the crucified Christ is the Trinity." For Moltmann, the cross is that which stands between the son and the father in the harshness of its forsakenness. Our salvation then lies in God's taking up all disaster, forsakenness by God, absolute death and sinking into nothingness in history. "The bifurcation in God himself must contain the whole uproar of history within itself" (Moltmann 1974, 246). Inextricably involved at the cross was God's full humanity and divinity as well as a serious contradiction of God's eternity and God's death on the cross.

The Trinity ceases to be speculative theology insofar as "our history" becomes the "history of God" and God's history is our own. Here lies the importance of the doctrine of the Trinity - it demonstrates how God - "physically" participates in history in order to redeem us from sin whose wage is death. Any serious liberation theology must take the cross as demonstration of God's "Personal" involvement in our suffering, political oppression, poverty, sin of all shades, and the like. The Trinity viewed through the cross, is God's expression as love - caring love that gets involved for the redemption of all creation.

It is through the cross that we feel and enjoy the love of God and thereby join the perichoresis of the Trinity. Thus, we are "taken up into this 'history' of God" (Moltmann 1974, 246). This way, rather than being led to theism and even atheism, we are led "into new creation and theopoiesis" (Moltmann 1974, 247). The cross is an instance where humanity is drawn into the communion of the Trinity thereby indicating that the Trinity is not about numbers but the power that creates, the love that saves, the holiness that sanctifies and the life which is the nature of God.

Furthermore, in order to tell the story of Jesus in Christian terms, Moltmann says one "must tell of the history of Jesus as a history between the Son and the Father" (Moltmann 1974, 247). Moltmann claims that if "God-talk" is so conceived then God is not viewed or thought of as of another nature or a heavenly being or a moral authority, but in fact, an event (Moltmann 1974, 247). Moltmann then argues that this being the case, i.e. God as event, "there is in fact not 'personal God' as a person projected in heaven" (Moltmann 1974, 247). However, "there are persons in God: the Son, the Father and the Spirit". This being so, no longer does one pray to God in abstract but one prays "through the Son to the Father in the Spirit" (Mackey Dictionary. 581). As, according to the Scripture, God is love (1 John 4:16), Moltmann argues that the doctrine of the Trinity can be understood as an interpretation of the ground, the event and the experience of that love. And one may add, viewed as a point of Divine intensity, the Trinity at the cross will have to be summarized as LOVE. Again, it is not about numbers! To talk about Father, Son, and Spirit as the Great Spirit Being with personal qualities such as love, compassion, power and so forth is more plausible than "Threeness-in-One and Oneness-in-Three". For instance, the love of the Father can be the same as that of the Son and the Holy Spirit. Thus one does not count three loves, but having been loved three times by the same love!

AN AFRO-CENTRIC VIEW OF THE TRINITY

The Trinity is likely to remain mysterious to many Christian believers, if we focus on "mathematics and the metaphysics" of God. However, if we seek to understand the meaning of this mystery, as exemplified on the cross, it is possible to comprehend God's will as well as activities in the world because God's unfailing intention is to reveal Godself for the purpose of communicating the divine purpose for us, both in this world and even in the world to come! The goal of the Revelation is to make known God's love for us (John 3:16). The Trinity presents itself to us as a model of unity in diversity and community. It is at this point that we attempt to share an African perspective of this aspect of the doctrine of God so that we may not only believe but understand and emulate God's communal lifestyle in our endeavour to live as one family under God. Though traditionally communal, some Africans may be tempted to trade off their religio-cultural values for "foreign philosophies" presented to them under the guise of civilization and "religious values". Be that as it may, most Africans are striving to interpret God's metaphysics in such a way that it makes sense to their concept of community and their egalitarian lifestyle.

Raymond Mosha's article "The Trinity in the African Context" (Mosha 1980), attempts to discuss the Trinity from its Christian traditional beginnings to its interpretation in an African context. Mosha, however, merely makes a beginning. The task still before us is to develop an African perspective on the metaphysics of God. To make ourselves clear, ours is not a "numerical quest" but a spiritual inquiry into the GREAT SPIRIT BEING. An African perspective is more utilitarian because it does not just relate to the mathematical metaphysics of the Divine but to the nature of the Divine in terms of character or "modes" of existence.

THE TREENESS OF GOD: AN ANALOGY

The Shona perspective of the ONENESS of God could be explained by way of an analogy. On a bright day , if one looks at a huge umbrella tree from a distance, one generally sees a silhouette of the One tree. On approaching more features with character may begin to appear. There may be one, two or three large branches constituting this tree. When one is finally under the tree where the stem touches "the ground of its being", only One huge stem is all one sees: That is a TREE! Such is the "TREENESS OF GOD". It would be unreasonable to argue that "each branch is a whole tree." Equally unnatural and unreasonable would be arguing that one branch is more senior than the other two when all three "emanate" from the same trunk at the same. Rather, it is more natural for one to say: I have seen "a tree" when in fact one has only seen branches or just one branch. It is also reasonable to say: there is a tree over there when one catches just a glimpse of a tree trunk. We do not normally say, there is a tree without branches because such a detail is generally not called for since normally, most people can distinguish between a stump and a tree.

To talk of the " TREENESS OF GOD" is more descriptive of the NATURE of the GREAT SPIRIT BEING than to talk of the "THREENESS OF GOD" who is "Three-in-One and One-in-Three" as God has been described in the Trinitarian language. The language of "three-in-one" has always created a sense of "numerical quantity."
Christian theologians want to be clear that they worship one God, not three. Then they also want to argue that each of these three is God: God the Father, God the Son and God the Holy Spirit. That just does not make sense, and since theology must be COHERENT, the Trinitarian formula has always left much to be desired on the matter of "mathematics."

To go back to our analogy, we could discuss the character and identity of the tree , the DNA of the branches and their trunk, the sameness of the nature of the tree, same name (including branches of course), non-gender status , fecundity, singleness of purpose, providential quality, personality, unmoving mover status, and so forth. No one would have any problem with all this. Moreover, the prefix"mu" is the Shona language pre-suppose singleness, not multiplicity. If each person of the Trinity is God, and since the Son is God, how come those who saw the Son did not perceive the Trinity? Or, did they? Since the Holy Spirit is God, how come those who were filled with the Holy Spirit in the Upperroom did not testify having seen the Father and the Son? Jesus clearly expressed his "oneness" with the Father when he said: if you see me you have seen the Father. He did not say: if you see me you have seen God the Father and God the Son. There is a difference in what these two statements mean.

I contend here that since the doctrine of God has been "unfolding" from the Creator alone, then to the Redeemer and the Holy Spirit. Then to the Creator, the Savior and the Sanctifier, what we have is ONE GOD who is revealing Godself gradually as we are being drawn nearer and nearer to God. The analogy of the tree helps me to explain to anyone how we can see "more" personalities in ONE essence. Thus, the TREENESS OF GOD, leaves no questions about 1. Origin, 2. The

Begottenness of the Son, 3. The presence (or absence/ escape) of the Father at Calvary 4. The chain of command - - who sends who! 5. The revelation "front" of God. 6. The identity of the three. 7 Unity, 8. Singleness of purpose 9. Unchangeableness of God/ Eternal nature and so forth. The sentiments with which we prefer to talk about God as a Person, are the very ones which "muddle up" our spiritual vision. As far as I am concerned, talking about the Great Spirit Being as numbers [Three-in-One and One-in-Three] is no less impersonal than using such an analogous language as we have done in this discussion. The language of "Father, Son and Holy Spirit" [creating three persons] is a departure from the language of the One Great Spirit God we meet in Deuteronomy 6:4 or John 14:6- 11 as well as other Scriptures . Before we move on to other matters, the question I have for my colleagues who want to maintain the "mathematical Formula" is, would the Great Spirit God deliver any more because of this Trinitarian attribute than otherwise? I think to regard the One God- - -the Great Spirit God- - the MWARI, MODIMO, JUOK, IMANA, LESA, NKULUMUKULU, INKOSI , YAHWE, THE GOD OF JESUS, THE GOD OF ABRAHAM as "Three-in-One and One-in-Three " borders on being heretical unless the language has made it clear that GOD is ONE.

The people of African descent have come to the point where they have had to "discover truth" for themselves. And, God has also chosen to reveal truth to God's own who "seek God in spirit and truth". People who rely on the Great Spirit God will receive Divine compassion, mercy, love, care and POWER, all for the people's liberation, empowerment and affirmation.

To offer people a GOD who is "three-in-one and one-in-three", is a way of both trying to distract and confuse those who "seek to worship God" in spirit and in truth. People of African descent choose to worship the Great Spirit God - - ONE GOD! Not three. The TREENESS of God gives us a picture of the one God, while the "trinity" clearly indicates "three."

THE REPRESENTATION OF GOD IN THE INCARNATION

The purpose of the Incarnation is to make the Trinity understandable. Christianity shares with several major world religions this idea that at some point in history a deity has made a contact with history in order to be known among humanity -- a supernatural happening which, in our case has resulted in a historical phenomenon known as the Christian religion. Our faith has specifically described what occurred as union, (not mixture of divinity with humanity) when the WORD became Flesh. As it is God who BECAME flesh, we can discuss how it is that God in God's Spiritness, incarnated. How could the Son (who is God) be the incarnation of God unless there is a difference between God the Son and God the Father? If there is, then Christianity has at least TWO (not One) Gods who happen to get along! When the Son says "...yet your will and not my will be done," the implication is two, not one person.

Furthermore, it is important to distinguish the term Incarnation from reincarnation. These two common religious and theological concepts can not and should not be used interchangeably. To sharpen the definitions more, we also have to draw a clear distinction between these and "resurrection." According to John Hick, one of the most widely read thinkers of our day, reincarnation

> ...is the idea that we live many lives on earth, being reborn as babies after interim periods of disembodied existence. In varying forms this is believed by hundreds of millions within the Hindu and Buddhist worlds, as well as various other smaller groups. In its more popular forms in which the belief also has a certain currency in the West, it is claimed that the same self that is now living has lived before and will live again, with continuity of character traits and occasionally with flashes of memory of a previous life (Hick 1980).

Thus defined, it is clear that this idea seems compatible with the Christian belief of the resurrection since both concepts "constitute re-embodiment." It is clear that reincarnation does not hinge upon belief in Christ, whereas resurrection is understood as a one-time phenomenon resulting from one's belief in Jesus Christ. Reincarnation assures material, temporal continuity while resurrection guarantees eternal, spiritual continuity. This is the decisive difference between the two concepts as we apply them here. These should be distinuished from the incarnation which we discussed earlier. Two of the three concepts (incarnation and resurrefcion) place Jesus in a very peculiar category of human-divine being. As a true human being, Jesus is the only one who can genuinely represent human beings to God in a sacrificial manner which consequently becomes salvific. At the same time, only he can adequately divinely mediate God to humanity without himself being reduced to the status of a creature. It is this Jesus who is God's only sacrificial " lamb" - again, "the Lamb of God that taketh away the sin of the whole world". As such Jesus has to be an inextricable part of the

Trinity since he is God, constituting the Trinity. Furthermore, since only God can save humanity from sin, Jesus had to be the expiation of our sin because he is God. Note that while we can not say it is Jesus' full humanity or his full divinity that makes him uniquely and singularly appropriate, yet such is the case.

According to the Gospel of John, Jesus was with God in the beginning in a spiritual existence. Therefore, the event of the Incarnation is a mystery which characterizes and distinguishes the Christian faith because of the element of Christ's pre-existence, if this is taken seriously in all its spirit-material forms. For Fred B. Craddock , the New Testament attributes pre-existence not to all human spirits nor to an elect few, but to *Christ alone*. It belongs to the exclusive area of Christology, not to the general scope of anthropology, although these two considerations are not mutually exclusive. Thus, these special qualities about Christ attribute divinity to him and to him alone among all spiritual realities that ever existed "in history."

St. Paul's writings allude to the pre-existence of Christ in many instances. The Letter to the Hebrews, for example, indicates clearly that God still operates with and through the Son (Hebrews 1:1-4). What is difficult to imagine is whether Christ was completely inactive from the time of creation to the Incarnation occasion. However, Old Testament biblical studies indicate that Christ has always been active in history since creation. Unless God opens humanity's spiritual eyes, we can walk and talk to ourselves unaware of God's presence. But African spirituality points to God's Omnipresence.

Judith M. Bahemuka's article *"The Hidden Christ in African Traditional Religion"* argues for the ever present Christ when she says:

> But the story of Emmaus can be brought to life in Africa. Christ walked with the disciples: He talked to them, 'but their eyes were kept from recognizing Him'. It was not until the end of the journey, by a simple un-obtrusive gesture, that their eyes were opened, and the unknown figure was the Lord (Bahemuka 1989,4).

There may be some truth in this claim if one believes in the Trinity because we cannot talk about the Trinity without implying by it (God), who is the Father, the Son and the Holy Spirit.

It therefore, seems logical to me that by implication the agent of creation has always been at work since the beginning of time although, according to the traditional biblical view, God rested on the seventh day (Genesis 2:2). Now the rhetorical question is: What has Christ, through whom everything was created, been doing from the seventh day to the time of the Incarnation when the Word became flesh and began to minister among humanity in a particular social context? It seems we cannot accord Christ an inactive role if he is an inseparable part of the Godhead, without whom there can be no talk about God or the Trinity. That he was "hidden" from us as he was to the two men of Emmaus does not make him an inactive participant. Rather, we should think that the world did not heed the presence of Christ until God "opened" our eyes to his presence in Christ in the Incarnation event. To account for this seeming "gap" is important for African Christianity because that may help us identify crucial sources of faith that furnish African theology with an indigenous spirituality.

The mystery of the Incarnation, like that of the burning bush which was not consumed, drew our attention to Divine Self-manifestation. Regarding the "burning bush, "are we to imagine the bush had been burning since creation? No! It "began to burn" in time for Moses to see it. Similarly, the Incarnation occurred in God's time (kairos) in order that humanity's eyes may be opened to God's presence 'Among us." Furthermore, although the "burning bush" had a 'beginning" so to speak, one could not equate that with the "origin" of Yahwe's existence, yet the voice said: "I am the God of your father the God of Abraham, the God of Isaac and the God of Jacob" (Exodus 3: 6). God had been in existence eternally before this incident in <u>Chronos</u>, occuring in Kairos. The Incarnation only revealed the Nature of the Reality that has always been , not the fact that such Reality exists. It was not about existence, but about the Nature of that which exists. Via the Incarnation, God's "physical presence" made a specific impact on the human race -- God with us. These are some of the "contact points" which enrich African spirituality and consequently theology. In sum, the central message is, in African spirituality, God is always present but humanity's eyes generally "close" and "open" from time to time (Gen. 28:16-17).

WAS THE INCARNATION INCIDENTAL?

Another issue raised especially by John Calvin's Reform Theology is whether the Incarnation would have taken place had the fall of the first man not occurred. Put differently, was the Incarnation incidental? Within Christian circles, Thomist theologians tended to believe that the Incarnation was contingent on Adam's transgression, while the Scotists maintained the opposite view. For instance, a mystic, Andrew Osiander maintained that even if Adam had not fallen, the Incarnation would have still taken place "because God had decided that the Son was to become incarnate. Thus the incarnation was God's eternal purpose, and not a response to sin" (Gonzalez, 1975). As Osiander's thinking did not seem to be consistent with the gospel, he met strong opposition to his hypothetical argument. The historian J. Gonzalez tells us that 'Calvin rejected it [Osiander's theology] as vain speculation. What we know of Christ according to the biblical witness is that he became incarnate for our redemption (Gonzalez 1975). The Christian doctrine of the Incarnation, as argued and developed through the numerous councils which met and debated Christology over the centuries, however, does not sufficiently address this point, probably because it is an "iffy" statement. Fortunately the Scriptures make it clear that God loved the world so much that God gave God's own Son in order to redeem the world from sin (John 3:16). It stands to reason that if the world was not "lost in sin", there would not have been the need for the "dramatic intervention" by God. So the Incarnation is a resurgence of God's work of the salvation of humanity in a form that humanity can comprehend and hopefully respond and relate to. The Incarnation is God's act of love for God's creation. Thus, Incarnational Trinity takes the initiative to be involved in the redemption of all creation. It is ludicrous to ask: what if God did not have a Son?

The Chalcedonian teaching has been adopted by theologians of various schools of thought through the centuries yet the results did not necessarily translate into faith. Each person still has to encounter Jesus Christ and make a decision. Could it have been that personal faith in Jesus Christ would have enabled these theologians to understand the nature and person of Jesus Christ better? It may very well be that their task was made more difficult because they sought "understanding" prior to "belief." It is, however, safe to assume that among these intellectuals there were some who sought an understanding of the Christ whom they believed in.

From varying schools of thought, the Church gradually discovered that the crucial thing was to affirm that Jesus Christ is to be believed in and known as the Son of God. This awareness has led some African Christians to prefer to believe that Jesus Christ was more divine than human as our Lord and Savior, although his humanity was not docetic. They argue that since Jesus' primary mission was to "save" us from sin, a function which only God can fulfil, therefore his divinity is very crucial-his nature which is appropriate for our salvation is critical.

In 1986 some of my students at the United Theological College in Zimbabwe actually protested against any talk of Jesus Christ as being fully human and fully divine. They feared that that would weaken their faith in the Risen Lord. They preferred to believe in Christ who, since he is God, is more divine than human in terms of percentage! They did not claim that he was less human than other human beings, although this could have been part of their rationalization. In fact, most of them did not deny his humanity at all, except those who held various versions of docetism.

These ministerial candidates were not interested in Jesus' metaphysics. Rather they sought to cultivate their faith and know more about the Risen Lord. For the purpose of their faith in Jesus Christ their Savior, their Christological point of departure is "Christ is Risen. Hallelujah!" and not "Where is the baby who is born in Bethlehem of Judea?" However, from either perspective, the Incarnational Trinity is: "Immanuel" -- God with us! (Matt. 1:23). Generally speaking there is emphasis among most Africans, on the divine presence rather than human reality. For these seminarians who probably represent a majority view, what is crucial is Christ's divinity (his spiritual presence today) because that is what they can preach and experience, not his humanity. His humanity is important in so far as they can anthropomorphize their Christology.

Perhaps what my United Theological College students were arguing has some validity for them. They were saying that- for their faith, they draw on Christ's divinity in order to strengthen their humanity, a nature they share with Jesus. It is pointless to preach Jesus' humanity because we all share that. However, Jesus was not a mere prophet! What is salvific is Christ's divinity and so it is at the point of him being a divine sacrifice that Jesus Christ in his fullness is Savior. This view certainly introduces a new dimension to our understanding and doing of Christology. It is soteriology though not divorced from Christ's ontological character, that makes Christianity unique at the same time that the intellectual character of Christian theology refuses to be torn from the totality of Christian spirituality. At the same time, our articulation of the Trinity including a discussion on the Incarnation also points to the religion's appeal to one's intellect and emotions. Christian theology in Africa cannot afford to lose this "wholeness."

Most orthodox theologians emphasize that the Incarnation was an act of the whole Godhead, and not One Person acting independently, for the Godhead is always interdependent as well as communal within its divine circles and for divine purposes. Therefore, God is named and known by what God is believed to be doing among God's own people. For most African believers it is not so much the metaphysics as it is God's work through Jesus Christ that draws them to worship the Holy One. Also, it is not so much that the Word became flesh than why the Word became flesh that draws most African believers to worship the Risen Christ as our Savior. Of course, that the word became flesh is a mystery but why it became flesh is the AMAZING GRACE!

The Incarnational Trinity considered wholly gives depth to our discussion on salvation (or redemption) due to the tangibility and indispensability of its purpose. Furthermore, the Calvary event touches our lives when we realize that God took the form of humanity in Jesus Christ, emptied God's self and empathized with our human plight, because God willed to save our perishing souls, without losing God's own Godhood. To accomplish this, the task called for a divine action which physically unfolded from the Incarnation to the Resurrection. Conceived spiritually, the unfolding of the mystery began with the pre-existence up until the present reign of Jesus Christ who "sits on the right hand of God."

The Incarnation sheds profound meaning on the significance of Calvary, which could not have been without it, because only one who is fully human and fully divine for the purpose of sacrifice, and without spiritual blemish (sin) could put oneself in the place of a divine sacrificial victim, (the Lamb of God). Only one who is "Word that became flesh" could redeem the rest of the human race without being overcome by any debilitating creaturely and demonic forces. In fact, it is this Divine involvement in history for the sake of the redemption of God's creation which by and large sets the precedence for Christian ethics (Matt. 25:31f). Many modern theologians under Kantian influence tend to be distrustful of metaphysics but seek to interpret the Incarnation in terms of morality. However, here our emphasis is the meaning of the Trinity though not at the exclusion of morality, which itself is one more lesson we can learn from this doctrine. What this section has attempted to do is to make clear what the role of the Incarnation is in a discussion on the Trinity. Now we move on to the meaning of the incarnate Trinity.

THE INCARNATE TRINITY

The subject of the Incarnational Trinity comes to the forefront naturally in our discussion on the Trinity because the Creator, the Redeemer, and the Sustainer are all involved simultaneously at all times. In *The Origins and Development of African Theology*, the author very briefly discusses the Trinity in the context of the "origins of African theology." In that brief discussion, he concludes that if the Creator was FULLY GOD before the birth of Jesus, and FULLY GOD during the life of the historical Jesus, and is still FULLY GOD after the crucifixion, death, resurrection and ascension, then for African theology "the meaning of the Incarnation, rather than its history, would ... become the essence of Christianity" (Muzorewa 1985, 146). In other words the meaning of what God did and does in God's involvement is more important than our momentary caption and description of the accounts, i.e. history. Thus, I perceive the Incarnate Trinity as a process involving creation, sustainance and salvation. In fact, the designation "Incarnate Trinity" seems to express best the idea of God's involvement in history. In this regard, I agree with Kenneth Leech that:

> what is central to this whole tradition (of the doctrine of the Incarnation) is not only the belief that in Christ, humanity has been taken into God, but also that this process of taking humanity into God is going on all the time, that reality is incarnational, and that therefore to hold an incarnational faith is of the greatest importance if we are to view humanity and the material order in a way that can lead to their sanctification and transformation (Leech 1985, 249-250).

The Incarnation goes on. Incarnate Trinity is the state of the Spirit who is always active. However, in Jesus Christ, the path of the Incarnation in history is marked with a huge "poster" which reads: "God among us." That is the sign every Christian must bear in their heart. But this poster "God among us" does not and cannot locate God as such. It can only be understood as the "wheel in the middle of a wheel" (Ezekiel 1:16). Incarnate Trinity means the creator, redeemer and Sustainer God is always with us. There is not a time when God is not with us. This points to the full meaning of God and Divine presence.

For the African faith today, the importance of the life of Jesus of Nazareth is that it provides the form in which God revealed God self to humanity as well as showing us God's will through Jesus' concrete actions and living faith actions. It is in this sense that we say the meaning of the Incarnation, rather than simply its historicity, is extremely decisive on the agenda of African theology today. For us, spirituality among African Christians takes both material and spiritual dimensions at once, all within a historical context. It happened then and it continues to unfold in our daily lives -- an endless process. God continues to incarnate in and among humanity. The Word is ever becoming flesh, and continues to dwell among us. If the incarnation is to be understood as an event, then it should be comprehended as an ongoing one, for there cannot be a time when God's presence ceases to be. When we talk of the Incarnate Trinity as the "once-for-all" revelation of God, we are merely trying to argue for Christianity as the supreme religion. Christianity ought to be conceived of as not just a religion but a life-style and repeated behavior of response to and adoration of God. The temptation to make "knowledge of God through Jesus Christ" into a religion reduces the "Christian faith" to the level of a *religion*, which by nature always has a tendency to preserve itself rather than serve the original purpose of pointing the practitioner to God. Teachings of Jesus the Christ pointed us to God, but when the Church institutionalised them it began to point us at best to culturally defined morality, at worst to the institutional church itself. Now, the error is not serious as long as Christ is understood as Very God and the Church as the Body of Christ but this is often not the case unfortunately.

The meaning of "the Word became flesh" can be very difficult to understand, let alone interpret. It is not clear whether, when the Word became flesh, the Word continued to exist in the same state (Logos) as it *became* the flesh that began to grow from being a baby to becoming a man (the man Jesus), who then was crucified, died, and rose after three days. It has to mean that the word allowed itself to be crucified, dead and buried to be raised on the third day. We have already discussed this elsewhere in this book.

Most Africans, however, would have no theological difficulty in accepting the fact that Jesus died and then was raised from the dead because in most African cultures, it is believed that after physical death, life continues in a spiritual form as an ancestor charged with some social responsibilities over the family. The new spiritual body is glorified in the sense that it acquires supernatural powers -- i.e. power to protect all the loved ones, the capability to be everywhere at once, and commitment to the well being of the living. This demonstrates how African cultures can readily appropriate the gospel message which promises that those who believe in God, though they die, yet shall they live eternally. Most Africans conceive a spiritual body as a perfect entity capable of super human precision in its execution of duties.

It is interesting to note that in the light of the Trinity, when modern Western theologians of the 1960's entertained the thought that God was dead, they did not single out any one member of the Trinity. Does that signify belief in the Unity of the Godhead "unto death" if that theology referred to God at all? Or did it signify other things? Maybe the exponents figured that since God once died in Jesus Christ on Calvary, it is possible that God is dead again.

The mystery of the Incarnation is about as unexplainable as that of the Trinity because the real subject at stake is the same - God, a Great Mystery. Consequently, if we articulate the doctrine of the Incarnation, the mystery of the Trinity will also become relatively apparent to us, but this is made possible when God self-reveals.

With respect to the Trinity as well as the Incarnation, we gain some illumination ironically from the African concept of death which we have discussed in detail elsewhere in this book. The majority of Africans believe that when a human being is deceased, only the flesh or the material dies. The soul continues; in fact, death frees up the soul. This means that the death on the cross makes sense to an African believer. Because the spiritual does not die, resurrected body has to be conceived of as spiritual. According to this African concept, ontologically speaking, both death and life are acknowledged at once as unquestionable realities, and there is no contradiction between them since "death" is thought of as consistent with "life," and life with death! In the case of Jesus' death and resurrection, we understand that the spiritual resurrection does not contradict the physical death. This means when Jesus Christ rose from the tomb, it was necessary that the tomb be empty since the emptiness of the sepulchre complemented the appearance of the Living Christ. When Jesus showed the doubting Thomas his wounds from the cross, the "wounds" on the new spiritual body served a real purpose for Thomas. They substantiated the fact that truly this was the Lord who had risen. It is no wonder, upon seeing the wounds, Thomas exclaimed: "My Lord and my God!" Thomas became the first person (disciple) to address Jesus as "God", completing the dialectic from doubt to unquestionable belief-the one who doubted the most becomes the one who believed the most. If Thomas called Jesus: Lord and God because he had seem the wounds (in order to believe), did it dawn on him that his God had wounds?

Although there are many versions of the resurrection, questions such as these arise: do we rise from death with our original body or do we acquire a spiritual one?   What kind of a body did Jesus have when he entered locked up rooms? Will I resurrect in my cancer-wasted body? My broken limb? My scar on my forehead? Or, will there be other ways we will be able to recognise each other "physically" in the new body? Did Jesus show the doubting Thomas his wounds in his palms only to help him to believe that he had risen indeed?

Some African theologians take the doctrine of the Incarnation very seriously. For instance Mercy Amba Oduyoye notes: "The unique theological factor that Christianity introduced into Africa was the Incarnation" (Oduyoye 1980). My own view as an African Christian is that we should focus more on the meaning of what God revealed to us through Jesus Christ than on "Christ's unique ontological status" as God incarnate. Theologians who value this doctrine agree that the significance of the Incarnation lies in the fact that it reveals how God cares, loves, forgives, and demonstrates continually God's presence among us, consequently symbolizing and manifesting our eternal spiritual security. Thus, the importance of the Incarnation is what it reveals rather than how it occurred because the how simply discusses how the what occurred. In the incarnation, we are given the "What" and we will comprehend the "How" as we eventually mature in the faith, although we can never exhaust the question. Of immediate concern is the question of the divine presence in the Incarnation: Was the Godhead present in the manger? This remains unanswered.

It is rather unfortunate that the Christian doctrine of the Incarnation has been described in such a way that it has served more as "a barrier" to understanding the faith, than as a means by which the ultimate purpose of the faith is articulated. In many ways, the doctrine has tended to become more of a point of unbelief and impossibility than a "doctrine" which teaches and facilitates our belief in God. More energy is spent on attempting to explain the doctrine than elucidating the content of the revelation which constitutes the Trinity.

On the other hand, ironically the claim of Christianity to authenticity and uniqueness (and even absoluteness) tends to rest on the two "impossibilities": the Incarnation and the Resurrection through which God has chosen to reveal eternal truth. Some theologians have argued logically that there would not have been the resurrection without the cross. And we may add that there would not have been the cross without the Incarnation! And since the Cross-symbolizes our salvation, we must conclude that the Incarnation is part of the unfolding of God's plan for our salvation. (We have already discussed the invalidity of the Osianderian hypothetical problem which says would the cross have been if we did not sin?)

For the African the meaning of the Incarnation is made clearer when the doctrine is interpreted in the light of our ancestral spirituality which is a major vehicle of communication with the *MWARI*, the Great Spirit God.

It appears to me that the Christian and the traditionalist knowledge of God as Creator before and after the introduction of the faith

(Church) is only slightly different. Otherwise the two religions are perspectives of the same God. This commonality signifies an important observation that both perspectives only differ basically in their cultural expressions but their object of worship is the One God. Furthermore, both religious traditions share the concept of the transcendence of God though they differ on the meaning of the immanence of God due to their respective spirituality.

If then the difference between the two religions is a cultural spirituality defined on the basis of respective functions (and not just its historicity), African spirituality ought to be utilized more extensively by people of African descent to explain Christian doctrine. African Christian spirituality ought to inform Christians who are interested in spiritual growth.

THE RELEVANCE OF THE INCARNATION FOR THE CHURCH IN AFRICA

The Church without the Incarnate Trinity is like a human body without vital organs such as the heart and the brain. The Incarnation is significant and relevant for the majority of the African Christian believers because it creates a "link" between the Creator and Creation. The doctrine means God made God's self known in the form which is most familiar with humanity. Humanity is reconciled to God through the process of the Incarnate Trinity. God can now be known by the believers of any intellectual levels. The teachings of Jesus Christ characterised by his divine authority, reveals significant insight into our knowledge of God the Creator. Greater spiritual intimacy and identity between God and humanity was facilitated when "the Word became flesh," AND the flesh became the Word again in the resurrection, thereby manifesting the reality of eternal life.

The Incarnate Trinity also creates a trend that reveals the phenomenon that God's fullness is actually involved in history both spiritually and physically. Furthermore, God can actually work through human beings to accomplish divine purposes. The visible divine presence and action in Jesus makes the word of God and God's promises a reality for the African who believes in tangible as well as spiritual reality. Put in different words, God who is the Incarnate Trinity, is real and our witness is experientially validated.

Since the crucifixion of Jesus Christ was fore-ordained according to the Scriptures, and since the reason for which Christ died was

God-ordained, the Incarnate trinity means God has intervened in human affairs which are imperfect in order to take away the sins of the whole world! Consequently, the Incarnation was a pre-requisite for the crucifixion and resurrection. No sacrificial victim could have been more adequate to pay off the human indebtedness to God than the lamb of God. Thus, the Incarnate Trinity means God delving into creation for the purpose of rescuing humanity. The church therefore can invite people to worship God the creator, redeemer and Sustainer-the God who gives life.

Through the Incarnation, God's plan for our salvation is made known in the form that humanity can recognise and even witness to others in history. Hence the Lord's designation: Jesus Christ is the Light of the World, the Savior of the World, the expiation of our sin. Incarnate Trinity means God saving humanity through the Church which is the body of Jesus Christ and in spite of ecclesiastical channels.

A VIEW OF THE INCARNATION IN THE LIGHT OF THE CROSS

Most theologians I have dialogued with seem to avoid having to deal with what happened to the eternal divinity of Jesus when he died on Calvary. My brother who is the bishop of the United Methodist church prefers to say that God the Creator was present when God the Redeemer suffered to death, but he is not willing to take the matter to its logical conclusion, namely: since Jesus is God, and since Jesus died, God therefore died on the cross when Jesus was crucified and died. Other theologians maintain that God died on the cross because Jesus was and is Very God (Dawe 1985).

It would seem that the purpose of Calvary was not for God to die or for God to be present to witness God's own son die, or for God to be there to witness Godself die, or for the divine in Jesus Christ to escape death on the Cross thereby betraying the reality of Christ's true humanity. That is not the purpose of Calvary at all. The most important happening is that the divine sacrifice was offered by God and was received by God, culminating in the provision for the redemption of the human race. The efficaciousness of that event does not depend on our articulation of the mystery at Mt. Calvary or in the Garden on Easter morning, but on the power of God who alone triumphs over all. According to the theology of death which we espouse in this book, God could do whatever God had to do even in God's death because death is nothing more than an ontological metamorphosis. Since God does not change, God's death means a state of existence God assumed in the process of expiating our sin in order to reconcile us to Godself. The death of God in Jesus at Calvary means an extraordinary transformation of creation. Yes, God died on the Cross-a liberating death that set all humanity free from sin.

The act of spilling that precious and unique divine-human blood as an offering (or as a ransom for many) was carried out by God through human hands and it was a successful operation according to God's plan. Incidentally by using the term "Redeemer" it is hoped that the reader begins to get a sense of the concept that the Redeemer <u>died</u> in the process of redeeming us. The death of the savior concept signified the process of liberating those who are dead in sin. For those who followed Jesus because he was a wonder worker, here lies the ultimate miracle: Christ died so that creation may see God's salvation. (1 Tim. 4:10). He died so as to transform the dead. And because God's death in Christ means life, the death of Christ culminates in his resurrection since to die is to live.

In African religion for a sacrifice to be successful, the the offering must be selected ritually, presented appropriately and by the rightful personnel. Note these: 1. The victim must be killed; 2. the offering must be acceptable to and accepted by the appropriate party usually deity; 3. the priest must acknowledge and confirm the efficaciousness of the sacrifice; and 4. there must be a cause and effect for the sacrifice; 5. most of all, the victim must be without blemish. In fact, it is how properly and appropriately the priest prepares the sacrifice that makes it efficacious. All these points were met satisfactorily on Calvary! We note that criterion number three refers to God. God is the priest for it is God who determined the suitability of and necessity for the sacrifice.

But God is also MWARI: THE GREAT SPIRITUAL BEING, to whom the sacrifice was offered. God is the Spirit being invoked by the priest. So when we ask: what role did God play in the Calvary event, the response is clear: GOD SAVED HUMANITY through God's perfect sacrifice. Another question might arise: What kind of a sacrifice is this where the lamb, the priest and the Great Spirit to which the sacrifice is offered are the same reality? Is this superficial? NO. The point of the sacrifice is to "Take away the sins of the whole world". Calvary did just that, and it took the type of a sacrificial entity as the divine/human nature of Jesus to cleanse the sins of the world.

When Africans practised human sacrifice, the reason the whole event was "peaceful and not violent," is precisely because: 1. the human victim was willing to die in order to "save" the rest of the community from impending disaster. Furthermore, it required a person without blemish.

Acceptance of the offering was guaranteed, too. In the case of human sacrifice, it was conceived of as a vicarious death; and   2. those who made the sacrifice felt they were doing the appropriate deed which met with everyone's approval, and it was done for the good of the whole. An evil could not result in a good for the whole. The efficaciousness of the sacrifice did not depend on everyone's belief either. This traditional concept is always important to bear in mind when we reflect on what happened on the Cross. Good Friday is "good" because what happened has made the salvation of all creation possible. That is a good.

It is for this reason that the heart of the gospel today is not what "mistake" was made (if indeed it is a mistake) by crucifying an innocent person; or the sin (if it is one) of Judas Iscariot who betrayed Jesus, his Rabbi (teacher). Unfortunately, both these are highlighted as sinful in Easter preaching, in many African churches, yet that is not the good news. The real message -- and it is good news -- is that an ultimate sacrifice acceptable to God was made, by God on behalf of humanity, and both humanity and divinity were integral components involved throughout. In other words, the good news is that God's purpose to have human blood spilled sacrificially in order to save all of humanity was accomplished. Consequently all flesh shall see salvation (Luke 3:6)! This is the good news we preach to all nations (regardless of their religions.)   Most importantly, this good news entirely depends upon God's act which finally became apparent to humanity through the soteriological activity of the redeemer.

CONCLUSION

For an African believer, soteriology is decisively more important than a mere metaphysical Christology (if this does not take Christ's work seriously.)   The most crucial concern is to acknowledge Christ's redemptive work, which itself makes it easy for us to understand his nature and mission, bearing in mind that the former was such that he might most adequately perform the latter. Similarly God created humanity in God's image so that humanity may best serve God, i.e. to worship God in spirit, freedom and truth. But when political, social, economic and other forces oppress and dehumanize us, "how can we sing the Lord's song" in a state other than the image of God? Thus, liberation -- total liberation of the person is a pre-requisite for a totally meaningful humanity in relation to God the author of being in its fullness.

It has been my observation that the majority of the African

Christian believers do not reflect as much on the metaphysics of God as they do on God's acts in history on the basis of which they "name" or claim to "know" God and seek to relate to God. The same is true of Jesus Christ. Furthermore, most Africans do not base their faith just on the historicity of Jesus Christ, or just on the resurrection, but on his authenticity and authority as God who directs the course of the history of salvation. This points to God's intention and will for all God's people to be truly and fully human.

This is not to imply that most African believers are not concerned about a sound theology which reflects on what is experienced in every day reality, as well as what is read in the Holy Scriptures. To the contrary, we appreciate sound doctrine. However, I am inclined to believe that most African theologians would not want to engage in a theological discourse if it did not have any bearing on reality as they understand it -- both in its spiritual and physical forms.

African Christology therefore brings a liberating theology, and an experiential perspective to the doctrine of the Incarnation. Thus a major theological shift has resulted from a merely academic, abstract and obscure discourse about the Incarnate Trinity to an experiential salvific focus on what the doctrine means for humanity.

Of course we may speculate in pursuit of truth. (I have argued elsewhere that African theology can be a political theology just as easily as it is cultural if politics became the most pressing issue threatening our survival and existence.) So, while for our Western counterparts, the Incarnation is important because it "expressed the union of humanity and divinity," and while the doctrine of the Incarnation is being challenged by some within Protestant churches relative to its centrality, truth and intelligibility, the African believer values the divine mystery due to its meaning deriving from its tangibility, concreteness, and authenticity which the doctrine brings to the Christian faith--liberating us from all forms of evil. This is marked by the holiness of the birth (the Word becoming flesh), and the death (God's sacrificial and salvific love), and the triumphant resurrection of Jesus Christ, all culminating in our salvation, wrought by God, through God.

Bibliography

AACC. The Struggle Continues. Nairobi, 1975.

AACC. The Drumbeats from Kampala. London Lutterworth Press, 1963.

Abraham, W M E. The Mind of Africa. Chicago: University of Chicago press, 1962.

Adeyemo, Tokunbo. Salvation in African Tradition. Nairobi: Evangel Publishing House. 1979.

Akwne, Francis. "A growing African Vision of the Church's Mission." Voices from the third World, vol. 8 no. 2, June 1985.

Amoah, Elizabeth, and Mercy Oduyoye. "The Christ for African Women." In Virginia Fabella and Mercy Oduyoye. eds. With Passion and Compassion: Third World Women Doing Theology. MaryKnoll, NY: Orbis Books, 1988.

Anderson, Gerald H. and Thomas F. Stransky. Eds., Mission Trends, Third World Theologies. New York: Paulist Press, 1976.

Anderson, Gerald H. and Thomas F. Stransky. Eds., Mission Trends, no. 4: Liberation Theologies. New York: Paulist Press, 1979.

Appiah-Kubi, Kofi. "The Ecumenical Importance of African Theology" Voices from the Third World, July 1986.

Appiah-Kubi, Kofi. "Jesus Christ - some christological aspects from African perspectives." Report. (June 8 - 14, 1976. 1977.

Appiah-Kubi, K. "Indigenous African Christian Churches: signs of authenticity." In Appiah-Kubi and Sergio Torres, eds. African Theology En Route. MaryKnoll: Orbis Books, 1979.

Appiah-Kubi, Kofi. "Doing Theology in South Africa: A Black Christian Perspective." Journal of Theology for Southern Africa. No. 31, June 1980.

Appiah-Kubi, Kofi. "Three Christological Models in Third World Theology." Theologia Evangelica, vol. 15. No. 2. September 1982.

Appiah-Kubi, Kofi. "Why African Theology?" AACC Bulletin. 7 (July -August 1974).

Appiah-Kubi, Kofi. "Indigenous African Churches: Signs of Authenticity." In Kofi Appiah-Kubi and Sergio Torres, eds. African Theology En Route. MaryKnoll, NY: Orbis Books, 1979.

Baesak, Allan A. "Liberation Theology in South Africa." In K. Appiah-Kubi and S. Torres, eds., African Theology En Route. MaryKnoll, NY: Orbis Books, 1979.

Baesak, Allan A. "Wholeness Through Liberation." Church and Society, May, 1981.

Baeta, C G. ed. Christianity in Tropical Africa: Studies presented and discussed at the sevent International African seminar. University of Ghana: April 1965, London: Oxford University Press. 1968.

Banana, C S. Theology of promise: The dynamics of Self-Reliance. Harare, Zimbabwe: College Press, 1982.

Barrett, David. Aschism and Renewal in Africa. London: Oxford University Press. 1968.

Barrett, David. African Initiatives in Religion. Nairobi: East African Publishing House, 1971.

Bascom, William R., and Melville J. Herskovits, eds Continuity and Change in African Culture. Chicago/London: University of Chicago Press, 1959.

Becken, Hans-Jurgen, ed. Relevant Theology for Africa. Durban: Lutheran Publishing House, 1973.

Beetham, T A. Christianity and the new Africa. New York: Frederick A. Praeger Publishers. 1967.

Behr-Sigel Elizabeth. "Woman Too is in the Likeness of God?" Unpublished Geneva: WCC. n. d.

Berg, Robert J., and Jennifer S. Whitaker, eds. Strategies for African Development. Berkeley: Uni. of California Press, 1986.

Beyerhaus, Peter. "The Christian approach to Ancestor Worship." Ministry, VI (July, 1966), pp. 137-145.

Bigo, Pierre. The Church and Third World Revolutions. New York: MaryKnoll: Orbis Books, 1977.

Blomjous, Joseph. "Development in Mission Thinking and Practices 1959-1980: Inculturation and Inculturation." AFER, vol. 22, no. 6, 1980.

Blyden, Edward Wilmot. "Africa for the African." In H. S. Wilson, ed. Origins of West African Nationalism. London: MacMillian, 1969.

Blyden, Edward Wilmot. "African Life and Customs." In H. S. Wilson, ed. Origins of West African Nationalism. London: MacMillian, 1969.

Boros, L. God is with us. New York: Herder and Herder. 1967.

Bourdillon, M F C. ed. Christianity South of the Zambezi. Gweru: Mambo Press. 1977.

Brown, David. The Divine Trinity: Christian and Islam. London: Sheldon Press. 1969.

Brunello, Anthony R. "Liberation Theology and third World Social Transformation." TransAfrica Forum. Vol. 4, no. 4, Summer 1987.

Brydon, Lynne, and Sylvia Chant. Women in the Third World: Gender Issues in Rural and Urban Areas. New Brunswick, NJ: Rutgers University Press, 1989.

Bujo, Benezet. <u>African Theology in Its Social Context</u>. MaryKnoll, NY: Orbis Books, 1992.

Busia, K A. The African Worldview. In <u>Christianity and African Culture</u>. Accra: Christian council of the Gold coast. (Conference Report). 1955.

Buthelezi, Manas. "An African Theology or a Black Theology?" In Basil Moore, ed. <u>The Challenge of Black Theology in South Africa.</u> <u>Atlanta</u>. John Knox Press, 1974.

Buthelizi, M. Toward Indigenous Theology in South Africa. In Sergio Torres and Virginia Faballa, eds. <u>The Emergent Gospel</u>. MaryKnoll, NY: Orbis Books, 1975.

Chipenda, Jose B. "Theological Options in Africa Today." In Kofi Appiah-Kubi and Sergio Torres, eds. <u>African Theology En Route</u>. MaryKnoll, NY: Orbis Books, 1979.

Clark, Leon E. <u>Through African Eyes: Cultures in Change</u>. New York: Praeger Publishers, 1970.

Cone, James H. "The Content and method of Black Theology." The Journal of Religious Thought, vol. 32, no. 2, Fall-Winter 1975.

Cone, James H. "A Black American Perspective on the Future of African Theology." In K. Appiah-Kubi and Sergio Torres, eds. <u>African Theology En Route</u>. MaryKnoll: NY: Orbis Books, 1979.

Cone, James H. "Black Theology: Its Origin, Methodology, and Relationship to Third World Theologies." In Virginia Fabella and Sergio Torres, eds. <u>Doing Theology in a Divided World</u>. MaryKnoll, NY: Orbis Books, 1985.

Cone, James H. "A Black American perspective on the Future of African Theology." In Kofi Appiah-Kubi and Sergio Torres, eds. <u>African Theology En Route</u>. MaryKnoll, NY: Orbis Books, 1979.

Cones, James H. <u>God of the Oppressed</u>. New York: Seabury Press.

1975.

Croatto, J. Severino. Exodus: Hermeneutics of Freedom. MaryKnoll, NY: Orbis Books, 1981.

Cullmann, O. The Christology of the New Testament. London: SCM Press. 1959.

Daneel, M L. Quest for Belonging: introduction to a study of African independent churches. Gweru: Mambo Press. 1987.

Daneel, M L. The God of the Matopo Hills. The Hague: Mouton. 1970.

Daneel, M L. Zionism and Faith-Healing in Rhodesia: Aspects of African Independent Churches. Mouton, 1970.

Daneel, M L. The Christian Gospel and the ancestor cults. Missionalia vol. 1, no. 2, August, 1973.

Danquah, J B. The Akan Doctrine of God. London: Lutterworth Press, 1944.

Desai, Ram. ed. Christianity in Africa as seen by Africans. Denver: Allan Swallow, 1962.

Dickson, Kwesi A. Uncompleted Mission: Christianity and Exclusivism. MaryKnoll, NY: Orbis Books, 1991.

Dickson, Kwesi A. "African Theology: Origin, Methodology and Content." The Journal of Religious Thought. Vol. 32, no. 2. Fall-Winter, 1975.

Dickson, Kwesi A. :"The African Theological Task.' In Sergio Torres and Virginia Fabella, eds. The Emergent Gospel: Theology from the Developing World. MaryKnoll, NY: Orbis Books, 1978.

Dickson, Kwesi A. Theology in Africa. MaryKnoll NY: Orbis Books, 1984.

Diop, Cheik Anta. The African Origin of Civilization: Myth or Reality. Westpoint, Conn: Lawrence Hill, 1974.

De Carvalho, Emilio J M. "Jesus Christ - Some Christological Aspects from African Perspectives." In John Mbiti, ed. African and Asian Contributions to Contemporary Theology: Geneva: WCC, 1977.

De Carvalho, Emilio J M. "Who do you Africans say I (Jesus) am?" Voices from the Third World, vol. 11 no. 2, December 1988.

De Carvalho, Emilio J M. "What do the Africans say that Jesus Christ is?" African Theological Journal vol. 10. no. 2 1981.

Dumas, Andrew. Political Theology and the Life of the Church. London: SCM Press. Ltd. 1978.

Dwane, S. "Christology in the Third World." Journal of Theology for Southern Africa. No. 21, December 1979.

Ekeya, Bette J M. "A Christology from the underside." Voices from the Third World, vol. 17 no. 2. December 1988.

Ela, Jean-Marc. African Cry: MaryKnoll, NY: Orbis Books, 1986.

Ela, Jean-Marc. "Le Role des Eglises dans la liberation du continent africain." Bulletin de Theologie Africaine, vol. 6, julliet-decembre 1984.

Ela, Jean-Marc. My Faith as an African. MaryKnoll, NY: Orbis Books, 1988.

Enang, K. "Concept of Salvation in the Nigerian Independent Churches." Nene Zeitschrift fur missionswissenchaft, 37. 1981.

Fabella, Virginia and Sergio Torres, eds. Irruption of the Third World: Challenge to Theology. MaryKnoll, NY: Orbis Books, 1983.

Fabella, Virginia, ed. Asia's Struggle for Full Humanity. MaryKnoll, NY: Orbis Books, 1980.

Fashole-Luke, E W. "The Quest for African Christian Theologies." Scottish Journal of Theology, vol. 29, 1976.

Fashole-Luke, E W. "Footpaths and signposts to African Christian Theologies." Scottish Journal of Theology, vol. 32 no. 5, 1981.

Ferkiss, Victor C. Africa's Search for Identity. New York: The World Publishing Company. 1966.

Fortes, Meyar, and Germaine Dieterlen, eds. Africa Systems of Thought. New York/London: Oxford University Press, 1965.

Frostin, P. "The Hermeneutics of the poor: the epistemological "break" - in Third World Theologies." Studia Theologica 39: pp. 127-150.

Garvey, Amy Jacques, ed. The Philosophy and Opinions of Marcus Garvey or Africa for the Africans, vol. 1 and 2. Dover, Mass: Majority Press, 1986.

Geertz, Clifford. The Interpretation of Cultures. New York: Basic Books, 1973.

Gelfand, Michael. The genuine Shona: Survival values of an African culture. Gweru: Mambo Press. 1973.

Gelfand, Michael. The Spiritual Beliefs of the Shona. Gweru: Mambo Press. 1970.

Glasswell, Mark E. and E W. Fashole-Luke, eds. New Testament Christianity for Africa and the Worlds. (Essays in honour of Harry Sawyerr). London: S.P.GK. 1974

Goba, Bonganjaol. "An Africanf Christian Theology: Toward a Tentative Methodology from a South African Perspective." Journal of Theology for Southern Africa. no. 26. March 1979.

Goba, Bonganjalo. "The Role of the Black Church in the Process of Healing of Human Brockenness." Journal of Theology for Southern African. no. 28, September 1979.

Goba, Bonganjalo. "Toward a Black Ecclesiology: Insights from Sociology of Knowledge." Missionalia, vol. 9, no. 2, August 1981.

Goba, Bonganjalo. "Toward a Quest for Christian Identity: A Third World Perspective." Journal of Black Theology, vol. 2, no. 2, November 1988.

Grelzer, David G. "Random notes on Black theology and African theology." Christian Century. 87. (September 16th 1970): 1091-1093.

Griklin, Marie J. "African Christian Theological Resources." In Regina M. Bechtle and John J. Rathschmidt eds. Mission and Mysxicism Evangelisation and the Experience of God. MaryKnoll School of Theology, 1987.

Groves, C P. The Planting of Christianity in Africa, I-IV London: Lutterworth Press, 1948-58.

Gutierrez, G. The Power of the Poor in History. MaryKnoll, NY: Orbis Books, 1983.

Hamutyinei, M A. And A B. Plangger. eds. Tsumo-Shumo: Shona Proverbial Lore and Wisdom. Gweru: Mambo Press, 1974.

Harjula, Raimo. God and the Sun in Moru Thought. Helsinki: Finnish Society for Missiology and Ecumenics, 1969.

Hastings, Adrian. "On African Theology." Scottish Journal of Theology . vol. 37, no. 3, 1984.

Hayward, Victor E W. African Independent Church Movements. London: Edinburgh House Press, 1963.

Hearne, B. ed. Revelation. Eldoret, Kenya: Gaba Publications. 1979.

Hick, John. ed. God Has Many Names. London: Macmillian. 1980.

Hick, John. ed. The Myth of God Incarnate. London: SCM. 1977.

Hodgson, Leonard. "The Doctrine of the Trinity: Some Further Thoughts." Journal of Theological Studies, New Series 5, part 1. 1954.

Hood, Robert E. Must God Remain Greek? Afro Cultures and God-Talk. Minneapolis: Fortress Press, 1990.

Hooker, J R. Black Revolutionary: George Padmore's path from Communism to Pan-Africanism. London: 1967.

Horton, Robin. "African Traditional Thought and Western Science." Africa, xxxvii (January, 1967), 50-71.

Hountondji, P. African Philosophy: Myth and reality. Bloomington, Ind: Indian University Press, 1983.

Idowu, E B. African Traditional religion: A Definition. MaryKnoll: Orbis Books, 1975.

Idowu, E Bolaji. Olodumare: God in Yoruba Belief. London: Longman's 1962.

Idowu, E B. "God." In Kwesi Dickson and Ellingworth eds. Biblical Revelation and African Beliefs. London: Oxford University Press. 1965.

Idowu, E. Bolaji. Olodumare: The Selfhood of the Church in Africa. Mushin, Lagos State: Methodist Church Nigeria, n.d.

Idowu, E. Bolaji. Olodumare: Towards an Indigenous Church. London: Oxford University Press, 1965.

Imasogie, Osadolor. Guidelines for Christian Theology in Africa. Achimota,Ghana: Africa Christian Press, 1983.

Institute for Contextual Theology. "Contextual Theology for Groups in South Africa." Women in a Changing World. No. 27, May 1989.

Institute for Contextual Theology. "What is Contextual Theology?" Part 1 A.A.C.C. Magazine, vol. 2, no. 3, December 1984.

July, Robert W. The Origins of Modern African Thought. London: Faber and Faber, 1968.

Kabasele, Francois. "Christ as Ancestor and Elder Brother." In Robert J. Schreiter, ed. Faces of Jesus in Africa. MaryKnoll NY: Orbis Books, 1991.

Kaberry, Phyllis M. Review of African Ideas of God: A Symposium, ed. By Edwin W. Smith. Africa, xxi (January, 1951), 76.

Kalilombe, Patrick A. "Self-Reliance of the African Church: A Catholic Perspective." In Kofi Appiah-Kubi and Sergio Torres, eds., African Theology En Route. MaryKnoll, NY: Orbis Books, 1979.

Kalilombe, Patrick A. "The Salvific Values of African Religions." AFER, vol. 21, no. 3, June 1979.

Kalu, Ogbu. "Church Presence in Africa." In Appiah-Kubi and Torres, 1979.

Kasper, W. Jesus the Christ. New York: Paulist Press. 1976.

Kato, Byang. Theological Pitfalls in Africa. Kisumu; Evangel Publishing House. 1975.

Kayama, K. No Handle on the Cross. London: SCM. 1976.

Kiruren, M C. The Missionary and the Diviner: Contemporary Theologies of and African Religions. MaryKnoll: Orbis Books. 1987.

Knox, John. The Humanity and Divinity of Christ: A study of Pattern in Christology. \cambridge: The Cambridge University Press. 1967.

Kubicho, S G. The interaction of the traditional Kikuyu concept of God with the Biblcial concept. Cahiers des religions Africaines 4. No. 2., 1968.

Lediga, S P. A Relevant Theology for Africa: a critical evaluationof previous attempts in relevant Theologh for Africa. Beckon, 1973.

Lienhardt, Godfrey. Divinity and Experience: The Religion of the Dinka. London: Oxford University Press, 1961.

Long, Charles H. "Structural Similarities and Dissimilarities in Black and African Theologies." The Journal of Religious Thought, vol. 32, no. 2, Fall-Winter 1975.

Lugira, Aloysius M. "African Christian Theology." African Theological Journal, vol. 8, no. 1, 1979.

Maimela, S. Salvationin African traditional religions. Missionalia 13, no. 2, 1985.

Martin, M L. The Biblical concept of messianism and messianism in Southern Africa. Moriah, lesotho, 1964.

Martin, M L. Prophetic Christianity in the Congo, Johannesburg, 1968.

Martin, M L. Kimbangu: an African prophet and his church. Oxford: Blackwell. 1975.

Mayatula, V M. "African Independent Churches' contribution to a relevant theology." In H. J. Becken. Relevant Theology for Africa. Becken. 1973.

Mbiti, John S. Concepts of God in Africa. London: SPCK, 1970.

Mbiti, John S. The Prayers of African Religion. New York: MaryKnoll. 1975.

Mbiti, John S. Bible and Theology in African Christianity. Nairobi: Oxford University Press. 1986.

Mbiti, John S. "Some African Concepts and Christology." In George F. Vicedom, ed. Christ and the Younger Churches. London: SPCK, 1972.

Mbiti, John S. "The Biblical Basis for Present Trends in African Theology." In Kofi Appiah-Kubi and Sergio Torres, eds. African Theology En Route. MaryKnoll, NY: Orbis Books, 1979.

Mbiti, John S. "Some African Concepts of Christology." In J. S.
    Mbiti, <u>Christ and the Younger Churches</u>: Vicedome. 1972.

Mbiti, John S. The Encounter of Christian Faith and African religion.
    <u>The Christian Encounter</u>. (August). 1980.

McVeigh, Malcolm J. <u>God in Africa: Concepts of God in African
    traditional religion and Christianity</u>. Cape Cod: Claude Stark, Inc.
    1974.

McVeigh, Malcolm J. "Sources for an African Christian Theology." Presence 1974.

Milingo, E. The World in Between: Christian healing and the Struggle for Spiritual Survival. MaryKnoll, NY: Orbis Books, 1984.

Mofokeng, T A. "A Black Christology: a new beginning." Journal of Black Theology in South Africa. Vol. 1. No. 1, 1987.

Mofokeng, Takatso A. The Crucxified Among the Crossbearers: Towards a Black Christology. Kampen: J. H. Kok, 1983.

Mofokeng, Takatso A. "The Cross in the Search for True Humanity. Theological Challenges Facing the South African Church." Voices from the Third World, vol. 12, no. 1, June 1989.

Moltmann, Jurgen. The Crucified God: The Cross of Christ as the Foundation and Criticism of Christian Theology. London: SCM Press, 1974.

Mosala, Itumeleng J. "The Use of the Bible in Black Theology." In I. J. Mosala and B. Tehagale, eds. The Unquestionable Right to be Free. MaryKnoll; NY: Orbis Books, 1986.

Mosala, Itumeleng J. "The Relevance of African Traditional Religions and Their Challenge to Black Theology." In I. J. Mosala and B. Tehagale, eds. The Unquestionalbe Right to be Free. MaryKnoll, NY: Orbis Books, 1986.

Mosala, Itumeleng J. "African Traditional Beliefs and Christianity." Journal of Theology for Southern Africa, no. 43, June 1983.

Mosha, Raymond. "The Trinity in the African Context." In Africa Theological Journal no. 9 (April, 1980): 40-47.

Motte, Mary and Joseph R. Lang. Mission in Dialogue. MaryKnolls NY: Orbis Books. 1982.

Moyo, Ambrose M. "The Quest for African Christian Theology and Problem of the Relationship Between Faith and Culture - The Hermeneutical Perspective." African Theological Journal, vol. 12, no. 2, 1983.

Mshana, Eliweaha E. "The Challenge of Black Theology and African Theology." African Theological Journal, vol. T, December 1972.

Mugambi, J.N.K. African Christian Theology: An Introdcution. Nairboi: Heinemann, 1989.

Mugo, Erasto. African Response to Western religion. East African Literature Bureau. 1975.

Mulago, Vincent. Un Visage Africain du Christianisme. Paris: Presence Africaine, 1965.

Mushete, Ngindu. "Authenticite et Christianisme en Afrique Noire. Le cas du Zaire." Le Monde Moderne, 12, 1976.

Mushete N. The figure of Jesus in African Theology. Christian Identity. (Concilium 196, Edinburgh), 1988.

Mushete, N. "The History of theology in Africa: frompolemics to critical irenics." In K. Appiah-Kubi and Sergio Torres, eds. African Theology En Route. N.Y. MaryKnoll: Orbis Books, 1979.

Muzorewa, G. Origins and Development of African Theology. MaryKnoll: Orbis Books, 1986.

Muzorewa, G. An African Theology of Mission. Edwin Mellen Press. 1991.

Muzorewa, G. "Quest for an African Christology." Journal of Black Theology in South Africa. 2 no. 2, June 1988.

Nasimuyu-Wasike, Anne. "Christology and an African Woman's Experience." In J.N.K. Mugambi and Laurenti Magesa, eds. Jesus in African Christianity. Nairobi, Kenya: Initiatives Publishers, 1989.

Nolan, Albert. God in South Africa: The Challenge of the Gospel. Grand Rapids, Mich. Eerdmans/David Philip, 1988.

Nolan, Albert. Jesus Before Christianity: The Gospel of Liberation. Cape Town: David Philip. 1976.

Novak, M. Belief and Unbelief: A Philosophy of Self-Knowledge. London:Darton, Longmann and Todd. 1966.

Ntwasa, Sabelo. "The Concept of God in Black Theology." In Moore 1973, pp. 18-28.

Nyamiti, C. "The doctrine of God." In John Parratt, ed. A Reader in African Christian Theology, London: SPCK. 1987.

Nyamiti, C. The Scope of African Theology. Kampala: Gaba Publications. 1973.

Nyamiti, Charles. "African Christolgies Today." In J.N.K. Mugambi and Laurenti Magesa, eds. Jesus in African Christianity. Nairobi, Kenya: Initiatives Publishers, 1989.

Nyamiti, Charles. "The African sense of God's motherhood in the light of Christian Faith." Voices from the Third World. Vol. 8, no. 3, September 1985.

Nyamiti, C. "Approaches to African Theology." In Sergio Torres and Virginia Fabella, ed. The Emergent Gospel. MaryKnoll: Orbis Books, 1978.

Nyamiti, Charles. The Way to Christian Theology for Africa. Eldoret, Kenya: Gaba Publciations, 1975.

Nyamiti, Charles. Christ as Our Ancestors: Christology from an African Perspective. Gweru, Zimbabwe: mambo Press, 1984.

Nyamiti, Charles. African Tradition and the Christian God. Eldoret, Kenya: Gaba Publciations, n.d.

Nyerere, Julius. Ujamaa: Essays os Socialism. Oxford: Oxford
     University Press. 1968.

O'Connell, James. "The Withdrawal of the High God in Wester Arican
     Religion: An Essay in Interpretation.:" Man, Lxii (May, 1962) pp. 67-
     69.

Oduyoye, Modupe. The Sons of the Gods and the Daughters of Men.
     MaryKnoll: Orbis Books, 1984.
Oduyoye, Mercy Amba. "An African Woman's Christ." Voices from
     the Third World, Vol. 11, no. 2, December 1988.

Oduyoye, Mercy Amba. Hearing and Knowing: Theological
     Reflections on Christianity in Africa. MaryKnoll, NY: Orbis Books,
     1986.

Ogot, Bethwell A. "The Concept of Jok." African Studies. XX, no. 2.
     (1961). 123-130.

Omoyayowo, Joseph A. "Christian Expression in African Independent
     Churches." In Presence 5, no. 3 (1972).

Oostheizen, G C. Post-Christianity in African: A Theological and
     Anthropological Study, London: C. Hurst and Company 1968.

Oostheizen, G C.: The Theology of a South African Messiah, Leiden.
     1967.

P'Bitek, Okot. African Religions in Western Scholarship. Nairboi:
     East African Literature Bureau. 1970.

Pannenberg, Wolfhart. Jesus - God and Man. Philadelphia: The
     Westminster Press. 1977.

Parrinder, Geoffrey. West African Religion: A Study of the Beliefs
     and Practices of Akan, Ewwe, Yoruba, Ibo, and Kindred peoples.
     London: The Epworth Press. 1961.

Petulla, Joseph M. Christian Political Theology: A Marxian Guide.
     New York: MaryKnoll. 1972.

Potholm, Christian P. <u>The Theology and Practiceof African Politics</u>.
Engelwood Cliffs: Prentice-hall, Inc. 1976.

Richardson, Alan. <u>The Political Christ</u>. Philadelphia: Westminster
Press: 1973.

Roberts, Deotis J. <u>A Black Polticial Theology</u>. Philadelphia:
Westminster Press. 1974.

Sarpong, Peter. "Christianity Should be Africanized, not to Africanise Christianity." In Afria Ecclesiastical Review (Winter, 1975).

Sawyerr, Harry. God: Ancestor or Creator? London: Longman Group, 1970.

Sawyeer, H. "Jesus Christ: universal brother." African Christian Spirituality. In Shorter, 1978.

Sawyeer, H. "Sin and Forgiveness in Africa." Lodnon: Frontier 7. (1964): 60-3.

Sawyeer, H. "{What is African Christian Theology?" In Africa Theological Jouranl 4 (1971): 1ff.

Sawyeer, H. Salvation Reviewed from the African situation. Presence 5. no. 3, 1972.

Sawyeer, H. "What is African Theology? A Case for Theologia Africana." In Africa Theological Journal 4 (1971): 1ff.

Schillebeeckx, E. Jesus and Experiment in Christology. London, NY: Collins/Seabury, 1979.

Schoffeleers, Matthew. "Folk Christology in Africa: The Dialetics of the Nyanga Paradigm." Journal of Religion in Africa. Vol. XIX - Fasc. 2, June 1989.

Schoffeleers, Matthew. "Black and African Theology in Southern Africa: A Controversy re-examined." Journal of religionin Africa, vol. XVIII - Fasc. 2, June 1988.

Schoffeleers, M. "Christ as the medicine-man and the medicine man as Christ: a tentative history of African Christological thorugh." Man and Life. 8 no. 1-2., 1982.

Schroeder, Edward H. "Lessions for Westerners from Setiloane's Christology." Mission Studies, vol. 2, February 1985.

Seligman, C G. Races of Africa. Oxford: Oxford University Press. 1966.

Setiloane, Gabriel M. "Where are we in Africa Theology?" In Kofi Appiah-Kubi and Sergio Torres, eds. African Theology En Route. MaryKnoll, NY: Orbis Books, 1979.

Setiloane, Gabriel M. "Theolgical Trends in Africa." Missionalia. Vol. 8 1980.

Setiloane, G M. "I am an African." In Mission Trends no. 3, Anderson and Stransky. 1976.

Setiloane, Gabriel M. Afrian Theology: An Introduction. Johannesburg Skotaville Publishers, 1986.

Setiloane, Gabriel M. The Image of God Among the Sotho-Tswana. Rotterdam: A.A. Balkema. 1976.

Shorter, A. Jesus and a witchdoctor: an approach to healing and wholeness. MaryKnoll: Orbis Books. 1988.

Shorter, A. African Christian Spirituality. London: Chapman. 1978.

Shorter, Aylward. African Christian Theology: Adaptation or Incarnation? MaryKnoll, NY: Orbis Books, 1977.

Smith, Edwin W., ed. African Ideas of God. London: Edinburgh House Press, 1950.

Sobrino, Jon. Christology at the Crossroads. New York: MaryKnoll. 1976. (Translation).

Soelle, Dorothee. Political Theology. Philadelphia: Fortress Press. 1974.

Steve Biko, "Black Consciousness and the Qeust for a true Humanity." In Basil Moore, ed. The Challenge of Black Theology in South Africa. Athanta: John Knox Press, 1974.

Stroumsa, G. "The Incorporeality of God." Religion 13, (1983) 345-58.

Sundkler, B. Bantu Prophets in South Africa, 2nd ed. London: 1961.

Tappa, Louise. "God in Man's Image." In Johns Pobee and B. Von Wartenberg-Potter, eds. New Eyes for Reading: Biblical and Theological Reflection by Women from the Third World. Geneva: WCC, 1986.

Taylor, John V. The Primal Vision. London: SCM Press, 1963.

Temples, Placide. Bantu Philosophy. Paris: Presence Africaine. 1959.

Thomas, George B. "Kimbanguism: Authentically African, Authentically Christian." In African religions: A Symposium. Ed. N.S. Booth, Jr. New York: Nok 1977.

Thompson, P.E.S. "Reflections Uopn the Afrian Idea of God." The Sierra Leone Bullentin of Religion, VII (December, 1965), 56-61.

Torres, Sergion, and Virginia Fabella, eds. The Emergent Gospel: Theology from the Developing World. MaryKnoll, NY: Orbis Books, 1978.

Turner, H. African Indepent Church: The Church of God (Aladura). Oxford, 1967.

Turner, Harold W. Profile through Preaching: A Study of Sermon Texts used in West African Independent Churches. London: Edinburgh House Press. 1965.

Tutu, Desmond. "Black Theology/AFrican Theology - Soul Mates or Antagonists?" In Gayrand S. Wilmore and James H. Cone, eds. Black Theology: A Documentary history 1966-1979. MaryKnoll, NY: Orbis Books 1979.

Ukpong, Justin S. Afrian Theolgies Now: A Profile. Eldoret, Kenya: Gaba Publications, 1984.

Van de Merwe, W. J. The Shona Idea of God. Fort Victoria: Morgenster Mission Press, 1957.

Vidler, Alex. Objections to Christian Belief. London: Constable. 1963.

W.S.C.F. A New Look at Christianity in Africa. ed. vol. 11. no. 2, 1972.

Wallerstein, Immanuel. Afria: The Politics of Unity. New York: Vintage Books, 1972.

Wallerstein, Immanuel. Afria: The Politics of Independence: an interpretation of Modern History. New York: Vintage Books, 1961.

Wambuta, Daniel N. "Savanah Theology: A Biblical Reconsideration of the Concept of Salvation in the African context." In Bullentin of African Theology. vol. II (1981): 137-153.

Wambuta, Daniel N. "Hermeneutics and the Search for Theologia Afriana." In Africa Theolgical Journal 9. no. 1 (April, 1980): 29-39.

Welbourn, F.B. and B.A. Ogot. A Place to feel at Home. Nairobi: Oxford University Press. 1966.

Wiles, M. The making of Christian Doctrine. Cambridge: Cambridge University Press. 1967.

Wilmore, G S. The role of Afro-America in the rise of Third World Theology: a historical appraisal. In Appiah-Kubi and Sergio Torres, eds. Afrian Theology En Route. MaruKnoll: Orbis Books. 1979.

Wilmore, Gayraud, and James Cone. eds. Black Theology: A Documentary History. 1966-1979. New York: MaryKnoll, 1979.

Young, Josiah U. "African Theology: From 'Independence' Toward Liberation." Voices from the Third World.